HOT WAR
ON THE
CONSUMER

Edited by

DAVID SANFORD

PITMAN PUBLISHING CORPORATION

New York • *Toronto* • *London* • *Tel Aviv*

A PITMAN / NEW REPUBLIC BOOK

TABLE OF CONTENTS

INTRODUCTION   *vi*

PART I.   A CLOSER LOOK AT FOOD AND DRUGS

What Are We Made Of?—Time for a Deep Look and a Steady Resolve BY RALPH NADER   *3*

To Market We Go . . . Like Lambs to the Slaughter BY ED DOWLING   *10*

Gamesmanship in the Supermarkets BY DAVID SANFORD   *21*

Segregated Food at the Supermarket BY JAMES RIDGEWAY   *26*

Studies in the Grocery BY JAMES RIDGEWAY   *30*

Ghetto Merchants: A Study in Deception BY PHILIP G. SCHRAG   *33*

Something Fishy BY RALPH NADER   *37*

We're Still in the Jungle BY RALPH NADER   *41*

Watch That Hamburger BY RALPH NADER   *45*

This Additive Age BY DAVID SANFORD   *48*

Unfoods: Do You Know What You're Eating? BY DAVID SANFORD   *53*

Unmilk: Cowing the Consumer BY DAVID SANFORD   *58*

Radio-Inactive Food BY DAVID SANFORD   *64*

Radiation Treatment A NEW REPUBLIC EDITORIAL   *68*

Bitter News about Sweeteners BY W. DAVID GARDNER   *70*

Safety of Sweeteners BY W. DAVID GARDNER   *74*

Sweeteners Emerge Again BY ARTHUR S. GROVE, JR., M.D.   *78*

Drug on the Market BY DAVID SANFORD   *81*

In Brands We Trust BY DAVID SANFORD   *86*

Get Well Cheaper the Hard-Name Way A NEW REPUBLIC EDITORIAL   *89*

Drugs: Deceptive Advertising BY MORTON MINTZ   *91*

The Quinine Caper A NEW REPUBLIC EDITORIAL   *95*

More about Thalidomide BY JAMES RIDGEWAY   *98*

Can a Woman Be Feminine Forever? BY NANCY SOMMERS AND JAMES RIDGEWAY   *104*

The Golden Pill: We Can't Yet Be Sure It's Safe BY MORTON MINTZ   *109*

Be Happy, Light Up A NEW REPUBLIC EDITORIAL   *115*

Squabble over Cigarettes A NEW REPUBLIC EDITORIAL   *117*

Filtered Cigarettes A NEW REPUBLIC EDITORIAL   *120*

Time for the Truth A NEW REPUBLIC EDITORIAL   *122*

Columbia's Filter BY JAMES RIDGEWAY   *124*

PART II.   BIG BUSINESS MALPRACTICES

Admen in Orbit BY DAVID SANFORD   *129*

Hear, Hear A NEW REPUBLIC EDITORIAL   *133*

Selling Encyclopedias BY ERIC GELLER   *135*

Business Crime BY RALPH NADER   *138*

The Money-Lenders BY JONATHAN KWITNY   *141*

Investing in Mutual Funds BY MORDECAI ROSENFELD   *146*

Eastern's Shuttle Service BY JAMES RIDGEWAY   *151*

High Flying Fares BY GILBERT B. FRIEDMAN   *154*

The Trans-Pacific Air Route Tangle BY DAVID SANFORD   *160*

Togetherness in the Air A NEW REPUBLIC EDITORIAL   *165*

Come Right in "Colonel," "Admiral," or Whoever
    BY DAVID SANFORD   *168*

Henry Fonda's Steak A NEW REPUBLIC EDITORIAL   *171*

PART III.   YOUR SAFETY IS AT STAKE

Safety on the Job BY RALPH NADER AND JEROME GORDON   *175*

They're Still Breathing BY RALPH NADER   *181*

Danger: Death at Work BY J. V. REISTRUP   *183*

"Black Lung": Mining as a Way of Death BY ROBERT COLES
    AND HARRY HUGE   *188*

X-ray Exposures BY RALPH NADER   *197*

The Dick BY JAMES RIDGEWAY   *201*

GM Hired the Dick A NEW REPUBLIC EDITORIAL   *206*

GM Comes Clean BY JAMES RIDGEWAY   *208*

The Nader Affair BY JAMES RIDGEWAY AND DAVID SANFORD   *211*

Bureaucracy and Highway Safety BY DANIEL POSIN, JR.   *216*

Highway Murder BY JOSEPH KELNER   *220*

The Infernal, Eternal, Internal Combustion Engine
    BY RALPH NADER   *223*

PART IV.   INSURANCE—ASSET OR LIABILITY?

Underground War on Auto Insurance BY JAMES RIDGEWAY   *229*

More on Auto Insurance BY JAMES RIDGEWAY   *235*

Taken for a Ride BY GILBERT B. FRIEDMAN   *240*

No Risks Preferred BY JAMES RIDGEWAY   *246*

Dirty Deal in Small Loans BY JAMES RIDGEWAY   *253*

The Repossessed BY GILBERT B. FRIEDMAN   *257*

Big Brother Keeps Tabs on Insurance Buyers
    BY STANFORD N. SESSER   *262*

The Unbondables BY GILBERT B. FRIEDMAN   *266*

Cheap Life Insurance BY JAMES RIDGEWAY AND DAVID WIGGINS   *272*

INDEX   *275*

LIST OF CONTRIBUTORS

Robert Coles, a *New Republic* contributing editor and research psychiatrist at the Harvard Health Services, is the author of *Children of Crisis*.

Edward Dowling, a student of propaganda, attended the Institut d'Etudes Politiques in Paris after serving in the Marines during the Korean War.

Gilbert B. Friedman is a practicing attorney in San Francisco.

W. David Gardner, a free-lance medical writer, recently compiled the medical information for the Grolier Encyclopedia Yearbook.

Eric Geller is a *New Republic* staff member.

Jerome Gordon was a staff member of Columbia University's Bureau of Applied Sociology Research when "Safety on the Job" was written.

Arthur S. Grove, Jr., a graduate of the University of Pennsylvania Medical School and a Clinical Associate with the National Institute of Health for two years, received a J.D. degree from Harvard Law School in 1969 and is a resident at Massachusetts Eye and Ear Hospital.

Harry Huge is studying poverty programs with the Washington Research Project while on leave from Arnold & Porter, a Washington law firm.

Joseph Kelner is a practicing attorney in New York City and a past president of the American Trial Lawyers Association.

Jonathan Kwitny is a reporter for the Perth-Amboy *News-Tribune*.

Morton Mintz, a *Washington Post* reporter and author of *By Prescription Only*, won the Heywood Broun, George Polk and Raymond Crapper awards for his reporting of the 1962 thalidomide disaster.

Ralph Nader is the author of *Unsafe at Any Speed*.

Daniel Posin, Jr., a Yale Law School graduate, is a practicing attorney.

J. V. Reistrup is assistant Sunday editor of the *Washington Post*.

James Ridgeway is editor of the weekly political paper *Hard Times*.

Mordecai Rosenfeld, a New York attorney and Yale Law School graduate, specializes in lawsuits on behalf of mutual fund shareholders.

Philip G. Schrag, an attorney with the NAACP Legal Defense and Education Fund, is chairman of the Consumer Advisory Council of the New York City Department of Consumer Affairs.

Stanford N. Sesser is a New York newspaper reporter.

Nancy Sommers is a free-lance writer.

David Wiggins is a free-lance writer.

INTRODUCTION

Just four years ago Ralph Nader was an obscure young man with conspiracy theories about the way consumers are treated by big corporations. He was incensed about automobile accidents and had the uncommon view that accidents happen not so much because of bad drivers as because of bad cars—structurally unsound, shoddily constructed, stylish but lethal. He had written a book which was not yet published, and he went about Washington trying to convince reporters he had a story for them. For the most part, he was turned away. Gradually, he was heard, and when his work came to the attention of General Motors they put a detective on his tail. They interviewed his friends under the pretense of a pre-employment check and began an expensive campaign of intimidation which, more than anything else, was responsible for making Ralph Nader a household word and perhaps the most powerful man without institutional backing in Washington.

General Motors was embarrassed to have to confess in public, before a congressional committee, that it had a detective inquiring into Nader's affairs. And GM was even more chagrined when the detective owned up to asking questions about Nader's sex life.

The Senate hearings caught the imagination of Americans because Nader was cast in the role of a giantkiller. One man had embarrassed the nation's largest corporation. He had got the best of them.

Since 1966 Nader has become publicly associated with the stories he had been peddling behind the scenes: tainted fish, meat, and poultry; mine safety; the hazards of X-rays; exploding pipelines. And more often than not his projects have resulted in controversy, public hearings, and legislation. Nader himself has become a lecturer, an author (his second book is in preparation), an editor (of the new weekly muckraking paper called *Hard Times*), a part-time instructor at Princeton, and the central figure in Americans' new interest in "consumerism."

A journalist profiling Nader after he had become a public figure asked the question, "Can Ralph Nader Crusader survive the transition to Ralph

Nader Incorporated?" The answer, now becoming clear, is that he has. Nader has found that his far-ranging interests are more than he can take on alone. Accordingly, he has enlisted a staff of smart young law students who spend their summers nosing around Washington looking for muck for the Nader rake. This staff of consumer lawyers is a part of Nader's dream to have a consumer law firm that will bring cases against organizations whose products are unsafe, fraudulently advertised, or shabby.

In 1968 Nader had some of his boys, who have come to be called Nader's Raiders, looking carefully into the affairs of the Federal Trade Commission, an agency which, with all its staff and resources and official status, does poorly what Nader alone does remarkably well—protecting and educating the consumer.

Nader's Federal Trade Commission project became a 185-page indictment of the FTC. The report charged that FTC people cave in too easily to Congressional pressures, serve regulated companies rather than the public, and even sometimes literally sleep on the job.

The report had the usual Nader failing (or virtue) of excess zeal, but it is nevertheless a remarkable document, if only because it has received attention usually attracted only by presidential commission reports and other official government bilge. As a result of the Nader report, the *Washington Post* mused editorially that the FTC might best be disbanded.

Nader has thus illustrated that it is possible, if somewhat flukish, for an aggressive person without institutional support to become an institution in himself and to wield a great deal of power. Ralph Nader Incorporated seems to be doing very well.

But he cannot do the whole job. There is still no organized lobby in Washington to represent adequately the interests of buyers of goods and services. The drug industry has the Pharmaceutical Manufacturers Association with lobbyists registered with Congress. The individual druggists are banded together in the American Pharmaceutical Association. Physicians have the American Medical Association to promote their often antediluvian interests. But who represents the man who takes his doctor's prescription to the pharmacist to have it filled with drugs manufactured by Upjohn? No one. He passively pays what is charged for what he is given. The consumer has no leverage, because for the most part he is unorganized, unrepresented and therefore helpless. Official regulatory agencies have had an interesting place in consumer protection—seeming to serve the public interest in safe air travel, wholesome food, safe and effective drugs, honest advertising and packaging, fairness in broadcasting over public airwaves, and so on while at the same time placating American business and keeping the airlines, the pharmaceutical houses, the TV networks and stations, and commerce generally in the black. Even in the eight years of Kennedy-Johnson, the regulators often seemed to serve the special interests they are in business to oversee rather than those of the consumer they exist to protect. The best indirect evidence of this is the careers of the regulators, who serve a short hitch in the public service and then take fat jobs in the private sector, usually with companies they have regulated. It goes without saying that tough regulatory agency men make more enemies than friends if they do their job well (a Transportation Secretary should be an unwelcome president of a railroad). But that usually is not the case. President Nixon plans to reduce the power and function of the regulators still further.

Studies by market researchers of consumer behavior and attitudes suggest that housewives are more naive than one would guess, given their long postwar experience with supermarkets and their exposure to saturation advertising on television and to food ads in the Thursday newspapers. When a woman (or a man) goes to the store, she probably goes there with a number of erroneous assumptions about food products: (1) They are wholesome. (2) They are safe. (3) They are what they are represented to be. We have deceptive practices laws that ostensibly compel fair and accurate claims. We have a Food and Drug Administration to ensure that food is clean and safe to eat, and a Department of Agriculture to put its USDA stamp on meat found to be fresh and free of disease. President Johnson (and now Nixon) had a resident special advisor on consumer affairs to ride herd on malpractices. But despite all the agencies and the laws and the officials, the consumer is still not well protected; consumer grievance cases proliferate.

The ways in which the consumer is buffeted about are explored in this book, a collection of articles which, with one exception, have appeared in the *New Republic* since 1965. The composite consumer these pieces describe does not know what is in the food he eats, how much interest he pays when he buys on time, whether cheap drugs really are "cheap." He is ill informed about the hazards of smoking, working in the mines, buying insurance, driving a car. It is certain that what he does know he didn't learn from the purveyors of goods, because *they* lie to him.

Hot War on the Consumer is intended to focus light on the dark corners of American commerce and to offer practical remedies for consumers to organize around and examples of guerilla warfare tactics that will help win at least some skirmishes.

DAVID SANFORD
Washington, D.C.,
May 27, 1969

PART I

A CLOSER LOOK AT FOOD AND DRUGS

What Are We Made Of?—
Time for a Deep Look
and a Steady Resolve

by RALPH NADER

The $100 billion food industry is in need of thorough public scrutiny and reform. The only difficulty is that it does not know this as it continues to increase its prices, its profits and its myths. This is an unfortunate delusion for this industry to be harboring.

The decisive motivations that drive the food processors are the maximization of their sales, profit (which includes progressive reduction of costs) and the avoidance of undesirable regulatory and consumer feedback. This all seems innocent enough until one observes more closely just how spacious an arena for maneuvering against the public interest has been staked out by the industry. This has been accomplished incrementally over the years by the rapid development of technologies, chemicals, merchandising and packaging techniques to deny the consumer the information for critical feedback, to divert his attention to wholly extraneous, emotional appeals having nothing to do with the quality or price of the product, and to mask the true condition of the foodstuffs from the consumer's natural detection facilities. Thus, the dimension of most people's reactions to the food they eat is narrowed to an appreciation of just those responses that the processors can manipulate so easily. These deal with palatability, tenderness and appearance *cum* acceptable or not repugnant odor. If the particular food product can satisfy these narrow evaluations, it is home free, quite apart from any serious lack of nutrition, wholesomeness and purity. Home free,

---

Remarks before the 1969 Convention of the American Society of Newspaper Editors, April 17, 1969, Washington, D.C. Copyright © 1969 by Ralph Nader.

3

that is, as far as the consumer is concerned. Try this test on yourself next time someone asks you how a particular meal was and see if your reaction is not restricted to one or more of these three responses. Such induced and meekly accepted conditioned response by most of us makes a mockery of consumer sovereignty and the disciplining force for quality in the marketplace implicit in an opportunity for intelligent choice or rejection.

•

What is the consumer consuming? A few representative illustrations:

1. The little consumer—the infant—is being exposed to nitrate residues from the heavy use of nitrogen fertilizers in various farm acreage. Professor Barry Commoner of Washington University in St. Louis reported in 1968 on the increasing incidence of nitrate poisoning among infants discovered by European public health officials and traced to the consumption of unrefrigerated American-processed baby food. The more precise extent of this toxic hazard to infants is not fully known in this country because no one is trying to find out in any systematic way. The food industry is not interested in being burdened with this knowledge.

2. The rapid rise in antibiotic utilization for artificial growth stimulation and health promotion in poultry and red meat animals is raising the risk of residual transfer to the human organism, particularly if antibiotics are applied a few days prior to slaughter. Even the placid National Academy of Sciences and the FDA are worried about this one. What are the direct and synergistic effects on humans of such ingestion and how effective will these drugs be when they are needed for medical purposes? Existing regulations are too weak and poorly enforced. But these antibiotics surely make for a growth industry.

3. Fat content in meat is an acknowledged major contributor to heart disease. Fat content in many processed meats has been going up in recent years, according to the US Department of Agriculture. Why? Because fat is cheaper than meat; and since they are mixed together, the consumer rarely can tell the difference. How bad is the situation? Well, the USDA issued a proposal in December 1968 to set a maximum fat content of 30 percent for the class of finished sausage products that includes frankfurter, wiener, vienna, bologna, garlic bologna, knockwurst and similar products. The meat industry, led by the American Meat Institute, is strongly opposing this requirement. Fat as a cost reducing technique is terribly congenial to the industry's tastes. Look how well it works with the most expensive breakfast meat product—bacon. Some people, it may be, may want to pay hard dollars for fat in their bologna, but they have a right to know how much fat they're buying; and other more fastidious consumers should not have to buy meat with a high degree of latent material that isn't meat at all.

4

4. Consumers Union went out shopping for fresh pork sausage recently. CU subjected the sausage samples to laboratory tests. Thirty percent of the federally inspected sausage and 40 percent of the infrequently inspected Illinois samples failed CU's tests for absence of filth or acceptably low bacteria counts. (In March 1969 sixty persons came down with trichinosis in Missouri.) CU also found that one-eighth of the federally inspected sausage and more than one-fifth of the other sausage contained insect fragments, insect larvae, rodent hairs and other kinds of filth. The sausage samples tested included most major brand names.

5. USDA reports in 1962 and 1967–1968 covering non-federally inspected plants (a category accounting for 25 percent of the nation's meat supply) showed evidence of selling 4D (dead, dying, diseased and disabled animals) for human consumption, repulsively unsanitary conditions in the plants (rodents, vermin, etc., having access to the meat preparation and storage areas, for example) and the use of illegal additives or untested additives to color, season and preserve the putrid meat so as to render it palatable. Other USDA reports on poultry preparation revealed substantial prevalence of diseased poultry being sold to unsuspecting buyers throughout the country. Much of this substandard meat and poultry is routinely funneled into city slums. USDA-inspected plants are not without their problems. The meat industry likes to throw away only bones; all meat, no matter what its condition, is a tempting subject for "reconditioning" or "doctoring." Not even the better companies, such as Hormel, are above doctoring such meat once rejected by the first retail buyer for subsequent resale to supermarkets in the slums and some in the suburbs. Millions of pounds of meat are destroyed by federal order every month but many more get to market. Bad meat is still good business.

6. The fish inspection bill is once again before Congress. The fish industry, backed by such law firms as Covington and Burling, is confident that the bill will go nowhere this year. The confidence is based on the industry's power to lobby, not on conditions in its plants. In 1967 FDA's Deputy Commissioner Rankin offered data, since re-confirmed, on conditions in the smoked fish industry: an examination of 15 plants disclosed that 13 were operating under conditions judged to be potentially dangerous and 6 of these were judged to be imminently hazardous to consumers of the finished product. The FDA, severely limited in resources for inspection, still manages to seize numerous shipments every month involving decomposed fish and fish products, the presence of coagulase, positive staphylococci and parasitic copepods. Frozen breaded shrimps containing bacterial filth, leaking canned fish, frozen whitefish with parasitic cysts, caviar containing borates and imported dried fish containing maggots are some other illustrations. Consumers Union has conducted several tests over the past decade and will conduct more shortly. Here is part of CU's

5

tally: 98 of 120 samples of frozen raw breaded shrimp tested contained coagulase positive staphylococci (1961); 55 of 120 samples of cod, haddock, and ocean perch fillets judged substandard quality (1963); 85 percent of 646 cans of salmon (51 brands) showed a tendency toward mushiness or discoloration (1966); 17 samples of 18 frozen salmon steaks (three brands) were so rancid that no cooking method could disguise the bad flavor (1966). Like so many foods that are unwholesome, they are bad bargains in an economic sense.

7. Water pollution—sewage and industrial waste—in bays and offshore areas where shellfish are harvested is a mounting peril. The FDA recently seized 21,000 pounds of frozen salmon from the Great Lakes because of dangerous pesticide levels in the salmon. Environmental pollution finds its way into other food products as well. Is the food industry pushing for pollution controls? No. Is the food industry adopting and developing techniques for detection of such pollution? Only very slowly, at best.

8. Every week, FDA puts out its little-known "Weekly Recall Report." It is little known because FDA does little to publicize it. Some food recalls of late include cookies (rodent filth), egg yolk solids (contamination, salmonella—a fast-spreading food-borne menace), imitation pistachio, lemon, mint, etc., flavors (contained decertified color FD & C green #1), candy (high acidity), a sugarless, presweetened drink (mislabeled, contained 24 to 30 percent dextrose), assorted frozen pastries (contamination, petroleum hydrocarbons), chocolate-flavored drink (contamination, mold and insect fragments), plain chocolate candies (M&M's, contamination, salmonella), peanut candy (contamination, Aflatoxin), kidney beans (insect-infested), evaporated milk (rusty, leaking and exploding cans).

9. Cyclamate, an artificial sweetener in diet soft drinks, is beginning to cause the FDA worry after years of assurances that it was safe. Tests have shown that it leads to chromosome breakage in rats; humans are just now being tested. Other less serious afflictions are known to result from not overly generous consumption of these artificially sweetened drinks. Like many other additives to food and drink, the FDA has permitted a sell-now, test-later posture by the companies. FDA has admitted that it has heavily relied on summary assurances by food companies about additives and has not checked in detail the raw test data. FDA now recommends that a child drink no more than two 10-ounce diet drinks containing cyclamates a day.

10. More and more additives are pouring into our foods. The growth of chemical additive use in foods is being stimulated by the fast rise of convenience foods—so-called. Joseph G. Jarrell of Hercules, a producer of additives, declared that convenience foods are more likely to require "special flavorings, flavor enhancers, color and other additives to make up for the partial loss of flavor, color, texture and other properties caused by

6

processing." The food industry is moving rapidly into developing food substitutes—simulated meats, simulated orange juice, simulated coffee—all of which will require a wide variety of food additives. The industry's attitude toward the consumer is epitomized by the following advertisement which appeared in the magazine *Food Technology*:

> With Western Dairy Products' new *tasteless* (their emphasis) sodium caseinate called SAVORTONE, you can now successfully use sodium caseinate as an emulsifier and binder for sausages, salad dressings, oil emulsions and egg substitutes. . . . You can use it wherever you like and never wonder for a minute what the consumers will think. They'll never know.

The industry's attitude toward its own responsibilities in testing the various effects, short and long range, of its additives is reflected in a tragically low research and testing budget, most of which goes to developing new convenience foods using more additives and not into testing the effects of these additives on the human organism. The level of technical competence in the food laboratories is low, as judged by the producers of food additives who sell to these companies.

One of this century's greatest geneticists, Dr. Hermann J. Muller, put this kind of problem in proper focus:

> What we are concerned with . . . is the possibility of [food additives, drugs, narcotics, antibiotics, pesticides, air pollutants and water pollutants] being mutagenetic, that is, producing mutations in the genetic material, and being thereby damaging not only to the directly exposed individuals but even to their descendants.
>
> It is now important to know what substances have such effects, how they may be recognized and dealt with, and in what ways the effects will be expressed in the exposed and subsequent generations.

•

Over the past several years, leading geneticists and biologists meeting at scientific symposia have expressed alarm at the lack of national policy and commitment to learning what the somatic and genetic impacts on people are from the thousands of chemicals, including food additives, that are confronting us. When scientists such as Dr. Rene Dubos, Dr. Richard A. Kimball (Oak Ridge Laboratory), Dr. Marvin Legator (FDA) and Dr. Matthew Meselson of Harvard show deep worry, it is time we all become concerned about the need for safety guidelines and monitoring procedures.

What permits the food industry to manipulate its products for sales-maximization (including preservation for nationwide distribution) and cost

7

reduction in ways that place the risk of harm on the consumer is the absence of comprehensive standards of evaluation and the difficulty of tracing the cause and effect of this silent type of violence to tissue and cell structure over long periods of time. Even in cases of food poisoning outbreaks, the search for the responsible agent is difficult because of the many variables or inputs. This very difficulty requires a strategy of prevention at the source, not a wait-and-see attitude resulting in disastrous consequences of the type foreshadowed in the thalidomide tragedy.

There is still a widespread impression that the government is watching out for the consumer ever since the pure food law was passed early in the century. The fact is that FDA neither has the resources, the regulatory dedication nor adequate authority to keep up with the proliferating abuses in the food industry. To conduct research and inspection, review test results and enforce the law, FDA was provided with $23,056,000 for 1969—less than one-fourth the cost of one atomic submarine. According to Dr. S. S. Epstein of the Children's Cancer Research Foundation (Boston), there are only three laboratories in this country specifically evaluating the potential health hazards of chemical mutagens—all small efforts. A 1967 Health, Education and Welfare report, "A Strategy for a Liveable Environment," bewailed the fact that unlike most government regulatory agencies, the FDA "does not have subpoena authority either to summon witnesses or to require firms to divulge pertinent records." Hundreds of firms, which the FDA is supposed to police, routinely refuse every year to allow the FDA to conduct inspections, refuse to furnish quality or quantity formulas or to permit the review of safety or health control records. In 1965, 216 firms refused to give the FDA permission to review shipping records. This prevents FDA from getting at hazardous situations early in their development. FDA has itself been unduly meek, failing to publicize its drastic needs for the protection of the consumer and reflecting a passive enforcement policy. Its educational function has lagged greatly, even with reports by the National Academy of Sciences and the AMA Council on Foods and Nutrition warning about the loss of essential nutrients in foods and the Report of the National Commission on Community Health Services warning about existing food hazards and inadequate public health controls that "have created the potential for massive nationwide outbreaks of food-borne illnesses."

The time has indeed come for the public to expect the food industry to shoulder the burden of proof of health and safety in its products, to end its secrecy and to extend its inspection, testing, research and packaging appeals.

Perhaps more than any other consumer issue, adequate coverage of the contamination and adulteration of the food supply—as the matter un-

8

folds in public forums—will be a major test of the ability of the press to withstand strong pressures against reporting and investigating in the public interest.

To Market We Go
...Like Lambs to the Slaughter

by ED DOWLING

Representing the canners, freezers, driers, millers, packagers and bottlers of edibles, the food lobby has spent close to three-quarters of a million dollars trying to prove that when products compete with each other, they get better and lead to lower food prices. The money wasn't spent on disinterested gamesmanship, but rather to reach a political goal: the suasion of a presidential commission.

In 1964, ranchers were complaining about a sudden plunge in the prices they were getting for beef. The drop was all the more disconcerting in that it was not reflected in retail beef prices, which continued high. Cattle-state congressmen agitated for an investigation and President Johnson asked Congress to set up a commission to study not just beef prices but the marketing of food in general.

No sooner had the National Commission on Food Marketing been set up than the food lobby, formally known as the Grocery Manufacturers of America, decided the moment had come to launch what food lobbyist Howard Chase has called "a monumental study of the way competition works" in the food industry. At the outset, the Grocery Manufacturers raised some $400,000 from lobby members and quickly hired the research firm of Arthur D. Little, Inc., along with a number of economic theoreticians, among them Professor Jesse W. Markham of Princeton, Dr. Charles C. Slater of Michigan State, and Professor Raymond Bauer of Harvard. Later, needing still more money to complete its *magnum opus*, the GMA put the touch on TV networks, women's magazines and members' advertising agencies—all of them dependent to some extent on food advertising—for about $225,000. The GMA was fearful the President's commission might uncover something in food marketing that, if made public, would be harmful to lobby members.

Perhaps another cause for concern was the presence on the commission of a few veteran champions of the consumer: Senator Warren Magnuson (D, Wash.); Representative Leonor K. Sullivan (D, Mo.); Elmer R. Kiehl, Dean of the College of Agriculture at the University of Missouri, and Senator Philip Hart (D, Mich.).

But if there were consumer protectionists on the commission, their presence was balanced by Republican Senators Thruston Morton of Kentucky and Roman Hruska of Nebraska, Democratic Representative Graham Purcell of Texas and William Batten, president of the J. C. Penney Co.

The political behavior of the remaining seven members of the commission seemed less easy to augur. If these seven commission members could be swayed, the Grocery Manufacturers of America might be able to transform the commission report into an endorsement of the status quo in the food industry.

For 18 months, from late 1964 through January 1966, the President's commission and the GMA pursued their studies independently of one another. The GMA had in mind a definite goal, which was to show how competition *works*. The Little firm went about making an elaborate mathematical model of the industry's structure, based on case histories of 20 products in five food categories. The case histories were supposed to demonstrate how well the products filled consumer needs. Meanwhile, according to lobbyist Chase, professors under contract were assigned "an examination of consumer sociology," the object of which was to show how the food industry develops new products only in response to "the genuine needs of the changing character of households in our society." (An example of such a product might be Kellogg's Toast'em Pop-Ups, "a tart with delicate crust and pure fruit filling" that one drops in a toaster to warm up. The need that one assumes is being filled by the Pop-Ups is a need for something to put in a toaster other than bread.)

In a scant year-and-a-half the GMA researchers managed to come up with quite a bit. One of their surveys produced information to show that "people like food advertising better than other advertising." As long as the consumer "likes" food advertising, the hypothesis might have gone, he has no right to gripe about paying for it.

Early in 1966, the GMA turned over its fat volume of researches to Dr. G. E. Brandow, executive director of the President's commission. The GMA expressed the hope that its studies would be of some assistance.

When the food commission's first, roughly assembled draft began to circulate on Capitol Hill in the spring of 1966, it appeared that the GMA's exercise had been academic, for indeed the draft report seemed to show no influence by the GMA's massive study. Letters of protest were written

11

by lobby officials deploring that the conclusions being drawn by the commission were contradictory to the conclusions drawn in the GMA/Little study. The GMA began circulating among its members lists of things to say to the press, to the public and to politicians in eventual congressional hearings, in refutation of the commission's conclusions.

During meetings of the commission to work up a final draft for the President, members wrangled over the proposed recommendations, and out of the disputes a clear minority emerged that would not endorse the proposals made to protect the consumer. In this minority were Senator Hruska, Senator Morton, Mr. Batten, and Representative Purcell. (The Texas Democrat made an eleventh-hour attempt to take the teeth out of the report by declaring that the commission had exceeded its mandate in choosing to term its recommendations, "conclusions," and therefore had stepped outside the law.) Later this minority was joined by Representative Catherine May (R, Wash.).

Weeks before the commission made public its report, the six dissenting members rushed out a minority report. The minority scored a public-relations coup: newspapers were running its version of the events long before any mention had been given to the report itself. In the text of the minority report—much of which was lifted verbatim from the GMA/Little study—and in the language of two other dissenting statements filed by minority members, the efforts of the GMA finally bore fruit.

Although the minority takes the majority's recommendations to task, the dissidents themselves make no proposals of any scope, other than watering down measures proposed to aid farmers.

•

In June 1966, the National Commission on Food Marketing presented to President Johnson the final draft of its report, "Food from Farmer to Consumer." As the food lobby had feared, the report damned food advertising as wasteful, urged that food companies be stopped from becoming near monopolies, and, perhaps most radically, proposed compulsory federal grade labeling for almost all foods as a way of counteracting the immense power of brands, and thus restoring price competition. Under the commission's grade labeling scheme, the Department of Agriculture would grade all but a few foods in which hierarchies of quality cannot be established.

Since World War II, retail chains have used federal grades in buying from wholesalers. This voluntary grade system was set up to simplify procurement of food for the armies. The shopper sometimes gets a glimpse of these grades on beef ("Choice" or "Prime") or on potatoes ("US No. 1"). But few chains print the grades on their store-brand processed foods, and brand manufacturers almost never do.

In the compulsory system, the top grade on every food would be "A,"

12

unlike the current system, based on century-old wholesaler usage, when top may be "Fancy" or "Extra Fancy" or "AA." ("US No. 1," for example, is second-grade potatoes; "US Fancy" is first.)

The measure would drag grades down from wholesale to retail and extend them to the gamut of processed foods, as is done in most Western countries.

Now why does such a simple proposal trouble the food processors? Because it would knock out most of their profits. Most of the big processors sell their products under two labels, their own and retailers' brands—the so-called "private labels." For example, in an A&P, a can of A&P's "private-label" peas may come from Del Monte and be part of the same batch as the peas under the Del Monte label nearby on the same shelf. Usually the private-label stuff sells for less than the national-brand stuff even when the product is identical. (The brand packer is forced to supply the retailer with the same product under the retailer's label because otherwise the retailer might refuse to carry the big-brand stuff.)

The private label, in such a case, is of the same grade and quality as the big brand. If both were stamped "Grade A," people would probably buy the stuff selling for less, and the price of the big brand would have to be lowered to stay in competition. The "Grade A" alone would knock the stuffing out of the advertising for the big brand. "The brands would be destroyed," said a lobbyist.

The brands may go, but the manufacturers would survive by turning out the same products and, unburdened by the heavy costs of advertising, selling them at competitive prices. Grading would bring down the prices of both the national brands and the private-label goods pegged to them.

Predictably, the minority fires on the grade labeling proposal, blasting it as a "sterile notion" that would "foster static uniformity and inhibit innovation." What they mean is that grading might knock out attempts to hoke up products by trivial differentiation, such as the six-sided French Fry ("Tasti-Fries") put out by General Foods.

Crying *"de gustibus non disputandum,"* the dissidents claim the grading won't work because grades are necessarily subjective. As evidence that compulsory grade labeling is impracticable, the minority cites the famous applesauce case, dear to the hearts of brand advertisers. In 1959 Cornell surveyed how a number of people liked applesauces graded by the Department of Agriculture. Most of them preferred Grade C to Grade A or B. This finding the minority interprets as *a priori* demonstration of the impossibility of fixing grades in accordance to popular tastes. But back in the forties, when Agriculture set up its applesauce grades, it sampled consumer preferences to ascertain what should be Grade A. And brand manufacturers themselves use similar tests in developing their recipes.

If grade labeling goes into effect, it won't have much bite if people aren't told about it. Unless grades are publicized by the government, it's unlikely

13

that brand advertisers will feature them in their ads. (Retail advertising is another matter. Some chains use the voluntary grades to spur sales of their private-label goods. In the summer of 1966 A&P, foreshadowing consumer awareness of grade labeling, ran an ad campaign stressing that its own brands are all "Grade A.")

To tell consumers about grades and about how to shop economically, the commission urges that the government set up a consumer agency as an executive department. Senator Hruska lambasted the consumer agency proposal, saying that "no consumer cataclysm demands the erection of another executive department to give home-to-market care to 200 million Americans."

But even with a system as rational as compulsory grading promises to be, and with a government department to make it effective, the charisma of the established brands will be difficult to dispel.

An advertising agency was dismayed to find in a survey that the average adult can remember only some 1,800 brand names "in unaided recall." Belief in brands has been promulgated as a kind of lay religion. A Boston housewife was reported by the *New York Times* as saying, "As prices go up, I don't go into cheaper brands, I just buy less."

Although the value of a brand exists only in the minds of consumers disposed to buy it, the brand-owners count on consumer credulity in brands as if it were money in the bank. Witness, for example, what was claimed in the Supreme Court case Borden *vs* FTC.

The case arose when two Ohio retail chains complained to the FTC that Borden refused to sell them private-label stuff. However, the dairy company chose to argue that although it supplies the same condensed milk for private labels as is sold under its own brand, the stuff carrying the Borden brand could legally go to retailers at a higher price because "consumer acceptance" of the Borden brand makes it worth more than physically identical milk under a private label. (In other words, the brand is worth whatever the consumer is willing to pay for it.)

The Supreme Court ruled in March 1966 that the Borden's brand adds no value to the condensed milk. (The decision caused ululation along Madison Avenue.) But if brands have no real economic worth, they continue to have an almost mystical significance for many. A beer baron once said of his brew, "The customer imbibes the image." And so it is with food.

Among those who find such images most palatable are the poor. A food industry spokesman remarked in an unguarded moment that "the poor put more faith in brands than does the rest of the population." Possibly food brands are status symbols for poor families who would be better off buying private labels.

In a decrepit neighborhood in Brooklyn the most popular item in a small mom and pop store was a national brand of dog food. Upon inquiry

14

it turned out that dog food was a mainstay of the local indigents. One wonders whether they would have bought the stuff had they not seen it continually advertised on their TV sets.

The National Commission on Food Marketing found that poor people pay more for food because they shop in mom and pop stores (supermarkets are fewer per population density in slums than in neighborhoods above the poverty line), and because they buy in small quantities, missing out on whatever savings are possible with the "large, economy" sizes.

Respectably enough, the food lobby suggests that the poor be taught how to buy economically. Such instruction has yet to appear in the ads.

•

In the spring of 1966, food prices for the first time in the US attained the distinction of leading the inflationary movement, in a reversal of what happens in classic inflationary patterns where food lags far to the rear. The food prices in the Consumer Price Index had climbed by 6.2 percent since spring of 1965, twice the rise of the overall CPI. As the general inflation has gone from trot to canter, food prices have begun to fall behind the classic indicia, but their upward spending movement is bound to continue; accelerated price rise is now built into the structure of food distribution, independent of flood, glut or famine.

The Food Marketing Commission points out that the excessive cost of advertising and other forms of promotion is the chief cause for the rise in food prices. In the past two decades the amount spent by food processors on advertising alone has quadrupled, while total food sales only doubled.

In 1966 the processors spent more than $2 billion on ads. Another billion was spent on merchandising, retail advertising, premiums and push-money (bribes to store clerks), and yet another billion on that part of packaging which should be accounted advertising. (Over $5 billion a year is spent on food packaging.)

Food advertising has swollen to such a volume that it has virtually eliminated price competition. It pushes retail prices continually upward. Instead of competing through price, food processors compete through advertising, and food retailers compete through showmanship, trading stamps, free parking and Muzak.

As if in echo of the Supreme Court's decision in the Borden case, the NCFM stresses that promotion adds nothing of value to the product. The consumer pays higher prices as a result of it, and yet gets nothing in return other than free TV shows and the like. The NCFM found that in 1964 the 22 largest food manufacturers spent an average of 16.3 percent of sales on advertising, with four of them—all breakfast cereal processors—spending around 20 percent. (On new products, promotion costs may *exceed* sales for the first year or so in the marketplace.)

15

Before the publication of the NCFM report, no government body had ever put the finger on advertising as a cause of jacked-up prices.

Advertisers talk about the need to spend enough to pitch their ads above the "noise level," the general din resulting from the heavy volume of all advertising. Whenever a new product is launched the noise level rises, and with it, prices, as competitors increase their spieling to shout down the newcomer. Up through the din the prices rise, behind a smokescreen of "specials," cents-off deals, and two-fers—momentary illusions all. (If a retailer loses a cent on a special, he recoups it by raising prices on non-specialed items.) Competing through advertising, and thus burdened with excessive promotion costs, manufacturers and retailers forswear undercutting their competitors.

As if in anticipation of the commission's charges, the Grocery Manufacturers had ready a theory elaborated by one of its consultants, Robert D. Buzzell of Harvard, attempting to show that in the "life cycle" of a product, advertising paves the way for price competition. According to Buzzell, whenever a heavily advertised new product succeeds in the marketplace, small processors and retail chains rush out imitations. By getting a free ride on the advertising already done by the innovator, the coattailers can sell their knock-offs for less, or so the theory goes. In practice, though, the coattailer usually pegs his price only a notch or two below what the original is fetching.

Professor Buzzell goes on to claim that promotion costs are not excessive in the long run, since once a new product succeeds, the heavy advertising expenditures of the introductory period ("Phase I") are trimmed and the price comes down proportionately ("Phase II").

The President's commission states flatly that Phase II is seldom reached. Price competition rarely comes into play and retail prices stay high. Whatever money has been spent promoting a new product has primed a pump for high markup and high profits throughout the product's lifetime.

Spinning wobbly in the wheelhouse of Buzzell's tinker-toy model is the battered old prayer wheel of admen, the claim that advertising is the *primum mobile* of the economy, that without the demand it stimulates mass production would be impossible, jobs fewer, unit costs higher and buying power lower.

There was a time when the price-lowering claim often held true. But that was earlier in the century, when advertising expenditures were a fraction of what they are today, and when the deluge of new products had not yet begun.

Yet, in the face of multiplying advertising expenditures, pro bono publicists continue to maintain that want creation is responsible for the vaunted American Standard of Living, forgetting that SOL is an expression of what wages and salaries will buy. In food, at least, the rising prices

16

resulting from hopped-up advertising tend to *depress* the SOL, since wages lag behind.

To bolster the standard-of-living claim, the Grocery Manufacturers Association boasts that Americans spend only 18 percent of their income for food, down from 23 percent in 1939. As General Foods president C. W. Cook preened in a statement to *Business Week* magazine, "We must be doing something right."

Although this statistic is indeed evidence of a rising standard of living, it is not, as the President's commission points out, "evidence of superior performance by the food industry." It's axiomatic in economics that the greater the prosperity, the less the share of income spent for food. In fact, it's surprising so much is still being spent on food. In some measure this may reflect substitution of steak for potatoes, but it may also reveal the ingenuity of food processors in wringing a number of wants out of a necessity (food).

Want creation is responsible for raising the prices of *all* food products. For example, a retail chain figures it can make more money on processed foods than it can on raw produce, so it limits the variety and quantity of raw stuff it will carry. As a result, the cost of the produce goes up.

No economist seriously opposes the fact that in today's economy wants are created by manufacturers who hope to satisfy the wants they create. Yet the food lobby piously claims that new products are "developed in response to consumer needs" as ascertained by market research. (In addition to sounding out markets for new products, it is also the task of "market research" to find ways to overcome any consumer resistance to a product a company has decided to launch.)

Profit possibilities are much higher on new products than they are on the old. Kellogg's Applejacks, a cinnamon-flavored corn cereal, sells for more than twice as much per ounce as Kellogg's Corn Flakes.

As a result of marketing new products—ever more fanciful, more highly processed, and more remote from basic food—profits of the large food companies have been rising through the past decade at the rate of 7.3 percent a year.

The market for staples, plain old peas and potatoes, is fairly saturated, growing only in relation to population gain. Companies could, of course, hang on in business by simply supplying the growing population. But to make the *big* money and pump up ever higher profits, they twist out new products.

In the food-processing industry, the failure rate for new products is half what it is in all other industries.

•

It's part of the contemporary American credo that big corporations are more efficient than small ones, that they can make and sell their products for less. However it may be with heavy industry, this assumption does not hold true in the food industry, where, as the commission report points out, there are no further economies of scale to be realized once a company has reached middling size. Yet processors in several food fields are well on the way to monopoly. Campbell Soups, with some 95 percent of the sales of prepared soups, is already there. Borden and National Dairy (Kraft) together sell most of the processed cheese; National Dairy and Corn Products together sell most of the salad dressing; four companies— Kellogg, General Foods, General Mills, Quaker Oats—sell over 85 percent of the breakfast cereals. Even in fields where monopoly is a distant prospect, as in "crackers and cookies" or in potato chips, the number of firms is shrinking as big corporations take over or merge with other food processors. Worse, some conglomerate firms—like National Dairy or General Foods—acquire quasi-monopolistic positions in a number of food fields.

The high costs of advertising and the problems of getting good distribution are central factors in the push toward merger. Small companies can't afford the costs of advertising on television and in other media, and without such coverage they find it difficult to persuade retailers to give them the distribution and favorable shelf space they need.

Big advertisers, on the other hand, get volume discounts from the media, and so spend less per pitch. The bigger the advertiser the more shelf space he can command from retailers. Once an advertiser has attained wide distribution he's fairly sure of shelf space for the products of any food company he happens to buy up—as long, of course, as he keeps up his advertising.

Thus, advertising helps put weight on those who are already fat, while trimming down the number of firms able to survive in competition. The fewer the survivors, the more remote any possibility of price competition.

For this reason, the National Commission on Food Marketing urges that a halt be called on mergers or acquisitions involving companies that are already "dominant" in a particular food field. "Dominance," by the commission's rule of thumb, exists if a company is one of four or fewer having half the sales in any one food field. (The criterion is clearly met in the breakfast cereals industry, where four companies do 85 percent of the business.)

To make it easier to determine who's dominant, the NCFM proposes that companies be required to report sales on each of their product lines. The minority insists that with modern accounting methods, any sort of product-by-product report on sales is impracticable. (It also protests that publication of such information would aid a company's competitors.)

To prevent oligopoly from becoming monopoly, the commission wants the Federal Trade Commission and the Department of Justice, in line with the Clayton Antitrust Act, to issue cease-and-desist orders on any mergers or acquisitions by dominant firms.

•

The Grocery Manufacturers declare that sales figures are no measure of monopoly, or oligopoly, or dominance. They argue that every food product competes against all other food products for the consumer's food dollar: *i.e.*, if one company sells 99 percent of the canned soup in the US it's still far from monopoly because the soup competes against every other existing foodstuff. The lobby calls this notion "substitutability." If a house-wife wants to serve ice cream for dessert and finds the price too high, she can, according to the theory of "substitutability," buy pie or cookies or cake, instead. (This is rather like saying that if you're in the market for a new car and find the prices too high, you can always go out and buy yourself a bicycle.)

As evidence that high concentration doesn't exist in the food industry, the minority report points to the fact that the four biggest companies (General Foods, National Dairy, Campbell's Soup and Corn Products) had altogether only 6.1 percent of the total food sales in the US in 1963. (Sales for these companies came to $4.7 billion, out of a total of $77 billion that year.)

After examining the figures on *processed* foods for that year, however, the President's commission pointed out that the four biggest companies did over one-third of the $11 billion business. (Even were this not so, the minority sidesteps the commission's point, which is to find out how much of the soup sold is Campbell's, how much of the processed cheese is National Dairy's [Kraft] and so on.)

There's a general anxiety throughout the country over what may be causing higher food prices and who's to blame for them. Milk distributors charged with collusion blame dairy farmers and drought. California fruit growers blame the jump in produce prices on the government's ban on *bracero* labor. Hugh Marius, assistant commissioner of markets in New York, attributes the higher food prices in slums to exploiters of the poor and ignorant. Some misguided urban politicians continue to point the finger at government farm policy and price supports.

Former Secretary of Agriculture Orville Freeman believes the fault for the rise in food prices lies not with the farmer but with the middleman. Mr. Freeman has read the commission's report. "Someone is profiteering along the line," he said, when he asked the Federal Trade Commission to look into the matter of food prices.

Such an investigation may seem superfluous in view of the voluminous evidence already assembled by the National Commission on Food Market-ing. However, the press has been curiously silent on the NCFM report, al-

19

though it has been accessible since July 1966. The *New York Times* and the *Washington Post* have duly noted the fact that the report was submitted to the President, but along with other media they've forborne to make public its contents, even when alarms over high food prices were page-one stories. Eleven volumes of evidence supporting the proposals in "Food from Farmer to Consumer" came off the presses of the US Government Printing Office. The findings were ignored by the news media, although the documents were in demand in advertising and food-marketing circles. Yet the commission's findings and the proposals based on them are an arsenal for any legislator looking for what Washington calls a "people issue," one that transcends party lines. But if a champion of the consumer comes forth to pick up the cudgels, he had better be stalwart. Opposition from the food lobby promises to be intense. Enlisted in the defense of the big food brands is the advertising business—in toto and wholeheartedly, along with its hand-maidens, the mass media.

Gamesmanship in the Supermarkets

by DAVID SANFORD

"It is one of the ironies of these confused times," began an incredulous *Washington Post* editorial, "that housewives are protesting against inflation by picketing and boycotting the chain supermarkets." What have the grocers done to make the housewives so angry? The answer the newspaper supplied was that the stores have done nothing to deserve what they've been getting from boycotters all over the country. Chains haven't been gouging the customers; their profits in 1965 were a mere 1.3 percent of sales. And as profits generally have declined since 1950, consumers have benefited from more services, more and bigger supermarkets, more convenience foods, more reasonable prices, more of everything. "If there is any fault to be found with supermarket operations," said the newspaper which in 1965 ran 4,004,090 lines of food advertising, "it is the concentration on trading stamps, games and other costly promotional gimmicks."

The Bureau of Labor Statistics says food prices rose 5.2 percent in 1966. The Consumer Price Index, which reflects fluctuations in food prices, is going up at the rate of 3.5 percent a year—twice the 1965 rate. Prices of bread and milk, reports the Federal Trade Commission, went up more than seven percent in 1966. In Denver, when the boycotts broke out in October 1966, bread cost 25.6 percent more than it had in 1965.

Supermarkets are the largest merchandising industry in the country, and the industry is not about to go under. Chain store profits based on sales are small, much less than the irate housewives get on their savings at the bank, but based on capital investment, supermarket profits are much higher—12.5 percent on the average. A&P has 4,625 stores; it is the second largest merchandiser in the US. Only Sears, Roebuck is larger. Safeway ranks third. Safeway's profits for its 2,080 stores in 1965 amounted

Reprinted by permission of the New Republic, © *1966, Harrison-Blaine of New Jersey, Inc.*

to 13.9 percent of capital investment. Standard Oil of New Jersey, by comparison, made only 11.9 percent. A&P's profits were 8.8 percent, higher than those of US Steel (7.6 percent).

The National Commission on Food Marketing's study of the retailing end of the food business, published in 1966, found that chain store profits were higher than those of other distribution industries for the period 1946–1962 (except for two years during the Korean War). At no point between 1945 and 1965 did the return on investment for food chains dip below the average for all industries.

Profits for supermarkets based on sales may be modest, but when the Grand Union Store in New York posted a sign in its front window saying "Grand Union Earns Less than 1½ Pennies on Each Dollar of Sales ... Not Much Is It?", it was not telling the whole story. It was not explaining how chain stores in Denver found it possible to slash food prices 10 to 15 percent under boycott pressure. It was not explaining how chains, despite their meager 1.3 percent profit, can afford to spend two to three percent of sales income on S&H and Top Value and King Korn and Plaid Stamps and the variety of games of chance they offer as a come-on to customers. According to the National Commission on Food Marketing, chains spend more on stamps, advertising and fun and games than they do on any other single item except employee salaries—more than for utilities, more than for store supplies, equipment depreciation and rental, interest, administration, and maintenance. They give more to the stamp companies than they keep for themselves in profits.

Esther Peterson, an assistant secretary of labor and Special Assistant to the President for Consumer Affairs, spent three hours in Denver in October 1966 talking to housewives and finding out as much as one can in three hours about the supermarket boycott. She immediately announced that she was asking the Federal Trade Commission to investigate the games and promotions which are rife in supermarkets in every state (except New Jersey and Wisconsin, where they are outlawed). Mrs. Peterson wanted to know how much games cost the consumer; how many winners there are; and if games are rigged. The FTC, which had been nosing around the trading stamp business and looking into rising bread and milk prices for Agriculture Secretary Freeman, quickly agreed that the games need study.

Anyone who browses around grocery stores is familiar with the gamesmanship that is going on (Bonus Bingo, Win at the Races, Play Happy Landing, Every Card's a Winner, Three of a Kind, Color Bingo, Harness Racing Sweepstakes, Fashion Game, Win-A-Check, Heads You Win and Tails You Win, Shower of Diamonds, and on and on). It is known, even without an FTC investigation, that the games are expensive.

Supermarket games come and go in two-year cycles. An estimated 200 firms churn out the imaginative money-makers, but about six companies have most of the game trade to themselves. Suppliers sell a game and its attendant paraphernalia to a store and control the number of winners (you can't have too many of the thousand-dollar kind). The games run for a few weeks and if they prove popular, that is, if they raise profits, they are continued or replaced with new, fresher games. Safeway's Bonus Bingo, for example, runs 13 weeks. (Customers receive a bingo book when they come into the store; each time they return they get a slip of paper with a number-letter combination corresponding to one of the squares on the bingo grids.) If Bonus Bingo is successful in a region, then another 13 weeks of the games are bought from the supplier, the W. J. Jeffrey Company of New York. John McDonald, public relations manager for Safeway Stores, Inc., says that 60 percent of his chain's stores have played bingo. In the first nine months of 1966 sales rose 14 percent, earnings 35 percent.

Stamps have become less popular because now that many stores offer them they don't pump up volume as they did. And if volume doesn't increase significantly, the stamps are a drag on profits as well as an expense to shoppers. According to the Food Commission, "there is a general belief among store executives . . . that trading stamps have been a principal cause" of higher costs and lower profits during the last ten years. And the cost has been passed on to the consumer. *Progressive Grocer*, a trade publication, is quoted by the Food Commission: "In most stores the cost of stamps (two to three percent of sales) has been added to retail prices."

•

The candor of the trade press makes it a good source of information about what motivates stores to choose certain sales promotions. "The third quarter in the retail food business is usually a low-volume one," revealed Andy Parker of Wilt's Food Centers, Elkhart, Indiana, in one journal, "and I have seen sales drop as much as 20 percent during this period." To avert the slump his store introduced a game called "WOW" which lifted third-quarter sales for 1965 by 25 percent. The explanation Mr. Parker gave his customers in newspaper ads the store ran was slightly different: "Our first half of 1965 was by far the most successful and rewarding in many years, and we want to share our success with you. . . ."

The magazine *Chain Store Age* ran an interesting article in 1966 on the big game business (subtitled, "More chains than ever are using the 'something for nothing' lure to cut a larger slice from the '66 sales pie.") The magazine quoted Robert Magowan, president of Safeway, as saying that with the added volume from Bonus Bingo "we can't help but show a big profit this year." The chains are "playing more games than ever before," says the magazine, "and making more money." *More money than ever before?*

Esther Peterson recommended certain things which housewives can do to hold down their food bills, such as sticking to a shopping list and not picking up unneeded items on impulse. Congress had a chance in 1966

23

to aid shoppers to make wise decisions and keep from being fooled by deceptive package weights and sizes. But although industry lobbyists managed to convince Senator Philip Hart (D, Mich.), the sponsor of the truth-in-packaging bill, that they had let him have a strong bill, the legislation Congress finally passed is not much help to shoppers. Under the bill the federal government can ask packagers to work out voluntary standard weights and measures. But if they don't comply, the Secretary of Commerce has to go back to Congress for authority to require standards. This is something Congress should have enacted. Hart said he thought "we'll get more done this way in two years than we would in ten" under the mandatory Senate bill that was rejected. That gave the lobbyists quite a laugh. "As far as the food business is concerned," said Harry F. Schroeder, vice president for packaging of the National Biscuit Company to the *New York Times*, "I think they have met practically all our objections."

The food industry has learned how to indulge its critics. The largely successful Denver boycott seems to have been a spontaneous "middle-class insurgency" of a kind no one remembers happening before. It was not politically inspired (despite Barry Goldwater's suggestion that the boycotts were run by Lyndon Johnson leftists trying to divert attention from government spending by making scapegoats of the businessmen). In other places where boycotts have been organized, notably Washington, D.C., they have centered around the complaints of residents of core city ghettos who, according to the Food Commission report and the shoppers themselves, often have to pay more than suburbanites do and for lower-quality food. The first meeting held to form the Washington Area Shoppers for Lower Prices was an unusual mix of ghetto residents and ladies from the upper middle-class Maryland suburbs of Bethesda and Chevy Chase, many of whom had never before been allied in activist organizations with their ghetto counterparts. The Washington boycotters organized buying clubs, with technical advice from the United Planning Organization (Washington's poverty war), to purchase food at wholesale prices. Washington and Denver have two of the highest rates of chain-store concentration in the country. Four chains in Denver account for more than 70 percent of food sales; in Washington the top four stores do 67 percent of the business. Where there is such monopoly control, a few chains have the power to raise (or cut) prices. Peter Barash, staff chief of Representative Benjamin Rosenthal's special inquiry on consumer representation in the federal government, was told by store executives in Denver that by tightening up on some of their administrative costs, by eliminating games, stamps, carry-out and other non-essential services, and by being more hard-nosed about cashing checks, they could cut prices 10 to 15 percent. Some officials, he said, were optimistic that increased volume made possible by lower prices might make up losses from price cuts. Stores which caved in to the housewives in Denver are attracting more customers, and individual customers are buying more items than before the boycotts.

For the first time, Mr. Barash believes, a genuine consumer constituency is forming—groups of people who study prices and are no longer willing to pay automatically whatever is asked. "A loud, organized, grass-roots consumer voice is being heard," he said, "and no one—in industry or government—can ignore it." Barash thinks this constituency will now begin to question and refuse to pay high prices for clothing, furniture, and other goods.

Segregated Food at the Supermarket

by JAMES RIDGEWAY

"What people spend their money on are the psychological differences, brand images permitting them to express their individuality," says Dr. Ernest Dichter, the well-known motivational expert. "When the Grand Union Markets labeled their peaches as 'gorgeous' and the co-ops called theirs 'reasonably good,' the housewife chose those sold by Grand Union. She had been trained by several decades to apply the same psychological disbelief to both statements. In other words, she felt that the Grand Union peaches were probably fairly good and that the peaches sold in the co-op stores were probably poor. Our recommendation to the co-op stores was to bring their labeling into line with the prevailing procedure of dramatization in order to meet the claims of the competition. . . ."

When asked by a member of the Senate antitrust and monopoly sub-committee, to whom Dr. Dichter was explaining these modern marketing methods, what he thought was the more accurate description of the peaches, he said, "reasonably good." He agreed that some people might regard as dishonest the practice of calling reasonably good peaches gorgeous, but said he preferred to view such labeling as "dramatizing honesty." Others might call it debasing the language.

The packaging techniques that Dr. Dichter extols make picking among 8,000 items in a supermarket tricky going. College-educated women recruited by a California survey were given $10 each and told to select from 14 basic packaged commodities on the basis of the largest quantity for the least price. The women failed to get most for the least in about half the purchases and took up to one hour to do the shopping.

Shopping is an inconvenience to many, but it is a nightmare for a poor person who must make a little money go a long way, while weaving through

Reprinted by permission of the New Republic, © *1964, Harrison-Blaine of New Jersey, Inc.*

the dreamed-up package slogans and occasionally contending with a retailer trying to palm off old eggs or elderly butter. This is a subject that bothers Mrs. Esther Peterson, President Johnson's adviser on consumer affairs. My friends who live in bum sections of town complain bitterly about the supermarkets. And so one Saturday I set off with half a dozen other people to make an informal survey of a large Washington supermarket chain's operations. I wanted to see whether the same quality goods were stocked in both the well-to-do and poor sections of the city, and whether, as I had heard, the poor pay more for inferior food.

In brief, the findings were these: Large stores with big turnovers in poor neighborhoods stocked a variety and quality of food comparable to that in stores in the most elegant neighborhoods. But in the numerous small stores of the chain, located in run-down sections of the city, whether white or Negro, the quality of perishable items diminished. The least expensive brands of some packaged goods were likely to be missing; in several instances, prices actually were higher.

Small branches of supermarkets are important in Washington as in other cities, for very often they are the only stores in a neighborhood. Where there are small corner groceries, the supermarket usually competes favorably. And it must be said that while some leave much to be desired, they are generally more pleasant places to shop than the small groceries.

In one cluttered little supermarket located in a down-at-the-heels section of northeast Washington, a good many food items (dried beans, sugar, lard, various vegetables, ice cream) carried no price tag. Nor did any baby food. I wanted to buy a two-pound box of granulated sugar. It was unmarked. The manager, who knew I was taking a survey, said it cost 27 cents. The checker charged 30 cents. One margarine brand was marked two packets for 55 cents. But as I was writing this down, the manager rushed up and said the price was wrong, it actually was selling for 53 cents, he hadn't had time to remark the packets. In other larger stores of this same chain, this brand of margarine all was marked two for 53 cents. In appearance the meat was not comparable with that displayed in fashionable Georgetown or downtown sections of the city. The beef was brown at the edges. Packages of jaded-looking hamburger were priced at 59 cents a pound—10 cents more than hamburger in a large downtown store of the same chain. And the latter was red and fresh-looking.

In checking meat prices in three markets of the same chain in this section of the city, one woman recently discovered she could buy ground chuck for 65 cents a pound in two small stores in Negro neighborhoods. The same meat sold for 55 cents a pound at a new large store in a white middle-class area.

In the big stores of this chain attractively displayed fresh packages of beef all bore little stickers stating they were US Department of Agriculture "choice." (Choice is a government grade, second to prime, which is the

27

top.) The beef in poorer sections carried no such labels, although on many cuts the prices were the same. This led one woman to believe she was paying a high price for inferior meat. She called the headquarters of the chain, and there was assured that nothing but choice or prime cuts were stocked in all stores, and that the manager of her store merely had run out of his little "choice" stickers. This was news to the woman, who had shopped in the store for a year and never once remembered seeing any sticker on any piece of meat. The mystery of the stickers remains unsolved, as does the mystery of where the old-looking meat sold in the small stores comes from. Perhaps these stores have a small turnover and it simply has sat there for a long time. Some Negroes, who refuse to buy it, say it really is left over, shipped from chic stores which must stock fresh to meet the demands of well-heeled customers. Although this is a widespread suspicion, there is no proof for it.

There was a significant difference in the variety and quality of fresh fruits and vegetables between stores in middle-class neighborhoods and those in the poorer sections of the city. Prices were usually the same. But in a store in a poor neighborhood, the lettuce would be wilted, the apples bruised, the green peppers shriveled. When prices differed, they were higher in poor neighborhoods. For instance, apples sold at 19 cents a pound in a large store in a good neighborhood; they cost 25 cents a pound in a small store in a run-down section.

Like most other cities, Washington doesn't require dairy products to be marked with a date after which they are considered bad and can't be sold. Nonetheless, the chain I checked marks its products with a code so it can keep track of them. Most of the milk in all the stores was well within the expiration date, though in one unpleasant small store in a Negro neighborhood milk sat in the display case that was six days beyond the expiration date set by the company. Eggs were a couple of days beyond their expiration date, and packages of margarine five months old were on display.

In a number of stores in poor neighborhoods, the cheapest items were not in stock. They would be out of the least expensive kind of butter, grape jelly, flavored gelatin and catsup. Many of the packaged goods were stocked in the smallest sizes, but this is probably because most of the people who shop there do not have the money to buy the large size, which over the long run would be cheaper.

Senator Hart's packaging legislation isn't going to solve the difficulties in these poor neighborhoods. The National Commission on Food Marketing, which was established to look into some of these chain store operations, may shed a little light on retail pricing practices, although its primary purpose seems to be to find out why farmers aren't getting more for their goods. In Washington, the poverty program may experiment with setting up complaint centers in poor neighborhoods where people can come when they feel they have had unfair treatment. But since one of the troubles in

28

chain stores in poor neighborhoods is that customers aren't willing to stand up to the store managers, it might be useful to put home economists in these stores to help people on tight budgets buy wisely and perhaps in the process get them to vary their diets. A home economist, familiar with the buying habits of the neighborhood, could well advise the store manager on his stocking procedures—it would mean better business for him— and could tartly remind him about the quality of meat, fruits and vegetables when need be.

Many of the people in these neighborhoods, however, live hand to mouth, purchasing tiny containers of food from corner grocery stores where they can get a little credit. The Washington poverty people are keen to get going credit unions so that low-income families can get enough money to shop more economically. But unless supermarkets in some of these areas change their policies, it might be best to bypass them altogether. Family groups could buy more cheaply and get better food by going directly to the wholesaler—or they could be taken free in buses to more expensive neighborhoods, to buy cheaply.

Studies in the Grocery

by JAMES RIDGEWAY

The June 1966 report on food pricing by the Bureau of Labor Statistics confirms what is widely known: Poor city people pay more for food because they often have no choice but to shop in small corner groceries which stock inferior merchandise at higher prices. They would be better off shopping in large supermarkets where there is a variety of quality goods at lower prices, but there are few supermarkets in the slums.

This BLS study coincides with an effort by Mrs. Esther Peterson, President Johnson's advisor on consumer affairs, to focus public attention on the high prices paid by the poor. When she took this inequity up in 1964, there was little interest in consumer problems at the White House. (Since then, consumer legislation has come to be viewed as a relatively inexpensive way, during an expensive war, of making hay before an election.) The poverty program was still trying to get on its feet and was no help. Congressional committees expressed no curiosity. Left with little political room to turn around in, Mrs. Peterson finally persuaded the National Commission on Food Marketing to hire the BLS to make a study, which at least got the matter out into the open.

The BLS performed this research in a most unusual way. One of the side objects of the study was to see whether food stores within a chain charged more in poor sections than in the better-off neighborhoods. Before making its survey the BLS got in touch with the headquarters of the various chains and asked their cooperation. The supermarket people were told which cities were to be surveyed and were given the dates of a two-week period during which the study would be done. The BLS arranged with the chains for its representatives to call at the individual stores at a time

Reprinted by permission of the New Republic, © *1966, Harrison-Blaine of New Jersey, Inc.*

when the managers would be free to show them around. While the Bureau alerted chain stores to what it intended to do, it did not so inform the independent stores. The BLS people walked in on them and noted prices. From the start, the research was loaded in favor of the chains.

Thus it is not surprising the BLS found no significant price differences among chain stores located in poor- and upper-income areas. What differences they did find were accounted for by the store managers, who said they had not had time to put up new price lists sent from headquarters.

The BLS conclusions are basically the same as those of the United Planning Organization, the Washington, D.C., poverty program. It made a similar price survey in district stores last fall. The UPO did not tell the chain stores in advance what it was up to, but on entering the stores to record prices the buyers presented the managers with letters of introduction from the UPO and the National Association of Food Chains, which helped sponsor the project.

In 1964, a few friends and I made a brief, unscientific survey of prices in some Safeway stores in Washington, D.C. Safeway is the largest chain in the city. Pat generalizations were hard to make, but the meat and vegetables looked shoddier in small stores of the chain in poor sections, the prices were sometimes higher than in Safeways in well-to-do sections, and there was less variety. But there was no doubt then that Safeway was a much better bet than the little mom and pop corner grocery stores. Since then Safeway has opened some new and larger stores in poor sections of the city; officials at the UPO feel that as a result of their inquiries on prices, the chain seems to have taken an added interest in keeping stores in the slums up to snuff.

A group connected with the poverty program and the civil rights movement in Washington has been hard after the Greenbelt Consumer Services, Inc., the biggest co-op of its kind, to open up some stores in the slums. (The Greenbelt co-op is located in the Washington suburbs.) They made their own quick survey which showed that a list of six small items could be bought at the co-op for 89 cents; at a chain store in the District for $1.06 and at a corner mom and pop for $1.58. However, the insurgent group who wanted the co-op in the District was badly beaten in a campaign for election of co-op directors. It will take some doing to woo the co-op from its safe, profitable suburban business into risking it in the slums.

People in the slums, of course, pay more for other things besides food. Mr. David Caplovitz in his book, *The Poor Pay More*, runs through a list of such items and describes merchandising practices. In New York City a citizens' group led by William Haddad found that consumers in low-income Negro areas paid more for medicines than those living in upper-income white sections. The Office of Economic Opportunity hired the BLS to make a survey of what prices poor people pay for clothing and household appliances.

31

While Washington has been intrigued since 1963 with the idea that the "poor pay more," it has produced little more than studies. Through its community action programs, the Office of Economic Opportunity is in a position to bring down materially the price of food and other goods in the slums. It can fund credit unions which provide cheap loans; start co-ops to stock and to sell products at lower prices. It can organize buying clubs where people on a block join together to purchase at wholesale markets. It can hire buses to transport people to good supermarkets. But the OEO moves at a snail's pace. In the two years after OEO began operations it funded but nine city co-ops and 25 credit unions. Out of 892 community action programs, there were but 30 buying clubs. The OEO goes in more for consumer education programs, of which there were 75 in 1966. Home economists and other specialists tell women on welfare how to pick out a good cut of meat or the bargain in a pound of apples. Sometimes they take an experimental buying trip. Sometimes they bake a cake. In this way the women on welfare learn how to pretend they are middle-class housewives —but they're not middle-class housewives; they have hardly any money, and the price of food is not coming down.

Ghetto Merchants:
A Study in Deception

by PHILIP G. SCHRAG

In 1968 the Federal Trade Commission released the results of a two-year study of deception by merchants selling to poor consumers in the District of Columbia. The Commission documented the expected: that unfair trade practices aimed at low-income groups are common and increasing. The two most prevalent abuses are false statements about merchandise and "bait and switch" advertising, in which the consumer is lured by an advertised bargain, then told that that product is unavailable or undesirable and switched to a higher priced item.

The Commission's study focused on the District, but it concluded that there was no reason to believe Washington unique among large American cities.

These findings are not new. They have been reported often, from David Caplovitz's pioneering study, *The Poor Pay More*, to the Kerner Report. But for the first time, government is becoming interested in the problem of consumers' remedies as well as consumers' rights. This approach may be more productive than past attempts to outlaw unfair selling techniques.

Fraud, after all, has been against the law for hundreds of years. The problem is enforcement. Nearly every page of the Commission's report reveals hand-wringing over the practical difficulty of compelling compliance. In the first place, many low-income consumers are unaware when they have been cheated. Of those who want to complain, two-thirds have no idea where to go. Others are afraid to complain, or do not want to become involved. The Commission "reached out" for complaints by sending lawyers to block meetings and publicizing a "hot line" for consumer gripes. But its staff is small, and it could only spare five lawyers to work on all the phases of the DC project. Because the investigation of each complaint consumes so much staff time, the Commission could not possibly respond to the needs of poor consumers across the country.

Even after the Commission staff accumulated the evidence to prove its cases, the work was far from over. Its cease-and-desist orders demanded written assurances of compliance from the merchants involved, but the Commission did not have the manpower to investigate whether the stores were indeed refraining from using misleading sales talk (and half of the merchants cited failed to submit acceptable written reports). The Commission estimated that securing compliance with its orders required "almost the same type of intensive investigatory work which was involved in uncovering and proving the violation in the first place." And even when this enforcement procedure works, the Commission only prevents future violations; it has no power to obtain compensation for the victims.

The FTC's frustrations are typical of governmental agencies charged with protecting consumers. Each case requires days or weeks of investigation to amass enough evidence to prove a violation; yet state consumer protection bureaus have few lawyers and fewer investigators. The volume of complaints—which is only the top of an iceberg of abusive practices—is so staggering that the agencies can do little more than tabulate grievances and beg legislatures for more staff and broader jurisdiction. In New York, for example, the Consumer Frauds Bureau of the Attorney General's Office receives 15,000 complaints a year, but in five years the Bureau went to court only six times to attack false advertisements. New York's Attorney General, like the FTC, has no power to obtain restitution for injured buyers. In one recent case, the Bureau put out of business a fraudulent food plan and freezer sales operation, but could do nothing about the $800,000 in time contracts that the seller had sold to a finance company, which is now enforcing them against thousands of defrauded consumers.

Normally, in the commercial milieu, individual rights are secured and enforced by those most directly affected, through individual litigation or the threat of it—by suits for damages, or defenses asserted in court to creditors' suits for payments due and owing. But consumers, particularly low-income consumers, are unlikely to go to court. Not only are they unaware that they have legal rights (which they do, despite the commercial law's severe slant in favor of sellers and creditors) but they are effectively precluded from asserting them because the cost of litigation is almost always greater than the claims consumers assert. No attorney can afford to spend two days investigating the operations of a store, two days examining witnesses such as salesmen and other buyers, and a day in court, over a $150 claim. His bill would necessarily be many times the client's recovery. Only a few middle-class consumers who go to court "for the principle of the thing" can be so extravagant.

The fact that legal aid societies and OEO neighborhood legal offices serve poor clients without charge does not change this; their attorneys, like those in the state agencies, can barely keep up with the tremendous volume of daily complaints. Most of them are forced, out of practical necessity, to make compromise settlements before trial in nearly every case, even when buyers have complete defenses to creditors' suits. In order to go to trial, anti-poverty agencies would require staffs and budgets many times larger than Congress or state legislatures are willing to provide.

Two reforms—which could be effected by either the courts or the legislatures (including Congress, acting through its commerce jurisdiction)—might give the consumer practical redress. One would be to provide that consumers who prevail in court are entitled to collect from merchants and credit companies all of the reasonable attorneys' fees expended in the litigation. A lawyer who felt sure of his case could spend whatever was necessary to prove it, and neither he nor his client would have to take a net loss. Legal aid societies could handle such cases in bulk and recover enough fees to avoid large budget deficits from consumer cases. This approach has worked successfully in the past: the public accommodations and fair employment sections of the Civil Rights Act of 1964 provide counsel fees to the prevailing party, and Congress also grafted a counsel fee provision onto the 1968 Fair Housing Act (the Senate debate even reveals a deliberate intention to permit legal aid societies to recover their expenses from discriminating owners or brokers).

A second reform would turn finance companies from friends of the merchants into allies of the consumers and would make them the policemen of the ghetto markets. Under the law in most states (Massachusetts, Vermont and California are the exceptions), consumer installment contracts may bind the buyer to waive his legal rights if the contract is sold to a credit company. Buyers neither read nor understand this clause, but it is the primary device for robbing them of their legal rights. If Greedy Merchant gets Ernest Black to sign such a contract for a "new color television," and the set turns out to be an old, battered black and white instrument, or *even if Merchant never delivers any set at all*, Merchant can sell Black's contract to Ghetto Finance, Inc., for a lump sum, and Black is out of luck. Ghetto has a right to payment in full from Black, and Black has no right to tell a court that he's been robbed. Of course, after paying Ghetto, Black can sue Merchant, but first he has to find a lawyer willing to sue on a small claim, and then he has to find Merchant, who is likely, after the year or so that has passed since the sale took place, to be operating as a different corporate entity or in a different city.

This 18th century doctrine of the "quasi-negotiability" of contracts has no place in the modern law of consumer sales, and should be done away with in the 47 states and the District that retain it. If the finance companies knew that defenses which might be raised against merchants could also be raised against them, they would insist that dealers from which they buy contracts deal fairly with the public. They would enforce the law in this industry because their continued profits would depend upon buying only contracts which would stand up in court, and they would stop doing business with dealers who sold them what is known in the trade as "garbage paper."

There is a potential army of private lawyers who could handle the volume of consumer cases if it became profitable for them to do so, and there are massive credit institutions which could impose a code of ethics and fair play on ghetto merchants if the profit motive required it. It may not be necessary to have more and bigger government agencies to protect the low-income consumer. With a few adjustments in legal doctrine, the free enterprise system could become a major force for dealing with some of its worst abuses.

Something Fishy

by RALPH NADER

During the very disturbing disclosures of conditions in the meat industry that led to the 1967 meat inspection act, some consumers began to take refuge in eating more fish. This shift was motivated more by lack of confidence in meat than by any positive attraction for fish. Over the past two decades, fish sales have not increased, in contrast to the steady rise in meat and poultry sales. Per capita consumption of fish and fishery products in this country amounts to an insignificant 11 lbs. a year—the same as 20 years ago. (Americans consume an average of 175 lbs. of meat and meat products a year.)

What accounts for this resistance to fish? Certainly, most seafood is less expensive than comparable meat servings. Excellence of flavor and texture has made seafood a staple for the most fastidious culinary preparations. Perhaps, one kind of answer can be seen in a 1963 survey by Consumers Union that concluded: "The general quality level of all frozen fishery products tested by CU in the past few years can only be described as dismal."

Consumers Union has made a habit of testing fishery products. Here is part of the tally: 98 samples of 120 samples of frozen raw breaded shrimp tested contained coagulase positive staphylococci (1961); 55 samples of 120 samples of cod, haddock and ocean perch fillets judged substandard quality (1963); 85 percent of 646 cans of salmon (51 brands) showed a tendency toward mushiness or discoloration (1966); 17 samples of 18 frozen salmon steaks (3 brands) were so rancid that no cooking method could disguise the bad flavor (1966).

The Bureau of Commercial Fisheries of the Department of Interior has made similar tests with disappointing findings.

The principal factors contributing to such low quality in fishery products range from the boat to the marketplace. Many ships are old and grossly unsanitary. But even the more modern portions of the domestic fishing fleet have yet to surmount the long time that elapses between the fish catch and its processing. Dead fish often rest 5 to 14 days in the hold pens with ice piled on top of them. The unique odors attendant upon decomposition aboard ship proliferate here. Deficient temperature control is the most serious problem. Storage at temperatures above the level of 0°F brings deteriorating havoc on this highly perishable commodity.

Sloppy processing practices, such as defective seams in many Alaskan salmon cans last year, can be highly dangerous. The Food and Drug Administration tested more than two million cases of that salmon to locate the defectively sealed cans.

FDA surveys of fish processing plants have revealed such situations as the following:

> The fish were hung on wooden sticks for the processing operation. The sticks and nails were encrusted with rotten fish scales and particles from previous batches. Debris from previous batches of fish was trapped in the nicked table top since no attempt was made to clean and sanitize the table between operations. These residues served to contaminate all batches of fish that passed over the table. No attempt was made to clean the rusty wire dip nets that were used to remove the fish from the thawing and brining casks. The nets had buildups of bits of rotten fish flesh and entrails.... A rusty perforated metal scoop was generally used to mix the brine solutions. In one instance an employee picked a stick off the floor and used it to mix the brine.... After smoking, the fish were allowed to stand at room temperature, for approximately 4½ hours before they were placed in a refrigerator.

The fish industry is very sensitive about such disclosures. The foregoing example was contained in an address by W. B. Rankin, Deputy Commissioner of FDA. He never had the opportunity to deliver his speech, however, because his industry hosts decided to cancel his appearance upon learning that he was planning to be mildly critical.

The commercial fishing industry has had less success in keeping non-public the outbreaks of illness and disease resulting from contaminated fish and shellfish. Botulism, salmonella, shigellosis and infectious hepatitis outbreaks have taken lives, made many people ill and contributed considerably to depressing the sales of fish products. In 1963, nine people died from botulism poisoning present in canned tuna. Tuna sales suffered for some months thereafter. During the 1966 Memorial Day weekend, nearly 400 cases of salmonella poisoning in New York City were traced to smoked fish coming out of filthy plants.

Very frequently, the difficulty of turning evidence into proof to show a direct link between seafood and disease or illness has kept down the toll collected by FDA. Hepatitis is such a case. The incidence of that disease is increasing sharply. Unremitting is the outpouring of industrial and domestic sewage on or near shellfish (oysters, clams and mussels) growing waters. Shellfish are often eaten raw or are only partially cooked. Other foods are eaten by the afflicted at the same time, to complicate further causal discovery. Few resources and manpower are expended to find the connections, except for significant outbreaks. The proper approach, therefore, must be one of prevention before larger disasters occur.

•

Prevention requires law—which at present is both inadequate and poorly administered. There are three main types of inspection. The FDA has a mandatory inspection program for domestically produced fishery products marketed in interstate commerce. Actually, the 2,200 fish processing plants in the US are inspected an average of less than once a year. By comparison, federally inspected meat plants have continuous inspection by "resident" inspectors. Virtually no fishing vessels are inspected. A huge gap involves imported fishery products, which totalled 1.4 billion pounds or 54 percent of total US human consumption in 1967. The FDA does not, except on rare occasions, inspect imports. And foreign producing vessels and processing plants—116 countries export fishery products to the US—are totally beyond scrutiny.

The second inspection system is a voluntary one offered by the Bureau of Commercial Fisheries, whose primary purpose is to promote the sale of fishery products. Firms which subscribe to this voluntary inspection pay the inspectors' fees. Only 40 processing plants have availed themselves of this inspection-plus-certification program. The Bureau has no condemnation authority, so products denied certification may still reach consumers.

Finally, the states have their nominal authority under general food inspection laws. Only Maine and California have specific programs of fish inspection, which concentrate on canneries. A number of states cooperate with the US Public Health Service in skillful water surveillance. There is even less activity on the state level for fish inspection than for meat inspection.

The inadequacy of legal controls over fishery product wholesomeness was brought out at a Senate Commerce Committee hearing in July 1967. The FDA testified on the pending legislation, saying that no additional authority was needed. All the industry trade organizations did the same. Yet under questioning by Senator Philip A. Hart (D, Mich.), and staff counsel William Meserve, the FDA spokesman, Kenneth Kirk, repeatedly acknowledged area after area where the Agency was doing little or nothing.

The FDA's concern was over the prospect of Senator Hart's bill giving more authority to the Bureau of Commercial Fisheries at FDA's expense. The bill, S. 1472, is eminently weak. It provides for the Secretary of the Interior to conduct a survey of the domestic fishery industry. Three years after enactment, the Secretary would issue "adequate sanitary standards and practices" which would not take effect for another three years. Vessels under 5 tons (comprising 25 percent of the domestic fish catch) would be exempted, along with wholesale establishments selling fish to retail customers. Willful violation of the standards, even if people die as a result, incurs no criminal penalties. Seizure of any products violating such standards is not even authorized.

Two witnesses came before the Senate committee and talked directly to the problems. John Nickerson of the Massachusetts Institute of Technology said that the "fishing industry has long been in need of some kind of continuous or semicontinuous supervision. . . ." He cited one fish plant operator who declared that "he could make just as much money selling bad fish as he could selling good fish." Some processors have this same attitude, Professor Nickerson added. He discounted any further reliance on industry voluntarily controlling its abuses and rejected the idea that an elaborate study is needed to find out what needs to be done.

It remained for a prosperous veteran of the Alaskan fishing industry, Lowell Wakefield, to etch the most discomforting truth. "Frankly," he stated,

> the segments of the industry that I have been familiar with need cleaning up very, very badly. The fishy stench that is characteristic of seafoods in the minds of so many customers just should not exist at all. There is no more excuse for an off-flavor or an off-odor in fish than there is in meat or poultry. The existence of such things results simply from low-quality standards and improper practices that are characteristic of much of the fishing industry.

In calling for "some harsh measures" and criminal penalties, Mr. Wakefield noted that wide differences in the quality of seafood products presented to the housewife in supermarkets each day "make shopping for seafood akin to playing a slot machine."

Whatever legislation is enacted, the authority should not go to the industry-indentured Bureau of Commercial Fisheries. BCF is a promotion agency. To give it a safety role would be too much of a strain. The Bureau has been grading samples of frozen fish bought at retail stores, at the request of a trade group, the National Fisheries Institute. In one typical test, 55 percent of the breaded fish portions were so substandard that they could not even be graded. BCF has refused to make public the specific brand information for consumers, saying that the surveys were "specifically designed to assist the fish processing industry." So much for the housewife. Presumably she is left with the one rule of thumb: "If it smells strongly fishy, don't bite."

40

We're Still in the Jungle

by RALPH NADER

Before he was elected to the House of Representatives in 1958, farmer Neal Smith (D, Iowa) noticed something curious about the numerous live-stock sales he attended. The same buyers seemed to be purchasing all the diseased, sick and maimed cattle and hogs. The destination of this miserable cargo was slaughterhouses not subject to federal inspection because the meat was sold only within the state. These meat-packing houses are outside the federal Meat Inspection Act of 1906. Since they do not have to incur the risk of having meat rejected by a federal inspector, the intrastate pack-ing firms manage to outbid other potential buyers. Once in possession of these animals, they are free, as Representative Smith points out, to cut the eye out of the cancer-eyed cow and send the rest of the carcass through the stream of commerce on its way to the dinner table.

Since 1961, Smith has been trying vainly to secure passage of strong amendments to the Meat Inspection Act—a law which has not been amended substantively since its enactment in 1906 following publication of Upton Sinclair's *The Jungle*. The proposed amendments would extend federal jurisdiction to all packing and processing companies operating intrastate but deemed to affect interstate commerce, as well as close glaring gaps which have absolved unscrupulous operators from legal sanctions. Until June 1967, Smith's bill was not even accorded a subcommittee hearing.

About 15 percent of the commercially slaughtered animals (19 million head) and 25 percent of commercially processed meat products in the US —enough meat for 30 million people a year—are not covered by adequate inspection laws. According to the Department of Agriculture, significant portions of this meat are diseased and are processed in grossly unsanitary

41

conditions, and its true condition is masked by the latest preservatives, additives and coloring agents.

Even in federally inspected plants, management is reluctant to resist the temptation of keeping costs down by keeping revolting meats on the sales shelf. In one year, the Department of Agriculture reported that its inspectors condemned over 22 million pounds of meat as tainted, rancid, moldy, odorous, unclean or contaminated. And consumers of meat sold *intrastate* have not been fortunate enough to have any such screening procedure by public specialists. Contaminated meat, horsemeat and meat from sick animals originally intended for dog and cat food has ended up in hamburger and processed meat. Eyeballs, lungs, hog blood and chopped hides and other indelicate carcass portions are blended skillfully into baloney and hot dogs. Hamburger embalmed with sulfite, a federally banned additive that gives old meat a deceptively bright pink color, abounds. One New York state survey found sulfite in 26 out of 30 hamburger samples.

A New York state official estimated that 90 percent of the uninspected processed meat sold in the state is deceptively labeled. Those big hams that you buy have 10 to 30 percent of their weight in water pumped into their veins at the supermarket's back room, meat is doped with Aureomycin as a substitute for sanitation, and detergents are applied to freshen up unfit meat. So the New York finding is not surprising.

It would be misleading to compare such intrastate operations today with those conditions prevailing at the turn of the century: As far as impact on human health is concerned, the likelihood is that the current situation is worse! The foul spectacle of packing houses in that earlier period has given way to more tolerable working conditions, but the callous misuse of new technology and processes has enabled today's meat handlers to achieve marketing levels beyond the dreams of their predecessors' avarice. It took some doing to cover up meat from tubercular cows, lump-jawed steers and scabby pigs in the old days. Now the wonders of chemistry and quick-freezing techniques provide the cosmetics of camouflaging the product and deceiving the eyes, nostrils and taste buds of the consumer. It takes specialists to detect the deception. What is more, these chemicals themselves introduce new and complicated hazards unheard of 60 years ago.

With conditions worsening year after year, the Department of Agriculture finally moved itself to dispatch a fact-gathering mission on intrastate meat slaughtering and processing operations. (There are 2,500 slaughterhouses and many thousands of meat processors operating solely within state borders.) The report, prepared by Dr. M. R. Clarkson, came in two portions. The public portion was presented in 1963 to a House appropriations subcommittee, while the non-public portion—said to be filled with sickening pictures, affidavits and other documentation—remains inaccessible in the department's files. Dr. Clarkson's public findings, however, were jolting enough without the pictorial assists. He criticized packers and processors for:

allowing edible portions of carcasses to come in contact with manure, pus and other sources of contamination during the dressing operations;

allowing meat food products during preparation to become contaminated with filth from improperly cleaned equipment and facilities;

use of chemical additives and preservatives that would not have been permitted under federal meat inspection;

failing to use procedures to detect or control parasites transmitted to man that could lead to diseases such as trichinosis and cysticercosis;

inadequate controls to prevent possible adulteration of meat food products during their preparation with substitutes such as water, gum, cereals or sodium caseinate;

use of false or deceptive labels on packaging;

failure to supervise destruction of obviously diseased tissues and spoiled, putrid and filthy materials.

The Clarkson report fell upon the states with all the force of a helium balloon. Only 41 states have any form of law at all related to meat inspection. Of these, 26 provide for mandatory inspection of animals before and after slaughter; the rest have voluntary programs. Twenty-five states provide for mandatory inspection of processed meat products. The legal authority on paper is weak enough, but its efficacy deteriorates to near futility because of grossly inadequate enforcement funds, personnel and laboratory facilities, and the omnipresent pressure of local packing and processing firms. Many of these firms are substantial business operations. Year after year, attempts to obtain bigger state legislative appropriations are tabled or defeated.

Probably the most effective restraint working to shield these packers and processors from inspection and safety standards is their common interest with both state departments of agriculture and the US Department of Agriculture in promoting the sale of meat products. Promotion is the categorical imperative animating these governmental agencies entrusted with the mission of insuring the safety of meat products. Despite the devastating evidence in its files, the US Department of Agriculture adheres in its policymaking to the avoidance of unfavorable publicity about meat products as the first priority. Consequently, years have passed without congressional hearings when all the department had to do was to request them.

Finally, in June 1967, chiefly through Representative Smith's urgings, the livestock and grains subcommittee of the House Committee on Agriculture opened hearings on bills to update and strengthen the Meat Inspection Act. The Administration's bill, HR 6168, is a pathetic response to the needs of effective regulation. The department's witness, Rodney E.

Leonard, took note of the hazards of "fast-curing processes, artificial tenderizing, artificial smoking, coloring agents and other additives that are potentially deceptive or dangerous to one's health." He added that there "are many opportunities for illegitimate operators to introduce into human food channels meat derived from dead, dying, disabled and diseased animals —commonly referred to as '4-D's'." Then he came up with the department's proposal—federal technical and financial assistance to the states if they desire to toughen their laws! If a state chooses to remain indifferent to its responsibilities, as there is every indication to believe will occur, the federal government remains powerless. (HR 6168 would eliminate some deficiencies in federal meat inspection authority but then proceeds to reduce the penalties for knowing violations from the 1906 Act's levels.) However, the number of seriously limiting amendments proposed by the National Association of State Agriculture Departments at the House hearings in July 1967 indicates that even such a weak legislative offering is too strong medicine for the states.

The administration's position on this entire matter is not being helped by the Department of Agriculture's determination to take over the Food and Drug Administration's powers over unsafe meat, principally seizure authority. The department's conflict of interest between its promotional and safety responsibilities does not merit such presumptuous preemption; nor does the department's record of indifference to the effect of drugs, including antibiotics, in animal and poultry feeds on human health.

The Department of Agriculture's laggard response to the intrastate contaminated poultry problem since enactment of the Poultry Products Inspection Act in 1957 further weakens confidence. A 1967 study, assisted by the National Institutes of Health, revealed that out of 2,057 samples of poultry taken from two representative plants, 11.2 percent contained the salmonella organisms. (The incidence of salmonellosis has increased sharply in the past 20 years.) The uninspected plant contributed a salmonella rate triple that of the federally inspected plant. The rapid growth of new frozen food products and "ready to serve" dishes that are eaten following short cooking periods is increasing the danger of trichinosis and other bacterial diseases. This trend is alarming scientists at various universities. Yet the department, apart from grudging recognition of the problem, does not rise to the challenge because of an aversion to unfavorable publicity for its clientele.

When Upton Sinclair's book came out on January 25, 1906, it was front-page news from coast to coast. Theodore Roosevelt wired the young author to visit him at the White House to discuss the problem. Now, with many more threats to consumers contained in the combination of old vices with new technology, the great hush-hush is the order of the day. Perhaps Upton Sinclair is needed once again to tell the Congress that the Jungle is still with us.

44

Watch That Hamburger

by RALPH NADER

The summer 1967 hearing by the House agriculture subcommittee on various meat inspection bills brought out as many facts as a seance. One by one, the three major trade associations and their faithful comrade in arms, the National Association of State Departments of Agriculture (NASDA), came before Representative Graham Purcell's subcommittee to pooh the bills down as unnecessary, undesirable and unreasonable.

The principal issue posed by the bills was whether to bring under federal inspection those plants which operate within state boundaries and produce 25 percent of all processed meat consumed in this country—nearly eight billion pounds. To the meat industry trade groups, there are no grounds for alarm. Americans, as every envious foreigner must know, can buy meat with confidence, knowing, in the words of L. Blaine Liljenquist, president of the Western States Meat Packers Association, "that it is the safest, cleanest and most wholesome in the world." Americans are in a meat-consuming Valhalla, according to industry groups which gave the appearance that they had come up to the House to describe the obvious in an exercise of public service tautology.

Both the trade groups and NASDA avoided any description of actual conditions in intrastate plants—the lurking *raison d'être* behind the Administration's proposed legislation. Aled P. Davies, vice president of the American Meat Institute, disposed of the matter by observing that the state meat inspection programs "have provided the kind of consumer protection in the various states that the people living in those states have thought necessary and have been willing to pay for."

Somewhat jolted by such a suave tour de force, Representative Thomas Foley (D, Wash.) initiated this exchange with Mr. Davies:

Reprinted by permission of the New Republic, © *1967, Harrison-Blaine of New Jersey, Inc.*

45

Foley: Do you think that I, traveling as an American citizen coming from someplace else, have any complaint if I am injured or made ill by tainted meat in that state? [Meaning one of the states without even a nominal inspection law.]

Davies: No more than the citizens of that state have.

Foley: Can you tell me a good way to determine what is interstate and what is intrastate in a hamburger?

Davies: Ask to see the package from where it came.

Foley: But you are a great deal more skilled in knowing what you are doing than most citizens.

Davies: I can smell.

It is quite clear from surveys of intrastate plants by the US Department of Agriculture (finally made public after four years of privacy) that Mr. Davies has underestimated the chemical ingenuity of some of his constituents.

A survey of conditions in Delaware records:

In addition to the very grave and urgent problem posed by the distribution of food derived from diseased animals, the attached report details extremely bad and revolting dirty food-handling methods without any regard for rudimentary sanitation. Rodents and insects, in fact any vermin, had free access to stored meats and meat products ingredients. Hand-washing lavatories were absent or inadequate. Dirty meats contaminated by animal hair, the contents of the animal's digestive tract, sawdust, flies, rodents and the filthy hands, tools and clothing of food handlers, were finely ground and mixed with seasonings and preservatives. These mixtures are distributed as ground meat products, frankfurters, sausages and bolognas. *Due to the comminuting process and seasoning of these products, most of the adulterations could not be detected by the consumer.* [Emphasis added.]

These USDA state surveys covered 48 states. It did not matter very much whether mandatory, voluntary or no inspection laws prevailed for intrastate plants. The conditions described by veteran USDA inspectors were repeated with revolting consistency in state after state. In fact, so overwhelming is the impact of these eyewitness accounts that the Department of Agriculture and the House committee have shown little desire in having their contents displayed before the public. Consumer skepticism might adversely affect the volume and type of meat products sold, it was believed. Senator Walter Mondale (D, Minn.) saw it another way. On Aug. 3, 1967, he read excerpts from the surveys directly into the *Congressional Record* to illustrate the need for his bill to bring all intrastate plants under the federal meat inspection service.

46

Meanwhile Representative Purcell asked the Department of Agriculture to make a new survey to see if conditions in the intrastate plants had changed. An Agriculture Department official admitted that there were some changes. The rodents and vermin were not the same, he commented; their descendants, however, were actively pursuing their daily rounds. Otherwise, the general situation remained unchanged.

The temptation open to intrastate operators to peddle "4-D" (dead, dying, disabled and diseased animals) meat, suitably masked by antibiotics, preservatives and seasoning agents, is continuous. Even plants under federal meat inspection find their owners reluctant to dispose of substandard inventory. Federal inspectors condemned and destroyed about 250 million pounds of meat and meat products in 1966 because of disease, spoilage or contamination.

There is a competitive advantage in "4-D" meat over more wholesome meat that has attracted not only marginal operators but also some of the larger meat packing firms in the country. A kind of meat industry's "Gresham's Law" operates here, with cheaply purchased "bad" meat driving out "good" meat.

The Department of Agriculture's surveys included reports of conditions at plants owned by Swift, Armour, Wilson & Co. which operate only within state boundaries. Swift refuses to divulge how many of its plants are not under federal inspection. The company says that 90 percent of its processing is federally inspected, however. The industry likes to speak in percentage terms because the absolute tonnage of non-federally inspected meat products has been growing. In 1966, 4.9 billion pounds of slaughtered meat were not federally inspected, compared with 4.3 billion pounds in 1950. Yet, with few exceptions, the large meat packers are against extending federal inspection.

This Additive Age

by DAVID SANFORD

Canterbury, England (AP)—A 23-year-old woman starved to death because she believed nearly all human food was produced by the suffering of animals, the Canterbury coroner's court was told.

Miss Brenda Holton, an office secretary, had a horror of meat and of other foods that she thought had been tainted by chemical sprays. She tried to live on a diet of honey, cereals and dandelion coffee, but her appetite faded and she wasted away.

Ralph Nader's stories about tainted pork, beef, poultry and fish have made more than one reader wonder exactly what Mr. Nader *does* eat and, by extension, what is in the food everyone consumes. The newspapers don't help to assuage fears when they report, as they recently did, that a Belgian scientist thinks man may soon be eating a by-product of gasoline (for protein).

There are a sufficient number of strange practices in the food industry and a sufficient number of casualties at the dinner table to fuel a morbid interest in food, although ironically it is true that food has never been better regulated by government agencies concerned with its purity, safety and esthetics than it is today. Still there are many unknowns, many mishaps, many mysterious chemicals added to edibles.

Flour, eggs, sugar, and butter are "ingredients." Monosodium glutamate is an "additive." The distinction, or rather *one* distinction, is between prosaic edible substances—the main constituents of food—and the less familiar, ancillary ones. *Safety* is a second distinction between ingredients and additives. Ingredients are assumed safe, if only because they are

---

Reprinted by permission of the New Republic, © *1969, Harrison-Blaine of New Jersey, Inc.*

familiar; additives frequently are not, at least in unlimited quantities. Many of the 2,000-odd chemical additives approved for use in the United States are toxic substances that must be kept at extremely low levels in food products, sometimes as low as four parts per million. The Food and Drug Administration publishes Food Additive Orders in the Federal Register, detailing in a precise way just how much of a substance is permissible in a food product. Orders are not granted when FDA considers an additive unsafe in any amount, and on rare occasion orders are withdrawn after it has been established that an additive already in use is unsafe. Safrole, a derivative of sassafras used as a flavoring agent in root beer, had its approval revoked when a committee appointed by the Secretary of Health, Education, and Welfare concluded it might cause liver cancer.

Another distinction that is made between ingredients and additives is *function*. Additives are frequently cosmetic in use. They are employed to make beer foam, oranges orange, or bread mold-free. They keep up appearances, which is important, but they are in many cases not absolutely essential to the product. Additives are in increasing use for a variety of economic, esthetic, nutritive, and frivolous reasons, and considerable debate goes on within the agencies concerned with food over how they are to be controlled and when they are to be permitted. The Flavor and Extract Manufacturers Association, for instance, maintains its own, quite unofficial list of "flavors generally recognized as safe." FDA is skeptical of the association's judgment. F. J. McFarland, chief of FDA's Petitions Control Branch, says the Flavor Manufacturers "like to think that every damn flavor that's ever been used is generally recognized as safe. Our view is that any material is unsafe until it has specifically been proved harmless." The current concern over the safety of artificial sweeteners has caused FDA to plan removing the cyclamates from its official list of substances Generally Recognized as Safe (the so-called GRAS list) and put them on its list of additives, with specific restrictions on their use.

•

The Food Additive Amendment to the Federal Food, Drug and Cosmetic Act was passed in 1958 because, in the words of McFarland, "a number of chemicals used in foods had not been adequately tested for safety." (One of the reasons the FDA was created in 1906 was to protect the consumer from then common but harmful preservatives like boric acid, formaldehyde and salicylic acid.) Under the amendment an additive was defined as any substance in food (or one which might get into food from packaging, processing or transportation) that is not known to be completely safe and which requires official clearance *before* it can be used. The definition excludes pesticides and coloring. These were for the most part covered by other legislation such as the Color Additives Amendment, the Pesticide Chemicals Amendment, and the so-called Delaney Clause which prohibits use of cancer-causing agents. Accordingly FDA put out the GRAS list; anything not on it must be cleared. FDA currently handles about 225 additive petitions each year and in 1969, 10 years after the law was enacted, is finally eliminating its backlog of unapproved petitions.

The brief history of the additive amendment has been a troubled one for many reasons. FDA has a hard time finding enough scientists to process petitions. And the ultimate disposition of additive applications rests with expert, but fallible, opinion. The true dangers of additives are difficult to ascertain with animal tests, and the variety of substances that must be looked at is immense. The package containing a food product, for instance, may contain chemicals ("indirect additives") that "migrate" to the food and, if toxic, may contaminate it and endanger the consumer. By the time the materials that go into making packaging emerge as paper, FDA's McFarland says, they are "pulped, beaten, deterged, slime-treated, colored, dried, finished, etc. into several hundred possible chemical combinations," any one of which could cause trouble. Chemicals added to animal feed are also considered additives under the law and add substantially to the problem of control.

The cyclamates have until now been listed as Generally Recognized as Safe, and except for the cryptic labeling requirement that they should be used only by those who must restrict their intake of ordinary sweets, no limits have been placed on their use. Because of possible chromosomal damage and birth defects and diarrhea that may result from excessive use of cyclamates, FDA has reversed itself and given notice that the sweeteners will now be viewed as additives, with restrictions on their use.

FDA has had other bad luck. In 1963 it approved the use of gamma radiation in the processing of canned bacon. Passing bacon through ionizing radiation sterilizes it and allows it to be stored for many months without refrigeration. Studies submitted to FDA and evaluated by the agency's scientists at first seemed to indicate that such bacon, and irradiated pork, were fit for human consumption. But in 1968, five years after the product had been cleared for commercial use, new animal studies cast doubt on FDA's approval. Laboratory animals fed irradiated bacon had higher mortality rates, retarded weight gain, reduced red blood cell counts, cataracts and tumors. The suggestion was that the same effects might be observed in humans and hence approval was withdrawn. Another preservative —a chemical known as NDGA—was put on the GRAS list in 1967 but was taken off in 1968 and reclassified an additive for which safety had yet to be established. Coumarin, a substance used in vanilla extract, had its approval withdrawn when manufacturers notified FDA that it had been found to have toxic properties. Cobalt salts used to make beer foam were banned in 1966 after it had been reported that heavy beer drinkers in Canada, where the substance was in wide use, had unusually high incidence of coronary disease.

50

A huge, little-known network of public and private organizations is concerned with food additives and related matters. It includes trade organizations such as the American Meat Institute and the National Canners Association, periodicals like *Food Chemical News* ("A weekly Washington publication for executives providing in-depth information regarding regulation of food additives, colors, pesticides, and allied products" at $175 a year), international bodies (the Food and Agriculture Organization of the UN and the World Health Organization have made recommendations on the safe use of cyclamates), the National Academy of Sciences (which studied cyclamates for FDA) and the Codex Alimentarius Commission, an interesting international body which meets now and then to determine how many peanuts there should be in peanut butter and other important matters.

•

George R. Grange, Deputy Administrator of the US Department of Agriculture, Consumer Marketing Service, is the US delegate to the Codex Alimentarius Commission. He says that on the international plane a great deal of the food regulation, particularly regarding additives, is arbitrary and hard to justify. The United States, for instance, permits use of additives in bread, chemicals functioning as stabilizers, emulsifiers, and antioxidants that among other things keep bread fresh and mold-free. "We wouldn't like it at all to go back to non-additive bread," says Grange. "France and Italy, however, don't allow additives in bread. But France colors the hell out of green peas, while the US, which colors many products, specifically prohibits coloring peas."

Codex Alimentarius is a mini-UN that brings together 52 nations who are members of the Food and Agriculture Committee of the UN and the World Health Organization. Since 1962 the members have been meeting periodically in places like Rome to iron out among themselves standards for food which, while not binding on any nation, are aimed at ensuring that products sold in international commerce have the same essential properties and can be relied on as safe. When a country agrees to a Codex Alimentarius standard, the country abides by it in domestic as well as international trade. The commission is broken down into a number of committees. There is one on additives that recommends international tolerances for additives in specific foods. Another works on labeling, a third on pesticide residues. There are Codex committees on honey, chocolate, fats.

Delegates from the Codex nations met on February 20, 1969, to consider a number of pressing issues, among which was a definition of "food hygiene" which, it was agreed, must be defined to be practiced. The General Principles Committee, at its second session, endorsed an English text definition of hygiene as "conditions and measures necessary for the production, processing and distribution of food designed to ensure a safe, sound, wholesome final product fit for human consumption." After heated debate the word "final" was omitted because it was pointed out that cleanliness was a virtue not only at the end of the production process but all along the way. Spain objected; its delegate thought the hygienic condition of a finished product was what mattered, not how dirty it might be at some interim point. It was also decided that in the Spanish version, the word "sound" would be translated "en buen estado." The French preferred "en bon état."

Later the commission was told by the Swiss delegate that his country would like to chair and pay for the work of the Codex Committee on Soups and Broths. The suggestion was tabled, however, for a number of reasons including the absence of any exact understanding of what is meant by "soup" and "broth." Then the representative of the International Olive Oil Council reported on new designations of olive oils worked out by the Conference on Olive Oils of the UN; the Chocolate Committee, chaired by Switzerland, asked the Commission to think about whether ingredients imitating milk and chocolate should be allowed in milk chocolate (that was referred to the Commodity Committee); the Fruit Commission discussed a new standard for dried prunes worked out by the Working Party on the Standardization of Perishable Foodstuffs.

The things that are done to the food we eat have long been under attack by food faddists and others who suspect every polysyllabic chemical causes cancer or some other horror and who are acutely anxious about what they don't know about what is in what they eat. Sodium silicoaluminate sounds like aluminium or glass, not the sort of thing one voluntarily puts in his breakfast coffee. But if he uses Coffeemate he does. And he needn't worry. Because the procedures worked out by FDA and Codex Alimentarius ensure the safety of additives and keep them at minimal levels, the dangers in most cases are negligible. Additives frighten people primarily because they are "chemicals" with unfamiliar names. Carnation, the maker of Instant Breakfast, a nutritious powdered drink, once played with the anxiety consumers often feel when they read product labels. Carnation's Los Angeles ad agency, Erwin Wasey, prepared a radio advertisement which listed the contents of Instant Breakfast. The spot sneered at the thought of greasy bacon, cold eggs and burnt toast while playing up the unparalleled delights of ammonium carrageenan, solium ascorbate, ferric orthophosphate, niacinamide, and thiamine mononitrate. The ad ran for a while on top-40 rock stations and teenagers, who have grown up with chemicals and can take the truth, thought it very funny. Erwin Wasey considered it one of its best jobs ever. But Carnation executives heard it, were aghast, and had it yanked off the air. As it happens the ad didn't hurt sales. In the age of additives, some actually prefer them to ingredients. Those who don't should remember the sad end of Miss Brenda Holton.

Unfoods: Do You Know
What You're Eating?

by DAVID SANFORD

The Thomas J. Lipton Company of Englewood Cliffs, New Jersey, has discovered an interesting new way to prepare soy beans—it's called beef stroganoff. It is a one-pot, main-dish meal, prepared by adding boiling water to dry ingredients and baking for 15 minutes. It would be stretching a point to suggest—as the company does in its advertising and in the picture of "tender beef" on the box—that the resemblance between the "beef" in this beef stroganoff and fresh meat is strong. A certain, unspecified amount of beef is said to be in the product, but the exciting thing about the new Lipton main dishes (you may also have "turkey" primavera, "chicken" baronet, or "chicken" la scala) is the isolated soy protein which gives the product its meaty bulk.

Soy bean simulates have long been familiar to food faddists and lacto-ovo-vegetarians. Companies such as Loma Linda Foods in California and Worthington Foods in Ohio have catered to those Seventh-Day Adventists who eat no meat, and to other vegetarians, with products such as Veja Links and Veja Burgers—soy beans prepared to look and taste like meat.

Since soy beans are very high in protein, as is beef, they make an excellent if somewhat inferior protein substitute. Vegetarians get along very well, what with all the attention they get from the soy bean people. If a diet of soy milk on cornflakes, ham-style vegetarian TV dinners, soy sausage, soy turkey and soy ham sounds monotonous—as vegetarians I have talked to say it is—you cannot blame Worthington Foods with its 60-odd products. The era of the uncolas and unfoods has brought a plethora of new things to swallow: nondairy creamers, instant mashed potato buds, ersatz orange juices, artificially sweetened soft drinks to reduce our intake of sweets and

Reprinted by permission of the New Republic, © *1968, Harrison-Blaine of New Jersey, Inc.*

animal fats, and our enjoyment in eating. At the same time they have enriched the Generals—Foods and Mills—and the food industry generally. A hypothetical meal could be constructed, beginning with a juice substitute and ending with simulated whipped cream, but until recently the ultimate meal was without a suitable mass-marketed main dish.

Lipton's entry and those of other companies eager to capitalize on the new market instruct us that soy beans can masquerade as practically anything (including fruits and nuts), that they are healthful, and finally that they are dirt cheap. A pound of isolated soy protein costs as little as 30 cents dry. Once it has been hydrated (i.e., pumped up with water, oils, flavorings, chemicals) it may increase three times in size. When one contrasts its price with that of beef, say 80 cents, it becomes clear why the food industry is excited about soy.

New processes for faking meat have been developed. If you can make a pound of soy protein into a pound of beef, advertise it as "beef," and sell it for a beefy price you have it made. The United States Department of Agriculture is watching this carefully. It has jurisdiction under the amended Federal Meat Inspection Act over contents of meat products sold in interstate commerce. USDA is reluctant to allow meal to masquerade as meat, soy as steak. Corned beef hash, for example, to be called corned beef hash must contain 35 percent cooked beef, no more than 15 percent fats, and a maximum of 72 percent moisture; no soy products, no nonfat dry milk or cereals. Beans and franks must be 20 percent franks; beef pies 25 percent fresh meat; beef stroganoff 45 percent fresh meat, 7½ percent sour cream and 5 percent wine, or without the wine 10 percent sour cream. Mr. R. H. Alsmeyer, head of the standards group of the technical services division of the consumer marketing service of the USDA, insists that USDA "will tell industry if in their formulations they are asking for a higher percentage of a less desirable ingredient than we permit. We permit only approved ingredients to go into a product." Alsmeyer explains that one way a manufacturer can avoid an encounter with the law is to inform the public frankly what it is getting in a product. A meatless hot dog labeled as containing no meat, for instance, does not run counter to USDA specifications for meat content.

This was never a problem for the vegetarian market since what attracts vegetarians is the *absence* of meat, and that is what Loma Linda Foods, for example, pushes. For the omnivores, however, the food processors may be less candid about their canned goods. Calling something "imitation" meat is anathema to them; they prefer more evasive descriptions. Thus Lipton lists the ingredients of its one-dish products in small print on the top of the box but otherwise fails to tell the consumer what he is getting; and not many customers know what isolated soy protein is anyway. General Mills, which recently began to market Bac*Os, a soy simulation of bacon bits for use in salads, soups, etc., labels it as having "a flavor like bacon."

54

Some companies market soy products only to institutional customers, restaurants and the like. They must tell their customers that soy beans are in the chili and the meat loaf, but, except where local ordinances require, the restaurant under federal law can be mum on its menus about the contents of its food. Swift & Co. markets a soy larded chili, salisbury steaks, canned meat loaf and sloppy joes to restaurants, which call them pretty much what they like.

•

The transforming of soy protein into edibles involves, in the case of Worthington Foods, General Mills and Ralston Purina a process licensed by Robert Boyer, an inventor and protégé of Henry Ford. Soy protein isolate is dissolved in an alkaline medium to form a viscous "spinning dope," which in turn is forced through platinum spinnerettes containing 15,000 tiny holes. The filaments which result are coagulated in an acid salt bath. The fibers, now called "tow" are more or less colorless and flavorless, and are at this point ready to be engineered into beef, pork, scallops, strawberries or pecans. (Worthington is particularly proud of its scallops which its promotional material says "are almost unbelievable.") All that is required once the processed soy is ready is some corporate imagination, a little artificial color and flavor, and a suggestible market.

Mr. Alsmeyer of USDA is unwilling to discuss specific cases that have attracted the attention of the standards people at Agriculture. He's not sure whether "this is information that can be released." When asked specifically, however, he will discuss the Lipton matter. Lipton's packaging, USDA found, "did tend to be a bit deceptive." USDA objected to the characterization of the product as beef, without any big-print information on the front panel of the box about the true role of soy protein. "After considerable discussion" USDA did approve the inner package in which the beef and isolated soy protein strips and sour cream are contained. The noodles are in a separate packet. But USDA has no influence over the labeling of the outer box, only the immediate package containing meat. FDA, Alsmeyer says, has questioned the outer packaging, but that "may be information which Food and Drug would rather not have in the press."

There's a jurisdictional loophole. A processor is permitted to label frankly the inner contents of a product, but label deceptively the package the consumer sees in the store. USDA has no control over the latter. Also, it seems to be legal for a product to be repackaged deceptively, *after* it has reached the state where it is to be sold.

Alsmeyer says he is confident that the problem with Lipton will be fully resolved and on the whole seems rather well disposed to the soy bean people. "I think we have some very good relations with manufacturers of soy products," he said. "In fact I almost daily get a call from one of the suppliers. We have very good rapport and have sat down trying to iron out our differences on labeling. If now and then they feel we're a little unfair we will review our position. . . ."

The director of Product Development at Lipton, Ray Franceschini, explained to me how the Lipton product meets USDA standards of composition. When Agriculture says that a beef stroganoff must contain at least 45 percent meat, what is meant is that the immediate package in which the meat component is contained must be 45 percent meat. In the Lipton stroganoff there are four containers—the box the housewife sees in the store and three inner packets, one containing noodles, one containing a bread crumb garnish, and one containing the beef, soy protein and sour cream. The law is interpreted in such a way that only the immediate container is relevant. The 45 percent figure is thus a percentage of the sauce mix, not the entire dish. Moreover, the standard "refers to the sauce component on an as-served basis, not on a dry basis. When the Department of Agriculture refers to a certain minimum meat content in a completed product they are historically and traditionally referring to the product as served or as used by the consumer which would be in its rehydrated state." Since soy protein rehydrates at roughly three-to-one, more than 45 percent of the product may appear to be meat. Lipton intentionally omits from the package, as it may legally, any mention of how much meat is actually in its product. Mr. Franceschini *didn't know* the proportion of meat in his products.

Under the Food, Drug and Cosmetic Act, a food is considered misbranded if it is an imitation of another, unless its label bears, in type of uniform size and prominence, the word "imitation." (Occasionally a product in imitation of another is accepted under a new name, as margarine was.) The Lipton box does not say that the meat is an imitation or that it is not all meat. This is an advertising half-truth, and while FDA reluctantly approved the packaging it nevertheless prevailed upon Lipton to redesign its package, mentioning soy protein each time the word beef appears on the package and deleting the picture of what looks like a big raw roast on the side panel. When asked whether the picture of meat is to come off the box, Mr. Franceschini said, "Not that I know of." He later rephrased this to "Well perhaps it is, to be very frank I'm not sure. . . ." He said that on FDA recommendation there would be a more prominent mention of the important role of soy protein.

Soy beans are the second largest agricultural crop in the US (250 to 300 million pounds of soy flour is used in food products a year). They are cheap and they hold some promise of answering the nutritional needs of the world. But Mr. Franceschini said none of these was uppermost in the collective Lipton mind. Lipton, he said, used soy protein merely to make it possible to freeze dry meat, which dried in any other fashion would be highly perishable and have an unpleasant texture. By combining dry pulverized meat in a dough with soy isolates, extruding the matter in a kind of macaroni fashion and chopping it off, Lipton has found a feasible way to prepare a dry meat. The result of this process is a simple-to-prepare, rather economical (79 cents at one store in Washington, D.C.), two-serving meal.

In 1966 a token quantity of Bac*Os, bacon-like bits test-marketed by General Mills in Denver, Buffalo and Sacramento, was seized by the Food and Drug Administration in Buffalo, and a case was brought in the US Federal District Court (Western Region) in New York to force General Mills to identify their product as "imitation bacon." Lipton's Mr. Franceschini admitted for General Mills that its package copy may have been a "little too loose." At the time of the seizure the Bac*Os bottles stated that they contained an amount equivalent to a pound of bacon fried and crumbled. It didn't say that Bac*Os were bacon, just that they were a lot *like* bacon. Before the case could come up, General Mills thought it discreet to change its label. It now reads "Crispy Bontrae bits with a flavor like bacon." Bontrae, the label explains, is a registered trademark for a vegetable protein product. Arthur Odell, manager of General Mills' isolated protein program, thinks that that is sufficient, that if margarine need not be called imitation butter (there is now even an imitation margarine) then Bac*Os should not have to go as imitation bacon. General Mills, therefore, petitioned FDA to develop a standard of identity for soy isolates that would allow the industry "to get around calling it imitation." It could then, for example, be called Bontrae (as in Bontrae stroganoff, and Bontrae bits) or under some other suitable coinage. Such a standard of identity would "be a consumer protection device." Bontrae would become a new entity, a new contribution to the quality of life, and in five years perhaps a $100 million market in the United States.

Unmilk: Cowing the Consumer

by DAVID SANFORD

American industry has improvised a way to produce an imitation milk which by some accounts is indistinguishable from the real thing, equivalent in nutrition, and, not least, very cheap to produce. It is white, comes in cartons, has a commercial name with lactic associations (Moo, Mello, *Mil-KAY*, Farmer's Daughter) and, where it has been introduced, has begun to steal the market from nature's most nearly perfect food. The producers of artificial milk already have 80 percent of the whipping cream market (with their non-dairy creamers) and in Arizona, ersatz milk one year after its introduction had 8 percent of the market on the way to 10. Imitation milk, and filled milk, which contains some milk solids but vegetable oils in the place of butterfat, may soon relegate milk to one of the lesser, but nevertheless genuine luxuries of life, something to be found with the specialty foods and as rare as fresh mashed potatoes in restaurants.

Imitation milk has become the single greatest preoccupation of the trade groups and industry societies concerned with dairy products—a matter for aesthetic, nutritional, and most of all economic discussions. And the talk provides an interesting case study in how businesses are able to rationalize making money.

Imitation milk typically contains water, corn syrup, vegetable fat (usually coconut oil), sodium caseinate (the ingredient common to all powdered coffee whiteners such as Pream, Coffee-mate, Cremora and derived either from milk or soy beans), potassium phosphate, salt, and various other chemicals, artificial color and flavor, vitamins and minerals. Filled milk is similar in composition but includes in addition a certain amount of non-fat milk solids. Where filled milk has been marketed it sells for between 10 and 15 cents less per half-gallon than the real thing, and because it is

Reprinted by permission of the New Republic, © *1968, Harrison-Blaine of New Jersey, Inc.*

still cheaper to produce affords a greater profit margin. In the spring of 1968, Robert F. Holland, the head of Cornell University's Food Science Department, made price comparisons to show the competitive advantage unmilk has over its dairy equivalent. Coffee creams sold in general for between 45 cents and 49 cents a pint, while coffee whiteners (industry prefers the term "non-dairy creamer" for its obvious connotative value) went for 24 cents to 29 cents. Whipping cream sold for 60 cents to 65 cents a pint. Synthetic whip, 35 cents to 39 cents. Butter 79 cents to 85 cents per pound; margarine 22 cents to 47 cents. Milk 26 cents to 27 cents a quart; "Moo, etc." 19-and-a-half cents.

"Not only are the wholesale or retail prices of these imitation products lower, but in general," Holland said, "profit margins are greater. For example, one company manufacturing the basic constituents of coffee whiteners claims an average retail price of 29 cents per pint, an ingredient cost of 6 cents leaving a margin of 23 cents to cover processing, distribution and profit. It is small wonder that imitations have gained popularity with both processor and consumer." Production costs for milk and other dairy products are such that they cannot compete and distributors are said to handle coffee cream, for example, at a loss. The PR departments of the food processing companies invariably can find a number of reasons to justify their interest in imitations, but the line of reasoning with the greatest suasion for their directors is the economic fact that there is more money to be made in chalk water.

Protectionist legislation in the dairy field is elaborate, and effective in inhibiting the incursions of ersatz products. Margarine was in the courts and in legislative battles for years, and persons over 25 are likely to remember the laborious process of squeezing plastic containers of oleo to disperse a little orange coloring spot to make it look like butter. There was little reason for laws prohibiting precolored margarine except in the eyes of the dairy men.

Filled milk, under current law, cannot be sold in interstate commerce, for no particularly good reason except that the law keeps Guernseys giving milk. (Its ostensible basis was a concern about adulteration of dairy products and the health and safety of the consumer.) Increasingly, the Filled Milk Act is being opposed both by dairy farmers and the more flexible processors, who would like to get into the imitation milk business, because it is now felt that it unnecessarily restricts innovations. Some dairy men would prefer that the law be amended and that the price of non-fat milk solids used in filled milk be raised so as to offset the competitive advantage filled milk would have over what is now "the more expensive drink." Imitation milk constitutes a greater threat since, without any milk derivatives, it is altogether outside the laws pertaining to milk. There are few compelling reasons for retaining the harsh milk laws (one is that they incorporate requirements of hygienic conditions in processing plants that do not apply

59

to the production of unmilk). Theoretically, the laws of the marketplace should prevail and the consumer should be given an option to buy either milk or something similar and cheaper. But the aestheticians of milk would protect the public from itself and from the diminishing quality of life as reflected in the food people consume.

Where imitation milk is already on the market—principally on the West Coast—housewives are buying it in ever increasing quantities. Not because they particularly like its taste, although it's okay, but because it helps their budget. And quite often its use seems to be among poor people with large milk-drinking families for whom a few cents a quart makes a big difference in subsistence. There is serious question whether artificial milk, particularly, approximates the nutrients in milk. Advertisements of the non-dairy products make claims for low cholesterol, protein equivalence, etc.—which many authorities say cannot be sustained. The National Dairy Council, which admittedly has its own interests to protect, has sponsored research showing that filled and imitation milks are inferior sources of protein and contrary to advertised claims are worse or no better for persons on "low cholesterol diets" than milk itself: "The fat used in many products is based on hydrogenated coconut oil, a fat notably high in saturated fatty acids. . . . Products identified as imitation milk are in no sense a nutritional replacement for milk in protein, minerals, and vitamins."

Those poor families who are unsophisticated in seeing beyond advertising claims and making the associations intended for them to make by market researchers thus are getting products which may do them a dietary disservice. In January 1968 the National Dairy Council convened "six leading nutritional authorities" and obtained from them unanimous agreement that "the imitation milks and certain filled milks as formulated today are unsuitable for infants and children . . . unsuitable not only from the standpoint of low content of protein, essential amino acids and minerals, but also because of the type of fat used, namely coconut oil. These products were also judged to be potentially harmful for other vulnerable age groups such as pregnant and lactating women, and persons on marginal diets such as those in low-income groups and the aged." Ersatz milk has certain distinct advantages over milk in that it is easier to control flavor stability, may be less vulnerable to spoilage and the action of microorganisms, meets Jewish dietary laws (which forbid the use of cream in coffee when meat is also served) and so forth. But such matters are secondary to nutrition and aesthetics.

•

Hugh Schwartz, president of San Francisco's Communications Research Center, did group interview studies for clients in the phony milk business, and documented the cynical assumptions of the unmilk producers. Schwartz worried about the challenge to "milk and motherhood" and wondered if

21- to 39-year-old housewives with children and a family income of less than $10,000 would go for white water. He found that "even with a product category as basic, as traditional as milk, the consumer was prepared for any kind of change as long as it looked like milk." The women were worried about cholesterol and were persuaded that if claims for the fats in unmilk were made they would purchase it. As one of Schwartz's respondents said about powdered milk: "At one time I used only fresh milk, but then this other is so much cheaper." The picture he draws is of consumers worried about money, who believe in progress, who fear heart attacks, and who trust the regulated food industry not to do them in: "I wouldn't feel concerned," one woman said, "because we know we have these drug and food laws which protect us. . . ." Schwartz concluded with his recipe for marketing success. "A creative merchandising policy could alleviate many of the consumer's hesitancies and doubts, by stressing perceived positives: a different kind of milk—a technological improvement; a new, improved processing permits longer shelf life; less cholesterol; less expensive, but just as nutritious; and by using supplemental descriptive phrases to alleviate the negatives in the word 'imitation.' "

If processors are successful in repealing or modifying the federal Filled Milk Act and the laws in at least 30 states which prohibit the sale of filled milk, the market will abound in facsimile dairy products. Already many companies are laying plans for entry of imaginative products into the grocery stores. Procter & Gamble is producing a poly-unsaturated fat that may replace coconut oil in filled milk and make claims concerning the cholesterol issue in chalk water more accurate. Loma Linda Foods of Riverside, California, is planning mass marketing for an imitation milk, using no milk products but rather soy protein, that the company hopes will compete with cow's milk. Marsh Food Stores, in Indiana, have introduced a frozen non-dairy "ice cream." Clover Meadow, Meadow Gold, Borden and Carnation all have lines of wholesome-looking chalk water.

The pressures and the profit picture are such that, as these examples illustrate, the dairy business itself is introducing lines of ersatz products. The processors, in theory, have no vested interest in cows, or at any rate are adaptable enough to retool and replace them with the mechanical bovine equivalents. And when the day comes when it is no longer profitable to put out dairy products at all they will probably not be too upset. It is the dairy farmer, the man with the cows, who in most cases will be left holding the bag. But the more enterprising dairy men themselves are providing for the future. *Farm Journal* reports that dairy men are enthusiastic about filled milk, since milk solids are an essential ingredient. And some of the more enterprising dairy men are themselves going into the manufacture of filled milk.

•

Once the nutritional snags have been worked out, as many predict they will be, and once soy bean milk can overcome *its* flavor problems, and once the consumer has been "educated," several other problems remain to be solved before the unmilk men can prevail in the supermarket and at the dinner table. The laws must first be amended, to permit interstate shipment and sale of filled milk. From the dairy farmer's point of view price controls must be established which would eliminate the competitive edge held by filled and imitation milk. And finally "standards of identity" must be devised that will give the products a name which is not deceptive, which does not trade on the good name of milk, and which will make the new foods sell in the supermarkets. Fortunately the antagonisms and the obstacles are so great as to make each of these problems difficult of solution.

The Milk Industry Foundation, whose name suggests that it cares about milk, is as ready as anyone to try electric cows. MIF has proposed a "model law" which would allow adding or deleting dairy and non-dairy substances from dairy-like products, and standardize the labeling requirements imposed by the states and federal government. MIF is also considering proposals to recommend changes in controls imposed by the Department of Agriculture, lowering the price of butterfat to make it competitive with coconut oil and raising the price of non-fat milk solids to drive up the costs of filled milk products. Such a scheme, while ensuring the continued professional lives of milk cows, is not likely to be supported by food processors who know very well that unless their simulates have a significant price difference they will be unable to find buyers. The whole history of new foods is of products similar but not the same, edible but hardly delectable, useful only when economy is the main criterion. What makes the difference is the convenience and the cost, and where economy counts, which is nearly everywhere, they are in use. Milk will go the way of cream if it remains more expensive. Changing the cost structure to eliminate the advantage in imitation dairy products would be to keep them off the market. Unless the Filled Milk Act is modified the dairy industry will be unable to push what it has to offer to the simulate business. So long as non-fat milk solids cannot legally go into filled milk, the sodium caseinate will have to come from soy beans, and the non-dairy imitation milk that results will be free of all the protectionist legislation originally patterned to the needs of the dairy farmer, but now outmoded.

It is more likely that the laws will be further strengthened to resist the incursion of ersatz. Representative Samuel S. Stratton of New York sponsors a bill which would (1). prevent imitation and filled milk from being packaged in milk cartons or other containers so similar to those customarily containing milk as to confuse the consumer; (2). prevent imitation and filled milk from being sold alongside dairy products in supermarkets; and (3). forbid the use of the word "milk" in promoting nondairy products.

The Food and Drug Administration has proposed standards which would require imitation milks to meet certain standards of composition and nutrition and would call them "imitation milk." Many who have commented on the proposal object.

In fact most everyone agrees that "imitation milk" is not the proper appellation for chalk water. It isn't milk, say the dairy men, and shouldn't ride on milk's good name. (After all the industry has spent a mint convincing everyone of the virtues of sweet fresh milk.)

The Milk Industry Foundation would allow the term "imitation" for filled milk but not for a totally non-dairy product.

The American Medical Association would reserve the term for products which are established to be nutritionally equivalent or superior to cow's milk, requiring other nomenclature for the rest.

The ersatz milk men, making for a consensus, reject "imitation milk" as a term, not because of the milk part but because of the term "imitation" which they know all too well translates "inferior."

The FDA's standard-setting action may have an effect on how the products are sold but will probably not keep them off the market. In about 20 states it is legal to market imitation dairy products and filled milk intrastate. There is probably no way to resist progress and there are, of course, those who in this case have no wish to try. But others feel that until the Rockies crumble and cows run dry they will side with the majority of Michigan cats who were offered their choice of moo and milk and turned up their noses at the former. The *Dairy Industry Newsletter* reports that "of an eight-cat panel, 37.5 percent completely rejected imitation nondairy milk; 75 percent prefer the natural milk to the nondairy imitation; and 25 percent seemed satisfied with a nondairy imitation."

Radio-Inactive Food

by DAVID SANFORD

The United States Atomic Energy Commission would like to have the American consumer eating meats, fruits, vegetables and grains that have been exposed to gamma radiation: a process the AEC believes will eventually be as useful and prosaic as refrigeration in preserving food well beyond its natural edible life. The Food and Drug Administration—whose spokesmen are as reticent to speak about irradiation as enthusiasts at AEC are eager in its promotion—is attempting to stay the day when much of the food we eat will have first been exposed to doses of radiation sufficient, if turned accidentally on a man, to be lethal. There have been too many examples of harm from radiation—from radium watch dials, shoe store X-ray machines, dental X-rays and (potentially) from color TV sets carelessly unleashed on the public—for one not to be interested in the outcome of the struggle.

The first constituency of the AEC is the atomic energy establishment—uranium mining, the military and industry. Sundry announcements of advances in irradiation emanating from AEC have in common three points, all in the service of that constituency: (1.) Irradiation promises to be a huge profit maker for food and related industries, as well as a boon to the consumer; (2.) processing food by passing it through a radiation source is safe; (3.) progress is retarded by FDA's insistence that it approve every single potential use of radiation-treated food. FDA, it is suggested, is withholding profit from industry by depriving the public of a perfectly safe new way to keep foods fresh. The statement must be looked at skeptically.

FDA for its part has insisted that AEC, the Army, and the corporate enthusiasts of irradiated food have not made their case for safety, except in a few isolated instances. The burden of proof rests on those who would

Reprinted by permission of the New Republic, © *1968, Harrison-Blaine of New Jersey, Inc.*

expose the public to these foods. FDA contends that although it has not been positively established that irradiated foods are unsafe, neither has it been determined beyond doubt that they are in general without hazard. FDA has approved the irradiation process for white potatoes (it retards sprouting), for bacon (which will keep for many months without refrigeration) and for wheat (as a pesticide). Some 76 other nations now have research and development programs in food irradiation.

Radiation "pasteurization"—exposing food to low levels of nuclear radiation—is useful in keeping strawberries firm and mold-free. Radiation "sterilization"—exposing food to higher levels of radiation, sufficient to kill bacteria—allows meat to be stored for months or even years without refrigeration. Potatoes can be kept from sprouting for at least 16 months. Wheat can be protected from costly insect damage by destroying eggs that pesticides don't affect. Unfortunately, radiation that will kill a bacterial cell will also destroy some food tissue cells. That may affect nutrition. And residual radiation in foods may be dangerous.

Applications for potatoes, bacon and wheat were accompanied by extensive data from animal experiments that at first assuaged FDA's qualms about safety. But it is conceivable that since varying amounts of radiation are used, the process may be safe for one commodity and not another. In April 1968 FDA approval was denied to ham because the Army (the petitioner) had in FDA's opinion not made a convincing case for safety. The Army, however, has an extensive experimental program which involves feeding recruits irradiated foods at Fort Lee, Virginia. And the food processing industry is eager to get radiation-treated foods into the supermarkets.

•

The Thomas J. Lipton Company wanted to use radiation on vegetables that go into its dried soup mixes. The process, in Lipton's case, would act as a preservative and speed cooking time, which Lipton feels would be commercially advantageous. Lipton officials found, however, that the texture of irradiated vegetables is not what it should be, and that radiation-treated vegetables have an offensive odor. The primary drawback, however, is that FDA would not permit Lipton to market the soups without undertaking animal testing Lipton estimates would cost $100,000. Lipton didn't want to do it, and hence withdrew its application to FDA.

An FDA spokesman informed about irradiated foods is wary of answering questions about the agency's position. FDA, he says somewhat cryptically, is the only interested party "without an ax to grind;" its only concern is "health." He fends off questions about responsible opposition to irradiation, refuses to divulge FDA's complex reasoning in rejecting applications ("They simply didn't make their case"), and will not discuss industrial applications to FDA.

The former FDA Commissioner, James Goddard, was somewhat more forthright. In a speech in 1967 to the Southern Interstate Nuclear Board and the Atomic Energy Commission in Oak Ridge, Tennessee, Goddard cautioned restraint by the atomic energy people, who, he hoped somewhat rhetorically, shared his emphasis on safety over profit. His most direct statement was that "those who are deeply involved in food irradiation must answer the hard questions of vitamin and mineral preservation, of the effect upon harmful and useful microorganisms in food, of teratogenicity among animals—including man—and of sterilization of the reproductive process."

Does irradiation do something to the vitamins and minerals in food that would adversely affect nutrition? Does it kill microorganisms that might be beneficial as well as those that cause spoilage? Does ingesting irradiated food over a period of years increase the likelihood of cancer? Could eating irradiated foods make a man sterile? Dr. Goddard dealt only indirectly with these questions; he merely raised the warning flag. But each time FDA rejects an application for irradiated foods it is saying, in effect, that it has not been established that these *are not* bona fide dangers. And until such dangers can be ruled out, applications will be denied. FDA has authority under the food additives amendment (1958) to the Federal Food, Drug and Cosmetic Act to refuse approval of any irradiated food where it has not been clearly established that the "expected advantages" of the process outweigh the disadvantages. A food must present "no known hazard to health." But Goddard is also concerned about the quality of life: "If we are to choose between irradiated foods and, for example, nonirradiated frozen or canned foods, we will, as consumers as well as regulators, choose what is better—better scientifically and, if possible, aesthetically as well."

Even the AEC admits that radiation creates some problems: "The first long-term feeding studies seemed to produce some abnormalities in experimental animals." But AEC believes that they resulted from poor experimental procedures (*e.g.*, feeding rats nothing but oranges, or keeping dogs locked in isolated cages). "A few have not been completely explained, so research continues." As for aesthetics, AEC contends that early problems with color, taste and odor have for the most part been solved or substantially reduced "by irradiation at very low temperatures, application of adsorbents as odor scavengers, skillful use of spices and condiments, and appropriate cooking practices."

The FDA quietly rejected the Army's application for approval of irradiated canned ham in April 1968. That decision and a nasty letter from Goddard to Glenn T. Seaborg, chairman of the AEC, cast a pall over the future of irradiated foods. Goddard's letter, which FDA refuses to release (but which is freely available from Dr. Seaborg) called the Army's animal studies "poorly executed" and "incomplete" and its evaluation of data

66

"inadequate." Whatever their shortcomings, the studies revealed, according to Goddard, evidence of adverse effects on the reproductive process, mortality, body weight, and red blood cell counts of experimental animals and incidents of tumors and cataracts. That might spoil a few appetites at Fort Lee.

The AEC and the Army contracted in 1967 with IRRADCO, an Allentown, Pennsylvania concern formed by Isotopes, Inc., Allen Products Co., Alpo (the dog food subsidiary of Liggett and Myers), Martin-Marietta and Uniroyal (whose connection is purely financial), to build a plant in Allentown to process 3,000,000 pounds of meat annually. The plant would start out with dog food and (it was hoped) canned ham which the Defense Department planned to feed its troops (300,000 pounds per year), starting in 1969.

Contingent on FDA approval, the plant, in which IRRADCO has already dropped half a million dollars, may never be constructed. Robert Kleiner, Vice President of Isotopes, Inc. and a member of IRRADCO's board of directors, said in June 1968 that if the disclosures in Goddard's letter were well founded, "then we have a very long way to go." "We're having a meeting in Washington with AEC, and hopefully with FDA although that isn't very likely, to determine our course of action. Building the plant is still quite up in the air." Kleiner was somewhat pessimistic although plans had been afoot to transfer FDA's regulatory function to AEC. In any case, "Dr. Goddard's departure can't do any harm."

It remains to be seen whether Dr. Goddard's successor at FDA will be any less zealous in safeguarding the public health against the AEC, the Army, IRRADCO and the irradiated food people. It is rather likely that FDA approvals already granted to irradiated potatoes, wheat and bacon will also be withdrawn by an FDA suspicious that there is something wrong with irradiated foods.

Radiation Treatment

A NEW REPUBLIC EDITORIAL

Some 26,000 American servicemen have eaten more than 15 tons of ir-radiated bacon, and smaller quantities of 17 other irradiated foods, as part of a 14-year, $6 million experiment. All the volunteers were told, in accordance with Army regulations, that there were potential hazards. However, since the Food and Drug Administration had cleared irradiated bacon (as well as wheat and white potatoes) for commercial use, the dangers seemed negligible.

Irradiation has long been considered a promising means of preserving highly perishable foods in an edible condition without refrigeration. But there has remained in many minds the fear that exposing foods to gamma radiation might affect nutrition and perhaps endanger life.

In looking at an Army application for approval of irradiated canned ham in the summer of 1968 the FDA reconsidered its position and suddenly withdrew approval of the process for bacon. It had evidence that the process destroys vitamins, and that treated food reduced the longevity of animals, and increased infant mortality rates. Also there was some in-cidence of tumors, cataracts and blood disease in experimental animals. The earlier approval of irradiated bacon had been based on test summaries that FDA later came to feel were poorly executed and incomplete.

Since consumers have not been offered irradiated foods of any kind, the change of mind at FDA caused no stir, except at the Army, the Atomic Energy Commission, and in the board rooms of various companies that hoped the process would prove profitable. The Army, however, is sticking it out and on its own authority is continuing to feed irradiated food to

Reprinted by permission of the New Republic, © *1968, Harrison-Blaine of New Jersey, Inc.*

human subjects. Its Natick, Massachusetts, labs plan to continue testing on military bases of irradiated beef, chicken and frankfurters. Congressional hearings planned for fall 1968 by the Joint Committee on Atomic Energy to further consider the safety issue were canceled.

Bitter News About Sweeteners

by W. DAVID GARDNER

Americans are using more and more of the non-nutritive sweeteners called cyclamates; two million pounds in 1957, perhaps 17 million pounds in 1968, and their growth is projected to continue at similarly rapid rates. Cyclamates are popular with dentists and their patients because they cut the incidence of cavities; they are popular with food processors who can save substantially by substituting cyclamates for sugar in their products; and they are popular with the public because of their low calorie content.

However, there is new evidence that cyclamate sweeteners—used primarily in diet sodas, drinks and desserts—may constitute a serious health hazard for some persons. That, at any rate, is the conclusion that can be drawn from a $46,000 study of cyclamates by the Institute of Experimental Pathology and Toxicology at Albany Medical College. The study was commissioned by the Food and Drug Administration, but it has a bipartisan tone to it since the two special interest groups most concerned with the production of cyclamates gave financial support to the study. Funds were contributed by Abbott Laboratories, and E. R. Squibb, drug companies which produce cyclamates, and by the Sugar Research Foundation, which represents sugar industry interests. Cyclamates cut into the sales of sugar.

The bulk of cyclamates are produced by Abbott, Squibb, Monsanto Chemical Co., Norse Chemical Co. and the Pillsbury Co. The biggest market for them is in the bottled soft drinks like Tab, Fresca, Diet-Rite Cola and Diet-Pepsi. They are also popular in presweetened powdered drinks like presweetened Kool-Aid and Funny Face. To a lesser extent, cyclamates are being used in diet desserts, ice cream and jellies.

The Albany group, in a three-month study of 32 prisoners at Clinton

Reprinted by permission of the New Republic, © *1968, Harrison-Blaine of New Jersey, Inc.*

Prison at Dannemora, found that some prisoners taking cyclamates experienced a change in the character of their blood. According to Dr. J. Henry Wills, the professor of pharmacology at Albany Medical College who directed the Dannemora study, the change—specifically, an increase in the level of protein-bound iodine—was one that could have misled physicians into thinking the prisoners were suffering from hyperthyroid condition (a high level of protein-bound iodine in a patient is one of the classic indications that the patient has a hyperthyroid condition). However, none of the prisoners with the high levels of protein-bound iodine had any other signs or symptoms to indicate they were suffering from hyperactive thyroid glands, and the scientists are satisfied that cyclamates do not cause or aggravate hyperthyroid conditions.

There is, though, another danger here: A physician orders, say, a series of blood tests on one of his patients. When the clinical laboratory test returns, it shows that the patient has a high level of protein-bound iodine —a signal that the patient has a hyperactive thyroid condition. Treatment for a hyperthyroid condition is begun. Sometimes the ailment is surgically treated. The problem is that the patient may not have a hyperthyroid condition. Dr. Wills believes that many physicians are treating patients with high levels of protein-bound iodine for hyperthyroid conditions when in reality they are simply taking too many cyclamates. Unfortunately, many physicians and pathologists are not fully aware of this possibility.

The Albany group is also disturbed, less because they have found an increase in the level of protein-bound iodine in prisoners taking cyclamates, but because they don't understand the mechanism of the production of the substance. The scientists are continuing their studies in humans and animals in an effort to learn more about the phenomenon.

In addition, nine of the 24 prisoners taking cyclamates (the eight prisoners in the control group were given placebos) developed "severe, persistent diarrhea" from the cyclamates. There seemed to be a direct correlation between the dosage and the result: The higher the dosage of cyclamate, the more severe the diarrhea.

The Albany group also found that 17 of 24 prisoners taking cyclamates converted the cyclamates into cyclohexylamine, a substance that raises blood pressure and causes vascular constriction in some people. If the cyclohexylamine is being produced in the blood or gets into the vascular system, the cyclamates obviously represent a potential danger to some cardiac patients, particularly those with high blood pressure who are trying to keep their weight down by taking cyclamates. At this point, the Albany investigators are unable to say where the cyclohexylamine is produced in the body. Dr. Wills says it is possible that it is produced in the blood or gets into the vascular system, although he found no evidence of this in the Dannemora study. Once again, the Albany group is interested in learning something about the fundamental mechanism of the conversion of the cyclamates into cyclohexylamine. Few physicians are aware of the potential danger of prescribing cyclamates to their heart patients who are trying to keep their weight down.

•

The findings that cyclamates can produce cyclohexylamine and can raise the level of protein-bound iodine are disturbing in themselves, and they raise a disturbing question: Why weren't these findings known when cyclamates were first approved for public consumption in 1955? In the light of the Albany study, it is now apparent that the initial cyclamate testing was incomplete or slipshod or both. Millions of pounds of cyclamates have been consumed since then. This is not to say that the drug firms or the scientific investigators involved in the development and testing of cyclamates did not comply with Food and Drug Administration standards; they did. But the situation illustrates the inadequacies of some drug-testing standards. (Standards have been tightened up as a result of the Kefauver-Harris Drug Amendments to the Federal Food, Drug and Cosmetic Act, and the amendments have prompted the FDA to begin to review older agents previously approved between 1938 and 1962.)

The history of the approval of cyclamates is interesting. The 1955 Food and Nutrition Board of the National Academy of Sciences report on non-nutritive sweeteners concluded there was no evidence that the use of cyclamates "for special dietary purposes is hazardous . . . ingestion of more than five grams a day of the cyclamates is capable in some adults of inducing the formation of soft stools, but this did not appear to be of physiologic importance."

In 1964, the Sugar Foundation commissioned a study that concluded that cyclamates can stunt the growth of rats. At about the same time, studies conducted by Japanese and English scientists claimed that cyclamates were responsible for harmful effects in animals. Nevertheless, in May of 1965, the FDA—after a review of the new accumulation of evidence on cyclamates—announced, "There is no evidence that cyclamates, at present use levels, are a hazard to health." That finding still stands.

Most cyclamates end up in the stomachs of Americans because advertising campaigns stress their low caloric content. The public equates a large amount of calories with obesity; a small amount of calories with a reducing diet. In their advertising, the food processors have been careful enough—and clever enough—to stress the low caloric content of their "diet" products, but not to say that their products will help anyone lose weight. There is no evidence that cyclamates—or any other non-nutritive sweetener, for that matter—have ever helped anyone reduce. Anyone who cuts his calorie intake with nourishment sweetened with cyclamates is likely to make up for the calorie deficiency unconsciously with other foods.

There is some speculation that the FDA will eventually relabel cyclamates to conform to new drug efficacy findings. Meantime, cyclamates will continue to be used by some for whom they are potentially dangerous, and by diet-conscious Americans who think cyclamate-sweetened products help them to lose weight.

Safety of Sweeteners

by W. DAVID GARDNER

"There is no clear justification for the use of artificial sweeteners by the general public as a weight-reducing procedure."—National Academy of Sciences-National Research Council policy statement on artificial sweeteners, 1962.

When the National Academy of Sciences-National Research Council studied the non-nutritive sweeteners called cyclamates for the Food and Drug Administration, it was felt cyclamates would be useful primarily for diabetics who must restrict their intake of sugar. It was emphasized that "the availability and consumption of artificially sweetened food-stuffs have no direct influence on body weight."

In spite of this, Americans are consuming annually 17 million pounds of cyclamates—the bulk in the form of 490 million cases of low calorie soft drinks—chiefly because they believe the cyclamate-sweetened food will help them lose weight.

Part of the problem is semantic. Most of the diet drinks are labeled with statements in large type like "flavored dietary beverage . . . dietary caloric beverage . . . special dietary beverage." Technically speaking, this means the drinks may be useful for diabetics or for others who have been advised by physicians to cut down on their sugar intake. To the typical consumer, however, the "dietary" statements mean that the soft drink will help him diet.

"Psychologically, people feel they will lose weight by taking cyclamate-sweetened foods," says Dr. Fredrick Stare, chairman of Harvard's Depart-

Reprinted by permission of the New Republic, © *1969, Harrison-Blaine of New Jersey, Inc.*

ment of Nutrition. "But I know of no evidence that non-nutritive sweeteners have helped anyone reduce. The problem is that they make up for these lost calories by taking extra portions of food and drink." As evidence, Dr. Stare cites what he regards as the classic study in the field—a 1956 survey of 247 obese persons by Harvard's Department of Nutrition and the Peter Bent Brigham Hospital. The obese individuals were divided into two groups—those who used non-caloric sweeteners and those who didn't. The study found no significant difference between the two groups in weight loss. Dr. Stare believes cyclamate industry interests would conduct a large-scale study of the effectiveness of their products as weight-reducing agents if there were any reason to believe cyclamates would be of such use. None has ever been done.

The issue here is drug efficacy. As a result of the Kefauver-Harris Drug Amendments to the Federal Food, Drug and Cosmetic Act, the Food and Drug Administration is reviewing some 3,500 agents previously approved by the FDA between 1938 and 1962 with an eye to determining whether they are effective for the uses for which they were originally specified. In the case of cyclamates, the investigation seems superfluous. Cyclamates were not approved as a weight-control agent in the first place, yet that is why most people use them. "I believe," says Dr. Stare, "that when the cyclamates were first introduced the FDA advised their use for individuals with diabetes. And why they haven't continued to insist upon this restriction I just don't know."

Then there is the issue of safety. Dr. Stare has been involved in one particularly frustrating incident involving cyclamates. In 1965 a Japanese doctor studying under Dr. Stare at Harvard called his attention to a Japanese study in which three non-nutritive sweeteners—cyclamate, saccharin and dulcin—were tested on pregnant mice (dulcin is prohibited in the US). The Japanese study found that all three non-nutritive sweeteners killed or retarded mice fetuses when they were administered early in pregnancy.

The study interested Dr. Stare and when he was in Japan the following summer he made a special trip to visit the Japanese investigator who had conducted the study. "I wanted to size him up," Dr. Stare recalls. "I found him to be honest, intelligent and dedicated. He was not looking for publicity and I remember that he was upset at the time with the Japanese sugar industry, which was using his studies to try to discredit artificial sweeteners."

When Dr. Stare returned home, he wrote an introduction to a translation of the Japanese study and attempted to get it published in US medical journals. After *Science* and *The Proceedings of the Society for Experimental Biology and Medicine* rejected the study for publication, he brought it to the attention of a Harvard scientist who is an expert on the human embryo. He agreed that it should be published here. But it never was.

Dr. Stare emphasizes that the Japanese study is no proof that cyclamates or saccharin are killing or retarding human fetuses. He feels, however, that it raises an important question that should have been brought to the attention of the American medical community and that should have prompted additional animal experiments. He believes the issue could be studied relatively easily in humans by reviewing records of stillborn babies at a large hospital in the South (where soft drinks are consumed at a high rate).

On the other hand, Abbott Laboratories, the biggest producer of cyclamates, and the Calorie Control Council, a conglomeration of manufacturers of low calorie foods and beverages, say animal studies have been conducted which indicate that cyclamates do *not* affect gestation or delivery of young. Other animal experiments also fail to confirm the findings of the Japanese study. In an "interim" report, the NAS-NRC committee backed off slightly from its earlier approval of cyclamates and emphasized that "totally unrestricted use of the cyclamates is not warranted at this time." The study committee, though, reaffirmed its earlier ruling that cyclamates are not hazardous to humans. Strangely, the NAS-NRC committee did not mention the issue of drug efficacy—whether cyclamates are helping people lose weight. In addition, important studies on cyclamates were not examined by the NAS-NRC committee; for instance, a study by FDA investigators, who found that a breakdown substance of cyclamate—cyclohexylamine—can cause genetic damage in animals. Hard on the heels of that report came another from a cytogeneticist at the Worcester Foundation for Experimental Biology in Massachusetts, that human cells in laboratory cultures could be damaged by cyclamate itself. Although neither study proves that cyclamates work the same way in humans, they have opened the way for additional genetic studies.

•

There is also new evidence that cyclamates can interfere with the effectiveness of other drugs. A University of Michigan scientist has found that cyclamate halted the absorption into the blood stream of about 75 percent of an antibiotic that was administered to humans. The trouble here is underscored by the fact that cyclamate is sometimes used as a covering to sweeten pills and is mixed with liquid medicines to improve their taste. This potential danger was picked up by the NAS-NRC committee, which said: "There is some concern that these binding processes of the non-nutritive sweeteners may alter the activity of drugs or other chemicals in the body." The committee called for more experiments to determine whether cyclamates interfere with drug therapy in humans.

In another study, a group of Austrian scientists reported that cyclamates were harmful to the livers and the blood coagulation process in guinea pigs and rabbits. On the basis of their own experiments and after reviewing the literature, the Austrians declared that some persons "appear to be particularly endangered by uncontrolled use of cyclamate." Those who were

76

warned about this potential danger included patients using anticoagulants and patients with a tendency toward decompensation with liver congestion.

One man who has been worried about the safety of cyclamates is Dr. Milton Rubini, editor-in-chief of *The American Journal of Clinical Nutrition*, who says:

> The fact that cyclamate-sweetened products may be used in copious quantities by children, pregnant women, and nursing mothers would make concern for long-term safety even more critical. The magnitude of the use of sweetening agents . . . is such that we cannot afford to find belated evidence of some subtle toxicity.

Sweeteners Emerge Again

by ARTHUR S. GROVE, JR., M.D.

In April 1969 Dr. Herbert Ley, Jr., Food and Drug Administration Commissioner, announced a proposed regulation which will require new labels on food products containing cyclamates, the widely used artificial sweeteners. This regulation calls for a statement of the amount of cyclamate contained in a normal serving of food or in a bottle of beverage. Manufacturers will also be required to specify the upper limits of cyclamate consumption that the FDA considers safe (3.5 grams per day for adults and 1.2 grams per day for children).

These maximum values, based upon the estimated amount of cyclamate that may produce a laxative effect, were suggested by the World Health Organization and the National Academy of Sciences-National Research Council. The content of cyclamate varies greatly among products, and in the case of certain soft drinks (Diet Pepsi and Fresca) the limit for children is exceeded by two 12 ounce bottles.

No official warning has been made regarding the possibility of dangers to unborn children, despite the fact that these sweeteners have been shown to enter the fetuses of pregnant animals. Two Italian scientists (Ghiani and Accame) at the University of Genoa have recently shown that cyclamates can produce club-foot deformities in developing chickens. Other malformations of the skin and extremities were found among young embryos that were similarly exposed. Abnormalities of this sort, known as teratogenic effects, correspond to some changes produced by thalidomide. Other animal experiments have suggested that cyclamates may destroy fetuses or produce abortions.

Most cyclamate is manufactured from cyclohexylamine (CHA), a toxic chemical, which has been implicated in chromosome damage and destruction of animal fetuses. The proposed regulation will limit the amount of CHA that may be present in cyclamate as a contaminant. Many humans, however, spontaneously convert cyclamate into CHA within their bodies. Pregnant women who consume cyclamate run the risk that they may be "converters" and that their unborn children may be exposed to CHA.

Cyclamate and saccharin, which are commonly used together for commercial purposes, have been described by the FDA since 1960 as GRAS ("generally recognized as safe"). This designation, by an act of administrative legerdemain, has meant that although they were added to foods, these sweeteners were not "food additives" for the purpose of the strict testing and safety provisions of the federal Food, Drug and Cosmetic Act. Current FDA actions will probably result in the removal of cyclamates from the GRAS list and in their becoming full fledged "food additives."

By the new regulation, the FDA suggests that people "count milligrams" to limit their consumption of cyclamate. This scheme presupposes that consumers are mathematically inclined and that they are aware of each cyclamate-containing product that they use. Many purchasers, however, buy and use diet foods by mistake. This fact was pointed out in the March 1969 issue of the *Progressive Grocer* (which calls itself "The Magazine of Super Marketing"). That publication described a technique of stimulating sales by removing low-calorie products from "diet departments" and grouping them with similar sugar-sweetened goods throughout the store.

Since low-calorie products are often used by all members of purchasing families (it is more convenient to serve one kind of food), many children are being exposed to cyclamates indirectly. Granulated sugar substitutes containing cyclamate and saccharin are now being actively promoted. They will probably be used by many children on their daily cereal. Because of the multiple routes by which cyclamates can enter the diet, the "milligram counting" that the FDA suggests will probably be either disregarded or impossible to follow.

In response to the FDA announcement Abbott Laboratories (the largest cyclamate producer) suggested that the new requirements may frighten the public without justification. Some other representatives of the artificial sweetener industry have reacted more favorably and support the proposed regulation. In any case, the current action is probably an interim measure, since investigations by the NAS-NRC should eventually produce relatively complete data regarding the safety and dangers of these sweeteners.

The FDA, in undertaking a long-overdue rewriting and tightening of its regulations, may actually block comprehensive reform by establishing limits that will probably not be followed and by directing attention away from areas of potential danger. The reports of malformations and abortions in some animals suggest that these sweeteners should not be used by pregnant

79

women until they are conclusively shown to be safe. The amount of cyclamate that could possibly be harmful to fetuses may be even smaller than the new FDA limits, which were primarily set by laxative effects. Similarly, until more data are accumulated, there seems to be no reason for children to be exposed to cyclamates unless their use is medically indicated.

Drug on the Market

by DAVID SANFORD

The real difference in aspirin products is the price. You can buy Bayer and pay for the name, or Brand X and save money. Aspirin, as doctors have known for years, is aspirin. The same is true for most drugs available only through prescription. One has a choice between an inexpensive product made by a company he's never heard of, or one made by Squibb or Upjohn that sells for 10 times more.

The brand-name hoax has hooked the public on all kinds of consumer goods. Two suits or TV sets are made by the same company but marketed under two different names—one expensive and familiar and one cheaper and unknown. The wise consumer, who knows the product as distinct from the label, buys the bargain. But when your health is at stake, you are less likely to take a chance. Quibbling over pennies or a few dollars seems senseless. The huge pharmaceutical companies exploit the fears of the sick, and of doctors who don't themselves have to pay for the drugs they prescribe. We pay heavily for a false sense of security.

Drug companies benefit from the lack of any central source of comparative data on drugs to prove that a brand-name drug and one called by its official or generic name and identical in chemical composition will have the same effect. In the absence of such comparisons, it seems less risky to buy the brand-name product. The only way a physician can compare drugs is to consult the Physicians' Desk Reference, a kind of doctors' yellow pages containing the puffed-up claims of the drug companies. The listings are advertisements, certainly not dispassionate or objective scientific reports; they have the credibility of the conflicting claims in newspaper and magazine ads for Anacin, Excedrin, and plain old aspirin. A physician can consult the United States Pharmacopoeia, a volume compiled privately but blessed by Congress, if he wants to know if a drug meets US standards for safety and efficacy, but he still does not know whether Miltown and meprobamate, identical in everything but name, are going to have the same therapeutic effect. This problem will be taken care of quickly enough if the Food and Drug Administration goes through with its plans to make such comparisons—but it is probably not worth the trouble.

An editorial note published in the *New Republic* suggesting that consumers might save money by boycotting drugstores that don't stock generics, and that they take their business to mail-order firms specializing in generics, join buying cooperatives, or do a little comparison shopping elicited a number of rebuttals from pharmacists. One registered pharmacist in Buffalo wrote:

> The overriding issue in the controversy, in my mind, is the question of therapeutic efficacy of generic brands. I had an opportunity to study the dissolution of a few generic drugs and found that they did not dissolve as readily or completely as the brand name. One generic heart tablet did not dissolve at all! Others will crumble or break with little or no effort. I have also seen brands of generic drugs with grease, dirt and paper imbedded in them; there is no charge for the added ingredients. Until the public can be certain of the therapeutic effectiveness of generic drugs the better value for dollar spent will be the brand-name drug.

His examples are alarming. But what he ignores is that even a brand-name drug affects different people differently, that it will not have the same therapeutic effect on the same person each time he ingests it. (His stomach may be empty or full, he may be rested or fatigued, nervous or calm. All these things make for variations in a drug's effects.) Moreover, two lots of the expensive brand-name drug may not be chemically identical (some lots have been found by FDA to be mislabeled, adulterated, too potent, not potent enough). Finally, the argument does not address itself to the fact that one is as likely to find bits of metal in a brand-name eyewash, rubbing alcohol mislabeled citrate of magnesia, and so forth in a brand-name product as in a generic. The recalls of drugs from the market by the FDA have involved one as often as the other.

The scandal of the pharmaceutical industry is that one is taking a risk whenever he swallows any drug—brand-name or generic. It would be as reasonable, though hardly economic, for the big drug firms to caution, "don't take any drug until we know that all drugs are safe and efficacious" as it is to warn specifically against the cheaper products of their competitors. From a consumer's point of view, so long as taking any drug is a calculated hazard one might as well take it with a less expensive drug.

Time magazine once had the bad luck to make a case for the superiority of Bayer aspirin on the very eve of a Federal Trade Commission announcement that it was taking action against the false and misleading claims that one brand of aspirin is in any way better than another. *Time* made a point of Bayer's practice of exceeding USP standards for aspirin. Under the Kefauver drug amendments of 1962, drugs must be proved safe and efficacious if they are to be sold. If, as in the case of antibiotic throat lozenges, the drug companies cannot prove to FDA's satisfaction that a drug does what its manufacturer claims, it can be taken off the market. The United States Pharmacopoeia sets standards for 900 drugs. If these are adhered to, as the law requires, then the drug is considered effective. Sterling Drug Company, which makes Bayer aspirin, goes to great, and as it turns out unnecessary, lengths to exceed USP standards. Says *Time*: "Before tableting . . . the basic chemical must be in tabular or needle-like crystals or crystalline powder; to produce a dependable dissolving rate, Bayer requires a special flake shape and needle shape (slender, tapered at both ends). USP permits .5 percent moisture and weight loss on drying; Bayer will tolerate none. USP allows up to .1 percent free salicylic acid; Bayer holds to one-third of that, and halves three other USP permissible deviations from absolute purity."

•

What the magazine did not say is that if a product is efficacious and safe and meets government standards, exceeding criteria may be gratuitous. Many brand-name drugs are alleged by their manufacturers to be superior to generics not because the active ingredients are any different, but because the sugar coating is different—cherry instead of vanilla. The difference between a bottle of tablets that dissolve in 30 seconds and one of tablets that take two minutes may be a price mark-up of 300 percent and little else.

The second example *Time* chose to make a case for brand names was Penicillin G, made by E. R. Squibb & Sons under the expensive name Pentids. Squibb sells Pentids to pharmacies for $6.62 per 100 tablets of 200,000 units. Pennex Products Co. sells the same drug by its generic name for 92 cents. Squibb runs more and lengthier tests than Pennex, tests not required by USP standards. *Time* did not note, however, that Squibb, for all its high standards and quality control, has had many mishaps. On April 15, 1965, the FDA recalled the company's Procaine Penicillin, which comes in disposable syringes, because the drug particles were too large to eject from the needle. Another Squibb Penicillin was recalled April 23, 1965, because of a labeling mix-up. In December 1962 a bottle supposed to contain Pentids Soluble was found instead to contain Diethylstilbestrol. Squibb has been involved in recalls for carton mix-ups, label mix-ups, foreign capsules, contamination, printing errors, excess potency, low potency, ingredient substitution.

Senator Gaylord Nelson's (D, Wisc.) drug hearings may go on, a legislative aide said facetiously, into the 1980's; there's that much ground to cover. Nelson's main objective is passage of a bill (with Senators Morse and Russell Long) to add to the Kefauver drug amendments of 1962. It would in effect require the federal government to buy drugs used in the Medicare program by their generic names—something which the military and many private hospitals already do voluntarily. The law's principal side effect would be to make generics more easily obtainable. It would dramatically reduce the $3.4 billion that Americans spend annually on prescription medicine.

The hearings of Nelson's monopoly subcommittee—not one of the more powerful Senate bodies—have already unearthed some interesting information. For example, the drug industry is the highest profit industry in the United States, with profits running as high as 31 cents on an invested dollar—despite the industry's moaning about the high cost of research.

Drug companies sell brand-name products abroad at highly reduced, competitive prices; they could reduce prices at home and not go out of business. (Recently Merck dropped the price of Prednisone overnight from $17.90 per thousand tablets to $2.20.) They set prices in some cities far higher than in others. William Haddad, a former investigative reporter, poverty warrior and chairman of New York's Citizens Committee for Metropolitan Affairs (an unofficial ombudsman) did a survey in which he found New York City paying $9.45 per 500 meprobamate tablets while Atlanta was spending $31.20. The bureaucrats of Atlanta are either stupid, in bed with the pharmaceutical companies, or bamboozled by drug company propaganda.

The hearings have also revealed that New Yorkers pay as much as nine times more for drugs (brand name) than they would have to (for generics). Ghetto Negroes in Albany were found to be paying more for brand-name drugs than residents of affluent white neighborhoods ($6.65 for the antihypertensive Serpasil that whites bought for $5.44).

Some large companies put their brand labels on drugs which they buy from smaller producers of generic drugs. Some sell their brand-name drugs to smaller companies to be sold generically and less expensively. Some brand-name companies themselves carry lines of generic drugs.

The contradictions of the drug industry were well stated by Mr. Haddad in his testimony and suggest the kind of action the government might take if it chooses to buck the powerful drug lobby:

> If generics are unsafe, as the drug companies charge, then you must ban their sale. You must stop doctors from prescribing these drugs generically. You must stop the hospitals from buying them.

84

And you must do it immediately. We are dealing with a life and death issue. If a drug sold generically does not meet its therapeutic potential, then a person may die. If, on the other hand, the arguments of the drug companies are not valid, they must be terminated. They must not be allowed to frighten Americans into paying higher prices for their medicines so the drug companies can increase their profits.

In Brands We Trust

by DAVID SANFORD

"Reputation. There is no generic equivalent. A reputation
is earned, not bestowed. Your Rx for a pharmaceutical
specifying a brand or manufacturer's name expresses confidence in the manufacturer's integrity, uncompromising
production standards, quality control, and his dedication
to the public welfare. There is no generic equivalent for
reputation; it cannot be bought or duplicated."

Pharmaceutical Manufacturers Association

"E. R. Squibb & Sons is one of the major drug manufacturers in this country. . . . It is unfair and detrimental to
the public at large, that this firm should have allowed
itself to operate under such extremely poor manufacturing practices that resulted in numerous mixups, recalls,
adulterated, and misbranded drug products. When a firm
of the stature of E. R. Squibb & Sons, a name trusted
by the medical profession, operates under conditions
whereby their entire output is open to question it is a
cause for serious concern."

The first message above comes to us, or rather the readers of *Medical
World* magazine, through the courtesy of the PMA, the official mouthpiece
for the drug industry. The second is a statement by a Food and Drug Administration official explaining a court indictment of one of America's most
reputable drug firms. In the quoted PMA ad is a bottle labeled "Reputation"—something PMA believes is the registered trademark of the high-
priced, well-known, expensively advertised and promoted prescription medi-

---

cine that PMA pushes. Reputation cannot be bought (even in costly magazine ads?) but it can be sold.

PMA has placed an ad in *Reader's Digest*, in *RD*'s editorial format, and disseminated reprints not identified as paid propaganda in behalf of brand-name drugs. PMA has paid five economics professors $40,000 to testify before a congressional committee. It has registered two paid lobbyists with the clerk of the House of Representatives, despite the statement in PMA's *Prescription Drug Industry Fact Book* that PMA "is not a lobbying organization." (That is a statement PMA has been making ever since 1958, when its executive vice president wrote the Commissioner of Internal Revenue that "there are no legislative activities carried on directly or indirectly by PMA. . . .") Early in 1968 Senator Gaylord Nelson (D, Wisc.) wrote several major drug firms for their opinions on a compendium of prescription drugs he hopes to have published. G. O. Lienhard, chairman of the executive committee of Johnson & Johnson, replied: "Since our products are generally not regarded as prescription drugs, few if any of them would be listed in a broad compendium you have in mind. We think it would be inappropriate for us to comment on a proposal that is of primary interest to the prescription drug manufacturers." Yet Johnson & Johnson is a member of the Pharmaceutical Manufacturers Association, which organization describes itself as the "representative of manufacturers of prescription products." J&J *owns* two companies that are in the prescription drug field in a rather big way—McNeil Laboratories in Fort Washington, Pa., and Orthopharmaceutical Corporation in Raritan, N. J. The latter firm puts out Ortho-Novum, the well-known contraceptive pill available only through prescription. McNeil Laboratories, a medium-sized drug firm (with annual gross sales of something under $50 million) produces about 50 different prescription drugs. And J&J told a US senator it is not in prescription drugs.

Johnson & Johnson has supplied Senator Nelson's monopoly subcommittee with scripts for 34 radio commercials for which the company bought time in Washington, D. C. Each describes a specific contribution by the pharmaceutical industry to health (*e.g.*, penicillin, tranquilizers, polio vaccine, epilepsy control, etc.). Each ad ends with the line—"Another great contribution to better health and longer life by men and women with the freedom to pioneer new medical frontiers." This soft sell for an unregulated drug industry disguised as public service announcements has rankled the subcommittee staff, since J&J has distorted the history of drug advances to play up the role of unfettered private enterprise (and play down government) in major medical breakthroughs. In script number one J&J touts the industry's role in the introduction of penicillin. Penicillin was discovered by the British bacteriologist Alexander Fleming in 1929. In the United States penicillin research was conducted by the federal Committee on Medical Research of the Office of Scientific Research and

Development. Production was coordinated by the Department of Agriculture. Dr. Vannevar Bush, director of OSRD, commented in 1943 that "the pharmaceutical companies have cooperated" but only "after a fashion. They have not made their experimental results . . . generally available. . . ."

J&J similarly touts industry's achievements in diphtheria and whooping cough vaccines, which were discovered in Berlin and Copenhagen respectively. Diphtheria research in the US was done at the Michigan Department of Health Laboratories and paid for with public as well as private funds.

Get Well Cheaper
The Hard-Name Way

A NEW REPUBLIC EDITORIAL

Pantheon Books published an unusual and valuable volume on drugs. Entitled *The Handbook of Prescription Drugs*, by Dr. Richard Burack of the Harvard Medical School, it tells how to save money by buying drugs by their generic names.

All drugs have an official, or generic name, but often are sold by an unofficial or brand name. New drugs and processes are protected by the patent laws for 17 years, during which period the manufacturer can do pretty much as he likes in setting up the price. But manufacturers seek to keep up the price long after the patent has run out, by hawking the medicine under a swell-sounding brand name. The drug companies spend $600 million a year in advertising, to din brand names into the heads of patients and doctors. As a result, 90 percent of all prescriptions are written for brand names, which sometimes are easier to pronounce, spell and remember, but often are expensive.

Dr. Burack's book lists the generic names, and prices (to the druggist) and manufacturers of drugs. By using his lists, it's possible to save money. Some examples:

Penicillin G, the basic penicillin, was introduced on a wide scale in 1942 and is unpatented. A number of firms sell it. Squibb offers Penicillin G under the brand name "Pentids" and wants $6.62 for 100 tablets. By contrast, a lesser-known company called Pennex will sell the same quantity of Penicillin G for 92 cents. Dr. Burack cites several other companies which offer the medicine at prices from $1 to $2 for 100 tablets.

People on diets often take the appetite suppressant they know only as Dexedrine. Dexedrine is the brand name that Smith Kline & French put

Reprinted by permission of the New Republic, © *1967, Harrison-Blaine of New Jersey, Inc.*

on a drug which has the generic name of dextroamphetamine sulfate. One thousand Dexedrine tablets cost the druggist $22.60. It is far cheaper to buy the drug under its generic name. For example, American Quinine sells 1,000 pills for $1. Ten other companies listed by Dr. Burack sell the medicine for less than $2 per 1,000 pills.

The ingredients in a gallon of phenylephrine nose drops cost the manufacturer $3.50. But to buy this common nasal decongestant, which is sold over the counter without a prescription, the customer must pay from 75 cents to $1 for a one-ounce bottle. That means that a gallon of the stuff whose ingredients cost $3.50 is sold at retail for as much as $120.

Digitalis is often prescribed to patients with heart trouble. It is the dried leaves of the *digitalis purpurea* plant which have been pressed into tablets. Made by Davies, Rose-Hoyt, digitalis is sold as "Pil-Digis" and sells for $18.40 per 1,000 tablets. McNeil makes a slightly cheaper digitalis tablet, selling for $17.55 for the same amount. On the other hand, the same amount of the same medicine can be purchased from American Quinine for $1.36 or from Corvit for $1.70.

Meprobamate is a widely used tranquilizer, probably best known to the public by Wallace Laboratories' brand name, "Miltown." Four hundred and fifty Miltown pills cost $6.50. Wyeth sells meprobamate as "Equanil" for $5.80. But you can buy 450 meprobamate pills from Pennex for $3.10.

Dr. Burack points out that another commonly used and inexpensive tranquilizer, Phenobarbital, costs the druggist between 50 cents and $1 for 1,000 15-milligram tablets. However, many druggists maintain a minimum prescription price and the patient frequently finds himself paying $2 for 50 or fewer tablets.

People suffering from iron deficiency sometimes are told to take an iron vitamin. This is known generically as ferrous sulfate. Smith Kline & French sell this medicine under the brand-name "Feosol" for $9 per 1,000. But Dr. Burack lists eight companies that sell ferrous sulfate for less than $2 per 1,000 pills.

The large drug companies sometimes suggest that it is better to buy their products at high prices because the product is reliable. However, as Dr. Burack's tables show, in half the cases where the government was forced to make companies recall drugs because of faulty manufacturing, the big firms were involved.

Dr. Burack provides a list of drug manufacturers that have been approved by the Defense Supply Agency. It buys drugs for the military and companies that do business with it are likely to be fairly reliable.

The patient can save money by asking the doctor to prescribe drugs by their generic names. Then, by using Dr. Burack's tables, he can ask the druggist to fill the prescription with medicine from the least expensive manufacturer.

Drugs: Deceptive Advertising

by MORTON MINTZ

"Drug manufacturers are obliged to and do fulfill their
responsibilities to provide the truth, the whole truth and
nothing but the truth regarding their products."

Howard A. Rusk, M.D.,
New York Times, May 5, 1968.

In few areas of our mass-marketing, technological economy is the medieval doctrine of *caveat emptor* less relevant than for prescription drugs. "He who orders does not buy, and he who buys does not order," was the way the late Senator Estes Kefauver described it. For a patient ("he who buys") the issue is more than economic: a potent medicine that is ineffective or less effective or safe than another preparation, may injure or even kill. In a woman, as thalidomide taught us, the consequence can be deformities in an unborn child. It is, therefore, of high importance to the public health that the physician ("he who orders") not be misled about the proper uses of the drugs that can be sold only if he prescribes them.

It can be extremely profitable to deceive physicans, however, and in Senate hearings, Kefauver established that they were deceived on a wide scale. He urged remedial legislation. This was achieved in 1962 in the Kefauver-Harris Amendments to the Food, Drug, and Cosmetic Act. "All advertisements and other descriptive matter" for prescription drugs, the amendments say, must carry "a true statement ... in brief summary" of efficacy, side effects and contra-indications (medical conditions in which a drug should not be used). The "true statement" must be faithful to the

Reprinted by permission of the New Republic, © *1968, Harrison-Blaine of New Jersey, Inc.*

labeling, or prescribing instructions, approved by the Food and Drug Administration.

The FDA devised implementing regulations which took effect in January 1964. Two years later, by estimate of FDA Commissioner James L. Goddard, the industry was spending between $600 million and $800 million annually to advertise and promote prescription drugs. With so much spent—about $3,000 per doctor per year—could Dr. Rusk be correct in saying that the companies "do fulfill their responsibilities to provide . . . nothing but the truth about their products"? In 1968 a significant record of performance is available to be examined.

Under the regulations against false and deceptive advertising, the FDA has taken 33 formal, public actions against 26 manufacturers. The target manufacturers have included some of the largest. Abbott Laboratories and the Upjohn Co. each were involved in three of the actions. The Armour Pharmaceutical Co., Geigy Pharmaceuticals and Wallace Laboratories each were named in two actions. All told, the number of separate drug products involved was 45, including some of the most popular.

Claims deemed by the FDA to be false have been made in letters and circulars and in the now much-reformed *Physicians' Desk Reference*, which is the most widely used prescribing guide. But the most common vehicle for their circulation has been medical publications—at least 16 of them by my casual count. These are either professional journals, including some of the most prestigious, or throwaways which, being supported entirely or almost entirely by drug advertising, are mailed free to doctors. Again by my informal count, the professional publication that has figured most frequently—15 times—in the FDA ad actions is the *Journal* of the American Medical Association. Among the throwaways the indicated front-runner is *Medical World News*, a McGraw-Hill publication. Second on the masthead, as Consulting Editor, is a physician who has a remarkable rapport with the drug industry. In his weekly column in a newspaper which has been discreet about his *Medical World News* connection he has praised the pricing policies of the industry that is the source of almost all of the revenues earned by *Medical World News*. After such a column was published on a Sunday in October 1966, an appreciative Pharmaceutical Manufacturers Association reprinted it to assure wider circulation. The column, of course, was signed by Howard A. Rusk, M.D. The *New York Times* has not reported most of the drug advertising cases and the remaining few negligibly.

Of the 33 actions by the FDA against false and deceptive advertising, 5 were criminal prosecutions. Two of these proceedings ended when pleas of no contest were filed. Such a plea was filed by Wallace Laboratories in the case of Pree MT, which was promoted for uses including alleviation of premenstrual tension, and by Armour Pharmaceutical in the case of Chymoral, which is used against inflammation and swelling.

In five civil cases the FDA seized interstate shipments of the drugs involved for false and deceptive promotion. The companies and the drugs in these cases were: Warner-Chilcott Laboratories (Peritrate SA, for the massive chest pain of the heart condition known as angina pectoris); Wyeth Laboratories (Serax, a tranquilizer/sedative); Upjohn (Lincocin, an antibiotic); Hoechst Pharmaceuticals (Lasix, a diuretic), and Ohio Chemical and Surgical Equipment Co. (Indoklon, an alternative to electroshock in some cases of depression).

With seizures and criminal prosecutions FDA fulfills its mandate as a regulatory agency. But these actions largely fail to fulfill the agency's mission to protect the public health. They are not directed at telling the doctor he may have been misled. Indeed, criminal prosecutions work *against* such disclosure. An inspired solution was devised by Dr. Robert S. McCleery, acting director of the FDA Bureau of Medicine's Medical Advertising Division, who won vigorous support from Dr. Goddard and his successor as Commissioner, Dr. Herbert L. Ley, Jr. The solution is the "corrective letter," a copy of which a manufacturer agrees to mail individually to more than 280,000 doctors. With this device, the FDA can compel a manufacturer to retract misleading claims quickly, before they become entrenched in the minds of physicians. In order for a "corrective letter" to be generated a major untruth must be involved. The alternative to the letters would have been still more painful—stopping sales through seizures of shipments.

•

Easily the most impressive "corrective letter" case is one involving Bristol Laboratories. In Dr. Rusk's *Medical World News*, in *Medical Tribune* (another throwaway) and in a promotional letter, Bristol Laboratories went beyond the FDA-approved labeling to promote its new Dynapen as a general purpose penicillin. This posed a grave danger: overuse of this semi-synthetic penicillin could imperil the whole class of these drugs as "reserves" against dread staphylococci germs. The possible consequences could be outbreaks, especially in hospitals, of severe and even fatal contagious staph infections resistant to the semi-synthetics. Despite pressures on behalf of Bristol exerted by well-connected Washington lawyers, the FDA embargoed shipments and sale of Dynapen pending publication in *Medical World News* and *Medical Tribune* of "corrective ads." Because Bristol's promotional letter had gone air mail, the FDA required that the "corrective letter" also be sent air mail.

The most contrite "corrective letter" was sent by Abbott Laboratories concerning the antibiotic Erythrocin. "We sincerely regret that the construction of [a promotional mailing piece] may have allowed interpretations extending beyond the limits of the approved package labeling and the full content of the cited references," the firm said. Usually, a company says that the material in question was considered by the FDA to be mis-leading. In sample "corrective letters," apologies were made by Ayerst, for implying a link between cholesterol-lowering Atromid-S and "a beneficial effect" on heart disease; by Geigy, in a claim "not supported by the data" for Hygroton in lowering blood pressure, and by E. R. Squibb for mis-interpreting a medical reference so as to denigrate a rival to its antibiotic Mysteclin-F. FDA's findings that hazards of birth control pills were misleadingly downgraded were reported by Searle (Ovulen-21), Mead Johnson (Oracon) and Syntex (Norquen and Norinyl-1). Several firms told doctors of a conclusion by the FDA that the provision of insufficient in-formation had jeopardized safe, effective use of a drug. This category included Pfizer for Renese and Renese-R, diuretics, and Lakeside for Norpramin.

In 1967, the FDA invited written comments on proposed new ad regu-lations embodying prohibitions against specific deceptions brought to light by the "corrective letters" and the criminal and civil cases. The responses came entirely from sources with special interests in drug advertising, and all were opposed to the proposed new rules. Not one physician, physician group or physician publication filed a statement in support of FDA. This suggests a certain apathy in the medical profession. Many physicians have a dependent relation with drug companies which begins in medical school, when they accept week-end trips and other gifts, and continues in later life with research grants and other help. They don't seem to mind too much being deceived. And so deception, remaining profitable, persists. For this, major news media deserve some blame. With few exceptions, they have failed to recognize the news value in "corrective letters" or in criminal prosecutions for deceptive advertising (which carry a tap-on-the-wrist maximum penalty of $1,000 per count). Adequate reporting might have a therapeutic effect not only on drug companies, but also on the medical profession. More physicians might come to identify with patients, the way airline pilots identify with passengers flying in the same airplane.

The Quinine Caper

A NEW REPUBLIC EDITORIAL

When those who buy quinine or quinidine (drugs commonly used in the treatment of malaria and heart disorders) plunk down their money at the local pharmacy, they pay a sizable hidden toll—amounting now to perhaps $5 million a year—to an international cartel dominated by Dutch and German interests. Since the turn of the century the cartel has systematically and almost continuously fixed prices, rigged bids, divided territories, artificially curtailed production. The members, as one participant crisply put it, work together "in an atmosphere of cooperation" so as "to keep prices high." While all of this has been widely known for some time to students of antitrust, Senator Philip A. Hart's (D, Mich.) antitrust and monopoly subcommittee turned its spotlight on the cartel and exposed its inner, and hitherto most secret, workings with the aid of a batch of documents—got on a tip—that contain the detailed minutes of cartel conclaves.

Usually members of this cartel hold a tight grip on supply, but back in 1962 they feared that the US might sell its huge stockpile of quinine to smaller, non-member buyers and thus undermine its position. American officials were aware of this possibility, too, but they took no precautions to see that the stockpile remained out of cartel hands and, in fact, passively acquiesced in its sale to the organization. The Justice Department, though disturbed about the "serious antitrust" implications, deferred to the State Department, and State, under pressure from the Dutch Embassy, was far more anxious to maintain "friendly relations" with The Hague (and the Queen, we might add, who is rumored to have a proprietary stake in Nedchem, the Dutch cartel giant). Consequently 14 million ounces of quinine fell easily into the hands of the cartel.

Although the Senate subcommittee has not come up with any hard

Reprinted by permission of the New Republic, © *1967, Harrison-Blaine of New Jersey, Inc.*

evidence of the cartel's operations since 1963, the elimination of the stock-pile threat unquestionably increased its leverage. And prices have been soaring. Helped along somewhat by unsubstantiated and inaccurate reports that the Defense Department would need umpteen tons of quinine to fight off malaria in Vietnam, prices of quinine and quinidine rose by five times between 1964 and 1966. Bulk quinine went up in value from 21 cents (the price at which the cartel bought from the stockpile in 1962) to approximately $4 an ounce in 1967. For the typical heart patient, this has meant that the cost of a month's supply of quinidine has climbed from $2 to nearly $10 since 1964—serious enough in itself, but especially so for the elderly who make up a large percentage of the drug's users. Moreover, the cartel does not exploit only Americans: it also levies a heavy toll on the poor of the tropics.

With the cartel now in control of most of the world supply of quinine, the US has very limited leverage. A portion of the existing national stock-pile could be released to non-cartel sources, but even with four million ounces on hand (far in excess of current and anticipated military requirements, incidentally), not enough is available to bring down the price for more than a short period of time. Then, with our reserves exhausted, the cartel would be the complete master. In the longer run, new sources of supply and substitute drugs could be developed (the Indonesian government might be induced to increase its quinine output and research on synthetics can be stepped up), but while these avenues should be pursued, they will provide no immediate relief.

The Antitrust Division of the Justice Department has shown little interest in the cartel (it shunted off responsibility for investigating the case to the Federal Trade Commission). The division could launch an inquiry of its own, then initiate criminal action or take steps to enforce a 1928 antitrust decree in which cartel members agreed to refrain from certain illicit practices "within the United States." However, if Antitrust does so, it is unlikely to obtain any meaningful relief, since the key members of the cartel are outside this country and make every effort to avoid carrying on any business within our borders. Even if an American court were to assert jurisdiction, it is extremely doubtful that it would be able to do more than verbally condemn the cartel.

The cartel's evils make wonderful newspaper fare (one story appeared under the banner, "The Dutch Quinine Blackmail: Pay or Die"). But they are only symptomatic of a larger, more complex problem. Monopolistic practices are by no means confined to quinine, nor are they exclusively the province of foreigners (two minor quinine cartel members are subsidiaries of American parent corporations). The United States cooperates in, initiates, and approves widespread monopolistic arrangements of its own. For example, our airlines participate in IATA (which sets international air fares) and our ocean shippers are members of rate-fixing conferences. Our companies can and do form export associations which fix prices and allocate markets exempt from usual antitrust prohibitions, with the result that just as we complain of the quinine cartel, so too do the Europeans assail our sulphur and potash cartels. There is only one way to control international monopoly: some sort of international cooperation. Here then is where the United States could make a major contribution by offering to police and suppress monopolistic practices of its nationals which harm the economies of other countries in exchange for equivalent protection from other states.

More About Thalidomide

by JAMES RIDGEWAY

Thalidomide never got on the market in the United States largely because of the obstinacy of Dr. Frances O. Kelsey, the Food and Drug Administration's medical officer, who had seen reports from other countries of side effects, and who demanded more information from Wm. S. Merrell Co., the manufacturer, before she would clear the drug for distribution in this country.

Nonetheless, she was under continuous pressure to pass out thalidomide from the time the new drug application was filed September 12, 1960, until it was finally withdrawn after its effects on unborn children were made plain in March 1962. The story of the efforts to get the drug approved by the FDA was slowly revealed.

Before a drug could go on the market, the manufacturer was required to furnish the FDA with certain information gathered from clinical investigations. In the case of thalidomide there appear to have been about 50 physicians who tested the drug for more than a four-month period; all in all, more than 1,000 doctors had been sent experimental samples.

One of the early clinical investigators in this country was Dr. Ray O. Nulsen, an obstetrician of Cincinnati, Ohio. He began testing thalidomide on pregnant patients in the late spring of 1959, and continued to do so until instructed to stop in late 1961. Dr. Nulsen is listed as the author of one of the two or three articles published involving the drug's possible effect on unborn children, and for this reason his article aroused unusual interest. It appeared in the June 1961 issue of the *American Journal of Obstetrics and Gynecology*. It states that thalidomide had no deleterious effect upon the babies delivered of mothers he studied who had been receiving thalidomide late in pregnancy. Dr. Kelsey remembers that the drug

Reprinted by permission of the New Republic, © *1966, Harrison-Blaine of New Jersey, Inc.*

company made references both to the Nulsen article and to the research that stood behind it, in its diligent quest for approval of this new drug; still, she was wary of the claims. The crucial period for deformities was early, not late pregnancy. Dr. Kelsey went back to the company for more information concerning this period.

Dr. Nulsen was named defendant along with Richardson-Merrell (The Wm. S. Merrell Co. is a division of Richardson-Merrell), in two million-dollar damage suits brought by two Ohio women who claimed the doctor gave them thalidomide in early pregnancy. Both women gave birth to deformed children. Attorneys for both the doctor and the company denied the allegations.

In a letter addressed "To all Physicians" on August 10, 1962, Merrell described chronologically the company's association with the drug and its precautionary action when possible ill effects were brought to its attention.

In June 1964 Craig Spangenberg, attorney for the women, took the deposition of Dr. Nulsen. This document provided an interesting view of the way research into new drugs is conducted in this country.

Over the years Dr. Nulsen had done clinical research in experimental drugs for several large firms, including Merrell. On April 20, 1959, Dr. Raymond C. Pogge, then director of Merrell's department of medical research, wrote Dr. Nulsen a letter asking whether he would be interested in testing a new sedative, "rather widely used in Europe for the symptomatic treatment of nervous tension." (Thalidomide then was called MER-32, and in Canada, Kevadon.) Dr. Pogge wrote, "I am anxious to confirm (or refute) in a statistically significant manner the claim that it is a useful preparation for the control of nervous tension associated with allergic disorders, cardiovascular disease, obstetrical and gynecologic conditions, gastrointestinal disease and a wide variety of ailments." He wanted to interest a small group of investigators in testing the product. Specifically, he wanted each investigator to select 20 patients suffering from almost any type of nervous tension and treat half of them with thalidomide and the other half with a placebo tablet. (A placebo is a medication which has no medicinal value.)

•

Dr. Nulsen agreed to the testing program. Dr. Pogge was encouraged by the initial results, and the studies were later expanded. Dr. Nulsen said he never received any fees for his work on thalidomide, no fees or honorarium for his subsequent article.

"I note, doctor," Spangenberg said in taking Dr. Nulsen's deposition, "that he [Dr. Pogge] asked you to start testing promptly and to send in reports. Do you have copies of the reports you sent in?"

"No, it was all verbal," Dr. Nulsen replied.

Dr. Nulsen later said he had passed on the testing information to Dr.

Pogge "by telephone, or it may have been that we had lunch together, or it may have been we played golf."

Spangenberg asked Dr. Nulsen about the details of his research:

Q. When you started giving patients doses of thalidomide at the hour of sleep, Dr. Nulsen, did you keep a record of who these patients were?

A. Yes.

Q. And how much you gave them?

A. Yes.

Q. Did you have any means of making any direct observation from the patients? By that I mean this, I know some clinical researchers wrote papers in which they said they would give the drug and every 30 minutes they would look at the patient and make some physical observation on what the patient seemed to be doing.

A. No, this was not done. The people took these in their own home.

Q. And would report back to you how often?

A. When they would come in for a visit or if they would call, by phone.

Q. Did you obtain consent from the patients in written form during this clinical investigation?

A. No.

But Dr. Nulsen explained, "We didn't give people this thing against their will. We always explained to them that this was something we were trying and it wasn't obtained, it couldn't be obtained in the drug-store, and that they should let me know how they liked it, how it worked."

By late 1960, Dr. Nulsen said, he had given thalidomide to some 81 pregnant women in their last trimester. This period of pregnancy was of particular interest to Merrell since it is a time women often are unable to sleep because of the discomfort. He had a list of the patients' names, and although they had not been observed in the use of the drug, the doctor had recorded from their later comments how they felt. Most of them said they had a good night's sleep. As he remembered it, there may have been one instance of side effects after taking the drug.

•

This information eventually was pulled together in an article published under Dr. Nulsen's name in the June 1961 issue of the *American Journal of Obstetrics and Gynecology*; the title was "Trial of Thalidomide in Insomnia Associated with the Third Trimester." It was a rather detailed four-page technical paper, laced with footnotes, which went over past research on thalidomide before discussing the doctor's own work. Its thrust

100

was summed up in the final sentence: "Thalidomide is a safe and effective sleep-inducing agent which seems to fulfill the requirements outlined in this paper for a satisfactory drug to be used late in pregnancy."

In taking the doctor's deposition, Spangenberg asked him: "Who wrote the article, Dr. Nulsen?"

Dr. Nulsen replied, "Dr. Pogge. I supplied him with all the information."

Plans for the article apparently had been underway for some time. In a letter dated January 25, 1960, Dr. Pogge had written:

> Dear Ray, Many thanks... for the splendid collection of 102 Kevadon reports received this morning. I think that I can have a very rough draft which we can go over together if it is convenient for you to have lunch with me on Thursday....
>
> In order to refer to your work in the handy file card, the text of which is included in the New Drug Application, I will need a very short note stating that you will authorize me to cite your Kevadon data as 'To Be Published.' After the journal has actually accepted your paper then I would like very much to have your permission to purchase reprints.

(The *American Journal of Obstetrics and Gynecology* states that "neither the editors nor the publisher accept responsibility for the views and statements of authors as published in their original communications.")

The article contained a diagram of thalidomide's chemical structure. Spangenberg asked Dr. Nulsen about it:

> Q. Now at the time you submitted the article and the diagram printed in it, did you really know what that diagram meant?
> A. No, I can't say I knew exactly what it meant so far as its chemical name was concerned or the breakdown....

At another point the attorney asked:

> Q. All right. In your article you cite many other researchers, and I will confess, if I may, when I asked you if you read German, your article cites about a half a dozen German magazines and German texts. [Dr. Nulsen had said earlier in the questioning that while he studied German in college he no longer read it.] Did you ever read these articles?
> A. No. That was supplied to me.
> Q. You also cite Mandarino, another doctor, and footnote the citation, and the footnote reads, 'To Be Published.' Did you ever see his article?
> A. I don't remember having seen it.

Spangenberg later asked:

> There was another sentence in this same article . . . there you are saying: "Studies on the metabolism, fate, and tissue distribution of thalidomide are being conducted with radioactive material but the data have not been published." This was information that was given you by Merrell and written in the article by Merrell, true?
> A. Yes.
> Q. Did they ever give you information on the metabolism and tissue distribution of thalidomide? By "they" I mean did Merrell ever give you that information?
> A. Not that I know of. I believe not.

On March 7, 1961, Dr. Nulsen wrote the drug company he had given between 500 and 750 patients thalidomide. Two hundred and fifty of these took the drug because they were unable to sleep. The remainder had taken doses for anxiety and tension or nervous indigestion with nausea. This group of patients would have taken the drug for a period of from one to three months, he said. An additional group of from 400 to 500 patients took an aspirin and thalidomide compound as needed for a variety of discomforts. He said none of these patients showed any symptoms of peripheral neuritis, a side effect that was reported in late December 1960 in the *British Medical Journal*.

In his deposition, Dr. Nulsen said he did not keep any detailed records of the number of pills he had received from Merrell, nor the exact totals he had dispensed. He could not remember how many the company had given him all told. Spangenberg asked him for more details on the testing records:

> Q. In the Kevadon program generally, doctor, there were certain report forms that the doctors were supposed to send, a standard form, or a standard form of case report form that would list a patient's name or initials, the age, the drug used, the dose used, and then a table of checklists as to whether it is better than the barbiturate or equal to it or less effective, whether side effects were experienced, and the indications for its use, that is, the reason you give it, associated with or resulting from a list of disorders, including obstetrical conditions. Are you familiar with that report form?
> A. We never filled out—so far as I know, I believe we never filled out anything like that so far as Kevadon is concerned, but we did fill out something like that for MRD-640 (an aspirin compound containing thalidomide).

Spangenberg asked: "Doctor, you recall your article, which you said they

102

wrote for you in draft form, listed a study of cases, and as I remember reading that article, there was quite a bit of detail as to the age groups and the effects and percentages of those who got as good relief and so forth. What kind of reporting or written detail was there to support those statements in the draft of the article Merrell wrote?"

"I don't remember," Dr. Nulsen said. "It may have been we filled out these original report things Dr. Pogge suggested or it may have been I put figures down on paper and stuck it in my pocket and gave those figures at lunch one time. I don't remember."

Since thalidomide the Kefauver amendments have helped tighten new drug testing procedures. The circumstances under which Dr. Nulsen's "clinical investigation" were carried out, however, have not altogether changed. As Congressman L. H. Fountain's (D, N.C.) 1965 hearings disclosed, drug companies still ghost-write articles for doctors, and medical journals publish them, without making clear their origin. The FDA now has authority to veto a drug company's plan of clinical investigation into new drugs if it does not seem adequate. But in practice the FDA is short-staffed and may well not get around to examining the details of a new drug investigation until the product is on the market. There is little to ensure that the investigators themselves have sufficient background in the research they undertake. And a doctor's patients still need not even be told they are the guinea pigs for a new drug. Under federal law, this is unnecessary if, in the "investigator's professional judgment, [it] is contrary to the best interests of the subjects."

Can a Woman
Be Feminine Forever?

by NANCY SOMMERS
and JAMES RIDGEWAY

"Must women tolerate castration?"

No, according to Dr. Robert A. Wilson, a Brooklyn gynecologist, who asked this question in his book *Feminine Forever*. In it he argued that if women take a prescribed dose of sex hormones they will not disintegrate into crones.

In his 40 years as a gynecologist, Dr. Wilson has had considerable clinical experience with menopause. Sometimes, his patients merely became deeply depressed on approaching this important time of change. In one instance, he had to take care of a middle-aged lady who was flinging herself from lover to lover in a final mad search for fulfillment before it was too late. Once a well-known Brooklyn gangster came into Dr. Wilson's office, pulled out a pistol, and demanded that the doctor do something to calm his wife, whom menopause had turned into a shrew. Dr. Wilson has been conscious of the sex revolution which is placing heavy demands on women to act younger as they grow older. And with an increasing number of women taking up important managerial positions in industry, he is worried about what can happen to their employees should the change of life turn the women into tyrants. Business could go down the drain. In his efforts to cope with menopause, Dr. Wilson has developed a hormone therapy which has received a good bit of attention. Half a dozen women's magazines have published rather complimentary pieces about his work. A paperback referring to his theories of estrogen treatment has come out. And then Dr. Wilson's *Feminine Forever* appeared.

An advertisement said:

Feminine Forever tells how to avoid menopause completely in your life, and stay a romantic, desirable, vibrant woman as long as you live. It shows how women who already have gone through the anguish of menopause can experience the phenomenon of Menopausal Reversal—and, without regaining the ability to bear children, grow *visibly younger* day by day until they are transformed into the exciting vibrant females they were before the "change"!

•

After dealing with hundreds of cases, Dr. Wilson concluded menopause is a deficiency disease, caused by the running down of female sex glands that produce two hormones, estrogen and progesterone. This imbalance, he concluded, can be corrected by giving women doses of synthetic hormones in easy-to-take tablet form which will have the effect of keeping them looking and acting young and in general good health. If a woman gets the proper amount of these hormones, Dr. Wilson says, she need not have sagging breasts, shriveled genitals, a dowager's hump, poor bones and itchy skin. Nor will she need to suffer postmenopausal gastrointestinal disorders, wretched headaches, hot flashes, night sweats, loss of memory, insomnia, all of which, he says often affect women in and after menopause.

Moreover, Dr. Wilson believes his estrogen therapy may well find a general application among younger women who feel they lack femininity, that is women who perhaps feel their breasts are too small, who tend to get fat or are frigid.

To get an idea of a woman's hormone needs, Dr. Wilson has devised a Femininity Index. He takes a vaginal smear on a slide and puts it under a microscope.

Three different types of body cells are visible on the slide: superficial, intermediate and parabasal cells. The cytologist in his laboratory makes a careful count of all three cell types. This count answers one of the most crucial questions that ever confront a woman. It tells whether her body is still feminine, or whether it is gradually turning neuter. If 80 percent or more of the total cell counts are superficial cells, you can still rejoice in your full femininity—your body still retains all the qualities that make you a woman. If the count of superficial cells is less than 80 percent, it is a clear warning that your femininity is waning.

Throughout much of his therapy, Dr. Wilson administered his estrogen treatments in sequence, giving women first an estrogen drug and then, later on in their cycle, changing this to a progesterone. It induces bleeding, and thus simulates a period in women after menopause. Later, however, he found that certain kinds of birth control pills may be a way of making up women's estrogen deficiency. He stumbled onto this quite by chance,

105

according to the book. Mrs. P.G., a woman of 52, came into his office one day in 1963 for a check-up. She had an erect carriage, good muscle tone, firm and supple breasts. Her skin was smooth and pliant as a girl's. Not even her neck was wrinkled. Dr. Wilson at once concluded she must be one of the relatively few women taking hormone treatment; he was wrong. She was, however, taking a certain birth control pill. "Soon, the logical connection between 'the pill' and the menopause prevention became clear in my mind," Dr. Wilson writes:

> Chemically, there is a close relationship between the contents of contraceptive pills and the hormones employed in menopause therapy. In some pills the hormones are identical. One brand of birth control pills contains a combination of an estrogen (mestranol) and an estrogenic progestin (norethynodrel), both quite similar to the hormones (estrogen and a progestin) I had been using all along for menopause prevention. It so happened that Mrs. P.G. had been taking that particular type of pill. Without realizing it, her doctor had been prescribing menopause therapy. . . .
>
> This estrogenic birth control pill provides a form of menopause prevention and treatment in addition to its contraceptive effect. The chief difference is that in the usual type of menopause therapy estrogen and progestin are given in sequence during different phases of the menstrual cycle, whereas the birth control pill contains both estrogen and progestin in combination.

Dr. Wilson was at once struck by the possibilities. This previously unsuspected property of certain birth control pills, acting as a menopause preventive, could perhaps prove even more important than its principal purpose, he wrote. Six million people in this country take oral contraceptives. He writes:

> Immediately after my encounter with Mrs. P.G., I began a systematic study of contraceptive pills as menopause preventives. On the basis of my findings, I can now confidently assert that no woman who uses estrogenic birth control pills [*i.e.*, pills containing norethynodrel] will ever experience menopause if she continues taking "the pill" beyond her childbearing years.

The basis of this assertion lies in the results of a study Dr. Wilson ran on 82 women, ranging in age from 32 to 57 years, with an average age of 45.8. Of 27 patients who took birth control pills specifically to avoid menopause, 26 were completely successful, he says. They never developed menopausal symptoms. The single exception experienced only mild symptoms. The other patients in this group took birth control pills to relieve menopausal symptoms that had already set in. This proved to be effective in 93 percent of the cases. In all the 82 cases, Dr. Wilson said, there were no instances of systemic, breast or genital cancer.

And he says it now appears that estrogenic contraceptive pills accomplish three goals: they keep women estrogen-rich and cancer-proof and they prevent menopause. However, Dr. Wilson does warn that under no circumstances should birth control pills be taken without a doctor's approval; the patient should be under a doctor's supervision.

•

In *Feminine Forever*, Dr. Wilson suggests that people who are interested in finding out more about menopause prevention inquire at the Wilson Research Foundation, Inc., a nonprofit organization based in New York City which he heads. His son, Robert A. Wilson, Jr., is executive director. This is an independent organization that makes available pamphlets about estrogen, arranges for lectures to be made and provides doctors with technical information about estrogen therapy.

In his book, Dr. Wilson did not name the birth control pill he used in his study of 82 women. But he said recently the drug was Enovid, the oral contraceptive made by G. D. Searle & Co. He said he personally felt it to be superior for menopause disorders because of its combination of estrogenic progestin; Enovid is cited by name in literature the foundation sends out to doctors. This literature also mentions other hormone preparations. Among them are Premarin, an estrogen preparation made by Ayerst Laboratories, a division of American Home Products, and Provera, a progestin put out by Upjohn.

In its application for tax exemption, filed January 19, 1965, the Wilson Research Foundation showed contributions of about $34,000 in 1964. Of this total, about $31,350 came from the following: Searle Foundation (set up by the Searle family), $17,000; Ayerst, $8,700; and Upjohn, $5,600. Robert A. Wilson Jr. said both Searle and Ayerst made contributions in 1965.

Dr. Wilson stresses, however, that the foundation is completely independent. He says it is approaching several major pharmaceutical companies in hopes of enlisting financial support. And it wants help from businesses in allied fields, *e.g.*, sanitary napkin manufacturers.

The Food and Drug Administration has not generally cleared Enovid for any use but as an oral contraceptive. However, G. D. Searle & Co. said it has an investigational license to test Enovid in menopause prevention. A spokesman for the company says Dr. Wilson is one of its investigators. He has been given a supply of Enovid for this purpose. The company spokesman says Searle is helping to sponsor the Wilson Foundation's research, but he would not disclose how much money is involved. The Searle spokesman says Dr. Wilson is completely independent, and received no support whatever from the company in writing his book or in getting it published.

Dr. Wilson said a doctor could extend the indications for a drug's use on his own responsibility and that Enovid simply had the effect of combining in one pill several different drugs already on the market and available for menopause disorders.

There is concern in the government about possible side effects from taking birth control pills. These include fatal clots, disabling clots and eye damage. In addition, there are fears that over a period of years the birth control pill may have a possible relation with cancer. One highly regarded expert at the National Institutes of Health says that in general Dr. Wilson's estrogen therapy presents very complicated medical problems that have not been resolved.

The Golden Pill:
We Can't Yet
Be Sure It's Safe

by MORTON MINTZ

"In her fresh, warm voice, she was singing a hymn of praise to God for inspiring mankind to invent the birth control pill." It is, she said, "shocking that the pill shouldn't be made available to everyone who wants it." She was known as the Singing Nun but is now, *McCall's* said in an article about her last May, "plain Jeanine Deckers." The name of her hymn was *"La Pilule d'Or"* —"The Golden Pill."

"If the instructions of the physician are followed ... I can imagine no danger whatsoever ... no condition in which these pills would not be safe to take." This from an interview of November 6, 1965 with Dr. Joseph W. Goldzieher, director of the Division of Clinical Sciences, Southwest Foundation for Research and Education.

"The excruciating pain increased until 10 o'clock that night when I experienced dagger-like, massive pains throughout my chest, screaming 'I'm dying.' A half-hour later, at George Washington Hospital, a dose of Heparin alleviated the condition. I spent two weeks in the hospital, and after seven weeks was taken off all medication and declared cured.... Last summer ... my 35-year-old sister, having taken oral contraceptives for about two months, had a severe thrombophlebitis which incapacitated her for several months."

Reprinted by permission of the New Republic, © *1968, Harrison-Blaine of New Jersey, Inc.*

This from a letter to the writer by a Bethesda, Maryland, mother of four sons who suffered a pulmonary embolism two months after starting to take The Pill. She was 44, had "enjoyed near-perfect health all my life" and had been rated a "good risk" by the obstetrician who had cared for her for 14 years.

On May 6, 1967, the *British Medical Journal* published a report of momentous significance, considering that The Pill was being taken by an estimated six million women in the United States and five million elsewhere. On the basis of three separate studies, the British Medical Research Council had concluded "that there can be no reasonable doubt that some types of thromboembolic disorder are associated with the use of oral contraceptives." The Council was positive of a cause-effect relation with thrombophlebitis, in which a blood clot forms in a vein, and with pulmonary embolism, in which the lung artery is blocked by a piece of a clot that has broken away at a distant site and moved through the circulatory system. Although firm evidence of a causal relation with strokes was lacking, the Council said, the preliminary results "support this suggestion."

The Food and Drug Administration's Advisory Committee on Obstetrics and Gynecology, in a report filed in August 1966, concluded that there are "no adequate data, at this time, proving these compounds unsafe. . . ." But at a press briefing on January 18, 1968, at the FDA, Dr. Louis M. Hellman, chairman of the FDA Committee, acknowledged what had up to then been heresy: a cause-effect relation had been demonstrated —by the British—between The Pill and thrombophlebitis and pulmonary embolism. FDA Commissioner James L. Goddard and Dr. Herbert L. Ley, Jr., director of the Bureau of Medicine, said that FDA had undertaken an "intensive review" of the labeling, which has been uniform for all brands of The Pill.

The death rate indicated by the preliminary British figures was three per 100,000 per year. For women who could use The Pill throughout the child-bearing age span, that is, from 15 through 44, the risk over the 30-year period would be 90 per 100,000. Efforts were made to make the risk appear trivial. The British Medical Research Council emphasized that in women of child-bearing age, the mortality rate "attributable to road-traffic accidents" is six per 100,000, or twice as high. This foolishness infected the lead paragraphs of dispatches from London by the wire services. United Press International reported that the Council found The Pill "far safer than a walk across a busy street." Reuters noted the Council's dismissal of the risk as "small compared to the number of deaths in childbirth or in traffic accidents."

Reuters' reference to maternal mortality was the result of more statistical non-science. Considering that it was engaged in by the Research Council

110

(and in this country by men with the credentials of Dr. Hellman and Dr. Joshua Lederberg, a Nobel Prize winner), not much blame attaches to the public for being taken in. Thus the Research Council cited an incidence of maternal mortality of 12 per 100,000 completed pregnancies, or nine more than among users of the birth control pills. The implication, of course, was that at a rate of nine per 100,000 The Pill saves the lives of women who use it. A preliminary objection to this is that it makes an unfair comparison—between women who are generally healthy (those using The Pill) and women who in large proportion have previously existing poor health which contributes to their maternal mortality. But there is a more fundamental objection which gets to the heart of the matter: the safety of The Pill is always *relative* and never absolute. Assuming the absence of medical conditions that contraindicate use of the estrogen-progesterone combinations, The Pill is safe in women for whom virtually 100 percent efficacy against conception is indistinguishable from safety—for example, mothers who cannot survive the birth of another child. The Pill is far less safe in, say, young women who want to work for a time before having children and who reliably will use another method of conception control, especially the diaphragm with spermicidal cream or jelly or vaginal foam (the intrauterine devices are not advised in women who have not been pregnant).

For the sake of simplicity, assume there are 10 million women who reliably will use the diaphragm or foam. Over the course of a year, the number who will become pregnant will be about 250,000 or about 2.5 percent, according to the best available estimates. It is this total—250,000 —and *not* the 10 million to which the maternal mortality rate must be applied, because 9.75 million of the women do not become pregnant. And so the number dying in childbirth would be 30. If all of the 10 million had taken The Pill, there would have been 10 times as many deaths, or 300 (the product of applying a death rate from clotting of three per 100,000 users).

Dr. Hellman termed the three-per-100,000 risk "very, very small." This contention is arguable on several grounds. *First*, it is a risk that, as already suggested, many women need not take. *Second*, it slights the unquestioned danger of serious and permanent disability in women who are not killed by clotting diseases. *Third*, Dr. Herbert Ratner, who believes The Pill should be removed from the market, recalls that at one time the government was ready to recall the Sabin vaccine "if cases of paralytic polio caused by the vaccine exceeded one per million inoculations." (He also points out that the death rate from polio in the United States has exceeded two per 100,000 in only three of the 57 years in which records have been kept: 2.4 in 1910, 8.4 in 1916 and 2.1 in 1952.) *Fourth*, the British calculation of the risk is almost certainly an understatement because it is based on *retrospective* studies; that is, not until after disease developed was inquiry made about use of The Pill. *Prospective* trials match patients

111

who are started on a drug with others who are not. Then the fates of the two groups are compared.

•

Dr. Arthur Ruskin, director of FDA's Adverse Reactions Task Force, said in *FDA Papers* that the "more scientific" prospective method "must be used when retrospective methods have failed to substantiate or disprove serious suspected adverse reactions, *e.g.*, thromboembolism." He went on to say that prospective trials with Parnate, an anti-depressant, uncovered 100 to 2,700 times as many cases of hypertensive crises as had been "originally suspected." The precise application of this experience to The Pill is speculative, but there can be no doubt that well-controlled prospective studies would unearth many more thromboembolic episodes than the retrospective studies, useful as they may be.

Finally, the supposed "very, very small" risk fails to take into account numerous other hazards. Plain Jeanine could not have known, when she expressed shock that The Pill wasn't available "to everyone," that FDA's labeling warns that in girls with incomplete bone growth the oral contraceptives can cause premature closure of the joints. Mothers using The Pill while breast-feeding, the labeling points out, produce milk containing "detectable amounts of the active ingredients. . . . The significance of this dose to the infant has not been determined."

In a pilot study in Great Britain sponsored by the Research Council, 118 women taking The Pill for the first time were compared with a "control" group. Almost one in 10 suffered symptoms of depression which in some cases was so severe as to call for psychiatric treatment (this indicates that such symptoms occurred in 1.1 million of the estimated 11 million women believed to be using The Pill worldwide). Minor side effects such as weight gain and nausea aside, there are risks of diabetes and jaundice. "Out of 13 significant side effects," *McCall's* said in a report on a survey it sponsored among 6,733 Fellows of the American College of Obstetricians and Gynecologists, the one "most frequently attributed to The Pill" was "the appearance in some patients of brownish facial skin pigmentation." There are reports of women who have become sterile after using oral contraceptives.

One question of utmost importance is whether The Pill causes cancer or prevents it, promotes a preexisting cancer or retards it. "It is to be emphasized that all known human carcinogens require a latent period of approximately one decade," the FDA Advisory Committee said in its report of August 1966. "Hence any valid conclusion must await accurate data on a much larger group of women studied for at least 10 years." The "much larger group" would be 20,000 to 30,000 plus at least 20,000 "controls." Similarly, a population of 100,000 children followed for six to nine years would be necessary to determine the relative frequency of abnormalities in the offspring of mothers who had taken The Pill.

•

How have we got into a situation in which 11 million healthy—not sick— human beings have come to take, 20 days a month, potent drugs about which so little really is known? A public predisposed to believe almost blindly in science and technology, deeply troubled by the desperate problem of overpopulation, and seeing "La Pilule d'Or" as the passkey to a new sexual convenience—such a public is not disposed to skepticism. But this public was badly served—by FDA, Congress, assorted experts, much of the medical profession, the press and manufacturers.

Years before The Pill, the pre-Goddard FDA had been captured by the drug industry it purported to regulate. Sometimes with disastrous consequence, the agency released dangerous new chemical agents despite inadequate testing. FDA was predictably incompetent when, in 1960, it concluded that "the evidence establishes the safety" of Enovid, the pioneer Pill; six years later, FDA's Advisory Committee recognized that the paucity of data "makes unreliable *any* assumptions" about a causal relation between *any* oral contraceptive and serious adverse effects. Although destined for millions, Enovid went on sale after being tested for a maximum of 38 consecutive menstrual cycles in an incredibly small total of 132 women. As to cancer, the experience was adequately documented for a mere 400 users, and in them for an inadequate four years. Until the adoption of uniform labeling in late 1966, identical compounds were labeled differently. Thus the FDA-approved instructions for Ortho-Novum said nothing about use in a woman with a history of psychic depression; the labeling for Norinyl said it was contraindicated in such a woman; both products were composed of equal amounts of norethindrone and mestranol. In a year when—on a purely statistical basis—1,200 cases of breast cancer were expected in women on the Pill, FDA's files had a report on one case.

In 1963, an advisory committee convened by FDA to look into initial reports of lung clots in women on The Pill made only one recommendation —for a well controlled prospective trial. Had it not been for the British studies, we would have today nothing more than what Dr. Roy Hertz has called "a statistically inadequate mass of scattered observations." FDA shelved the 1963 recommendation for prospective testing. It did not even ask Congress for funding, and Congress never asked why not.

In the absence of proper tests, such Pill advocates as the late Dr. Gregory Pincus could and did keep chanting that it had not been proved unsafe. Dr. Alan F. Guttmacher, president of Planned Parenthood-World Population, was urging prescription of The Pill "two cycles before marriage so that the relatively transient, minor effects will . . . disappear before the honeymoon," *i.e.*, before the girl knows whether her marriage is among the approximately 10 percent that prove sterile. The first reports associating The Pill with strokes were published in the *British Medical Journal* in 1962,

113

but in April 1965 Dr. Joseph F. Sadusk Jr., then FDA's top physician, said as to a possible cause-effect relation, "the information at hand is to the contrary." The assurance had hardly crossed his lips before a series of such associations began to be reported in the United States. The influential, ubiquitous Dr. Sadusk was a member of a World Health Organization task force that, in 1966, issued a highly reassuring report. But, the *Ladies' Home Journal* reported, one member said that unanimity was achieved only after an initial six-to-five split, under pressure from population-control forces to "deliver a whitewash" and with the help of an Iron Curtain delegate who liked being invited to "conferences in the West." In October 1965, in a major report in the *Journal* of the American Medical Association, an AMA committee said that if the safety of The Pill had not been assured, FDA would not have let it go on the market. Recently, both the AMA and FDA Commissioner Goddard have become commendably cautious, although as late as January 1967, on CBS' *Face the Nation*, Dr. Goddard insisted that The Pill was safe so long as its use was carefully directed by a physician who had carefully considered his patient's medical history. How could the prescribing physician know from a favorable examination and history whether a woman was predisposed to clotting? Whether a latent cancer existed? Yet the famed Dr. John Rock was telling the millions who read *Family Circle* that with precautions of the kind counseled by Dr. Goddard, The Pill "is perfectly safe." No drug is "perfectly safe."

Be Happy, Light Up

A NEW REPUBLIC EDITORIAL

The Senate Commerce Committee was treated to the world premiere of the Warner Brothers film, *World of Pleasure*, planned for release in theatres in 15 nations. It will not win an Oscar, but the Department of Agriculture will be happy if it just hooks a few new cigarette smokers. While the Surgeon General was reporting a causal connection between cigarette smoking and lung cancer, and while Congress was enacting a mild law requiring health warnings on cigarette packs, the Department of Agriculture was spending $106,000 to make a 20-minute film, in five different languages, touting the pleasures of smoking.

The film's existence was discovered by Don Oberdorfer, a reporter for the Knight newspapers, who wondered what the Department was doing for tobacco growers. He found that Agriculture spent $210,000 in 1965 to subsidize cigarette commercials in Japan, Thailand and Austria, and that it was about to release *World of Pleasure*, a fatuous travelogue. Everywhere one goes, a young couple is lighting up—at Hollywood and Vine, in the shadow of the Sphinx, in a Parisian cafe, in Winston-Salem, N.C. Ephrem Zimbalist Jr., the English-language film's narrator, delivers the cigarette message: "Capture the flavor of the land and one of its most pleasurable products. . . . Tobacco is a part of the lives of millions of people throughout the world—the pure joy part. . . . A symbol of pleasure within the reach of everyone. . . . An odyssey of global enjoyment."

Nowhere in the credits is the hand of the Department of Agriculture visible. Nor is it explained that the Burley and Dark Leaf Tobacco Export Association, the Leaf Tobacco Exporters Association, Tobacco Associates, Inc., and the Virginia Dark-Fired and Sun-Cured Tobacco Export Association were parties to the contract with Warner Brothers. (Senator

Thruston Morton of Kentucky, who approves of the film, speculated at last week's hearing that it would spoil the film's "soft sell" to disclose that the US government was responsible for it. If you labeled the film, he said, it would automatically be called propaganda. People would be saying "the Department of Agriculture is giving us a lot of bunk.")

The Department of Agriculture says it cannot discriminate against one commodity when it makes similar films promoting the sale of others— lard, for example. Moreover, the film will only be shown in countries which welcome it. (The film contract calls for distribution in England, Belgium, Denmark, Sweden and Norway, all of which according to Senator Warren Magnuson (D, Wash.) have government campaigns against smoking. England, Magnuson said, prohibits cigarette advertising altogether.) Anyway, explains the Department, the film was paid for out of counterpart funds amassed in the Food for Peace program which must be spent abroad.

David L. Hume, assistant administrator of the Foreign Agricultural Service of USDA, defends the Department for looking after the interests of the "700,000 farm families engaged in tobacco production" in the US. In a letter to Senator Magnuson, Secretary of Health, Education and Welfare John Gardner calls attention to broader interests: "The overwhelming weight of scientific evidence indicates a strong link between cigarette smoking and lung cancer. We consider it essential to make that fact known as widely as possible."

Squabble over Cigarettes

A NEW REPUBLIC EDITORIAL

The controversy over smoking and cancer is taking a new turn. In 1965 the tobacco companies got Congress to keep the government from tampering with their advertising; now they're in a violent squabble among themselves over how best to sell their cigarettes.

One of the big companies, P. Lorillard, quit the Cigarette Advertising Code and rushed to the market with a new brand called True. It is designed to deliver reduced tar and nicotine in the smoke.

The advertising code was drawn up after the Public Health Service's report, linking cigarette smoking to cancer and heart disease, came out in 1964. It took effect January 1965; all nine major cigarette companies were members. The code was meant to show Congress that the tobacco industry could police its own advertising. The first major change was to rule out tar and nicotine statements on cigarette packages: Robert B. Meyner, former Governor of New Jersey, who administers the code, felt these claims were without significance. However, the Federal Trade Commission in effect overrode the code and declared there was nothing illegal about making statements on amounts of tar and nicotine. Lorillard at once announced its new cigarette.

The chances of one's getting cancer from smoking are believed to be lessened as the amount of tar in a cigarette is reduced. In 1964, Dr. James Hundley, an Assistant Surgeon General of the Public Health Service, told a congressional committee: "We are convinced you can make a safer cigarette, much safer. Some cigarettes have been developed that have about one-tenth of the nicotine and tars of the ordinary cigarettes."

However, there are several reasons why cigarette companies might not want to put tar and nicotine statements on packages. The companies could end up spending millions competing against one another on this score, and in the process be constantly calling attention to unpleasant health hazards. Also, the less tar and nicotine in a cigarette, the worse the taste. So if competition were to result in lower quantities of tar and nicotine and less flavorsome smoke, sales might suffer.

A group of cancer experts, representing government and private agencies and called the National Interagency Council on Smoking and Health, has urged that tar and nicotine statements be included on cigarette packages. So has the American Cancer Society. In March 1966, the ACS told the FTC that:

> All studies of cigarette smoking show that its harmful effects are related to the number of cigarettes smoked and to the degree of inhalation; in other words to dosage. There is clear evidence also that tars in cigarette smoke contain chemicals which produce cancer when applied to the skin of animals and to the bronchial mucosa of dogs, and it has long been recognized that nicotine is one of the most powerful poisons known.
>
> We are convinced therefore that it would be in the public interest to let people know how much tar and nicotine they are taking into their bodies when they smoke cigarettes. The customer is given this information concerning the drugs he takes, the food which he eats, the beverages which he drinks. Why not concerning the cigarette smoke he inhales?

It was after having received several similar statements from other experts that the FTC decided to permit tar and nicotine statements. Governor Meyner was unmoved. He said this was stale information. "There is no adequate, relevant and valid scientific data," he said, "demonstrating that any specific amount of tar and nicotine is significant in terms of health, and in the absence of an adequate disclaimer of such significance to health such representations would reasonably be regarded as false and misleading." If Lorillard is successful with True, then Meyner either may be forced to change his mind and allow tar and nicotine statements in advertising, or the code is likely to fold up, as other companies follow Lorillard's lead.

The effect of the code in areas other than health is negligible. Meyner has been concerned to make sure cigarette advertising is not directed primarily at youngsters. This doesn't appear to be working out. In February 1966, *Advertising Age* analyzed the most recent Nielsen ratings. It showed that five of the ten most popular programs of twelve- to seventeen-year-olds carried cigarette commercials. These included the two best-liked shows, *Get Smart* and *The Man from U.N.C.L.E.*, both shown over NBC.

In all, nothing much has come of the Surgeon General's report on smoking and cancer. According to the Agriculture Department, Americans in

118

1965 consumed 529 billion cigarettes, a 3.5 percent rise in consumption over 1964. The industry won its battle to keep the FTC from regulating cigarette advertising until 1969. In exchange, it settled for the meaningless label on packages. The President never has said a word about the dangers of smoking cigarettes. In 1966 the government spent $106,000 in Food for Peace funds to make a movie *promoting* cigarette smoking abroad.

Filtered Cigarettes

A NEW REPUBLIC EDITORIAL

In his study of filter-tip cigarettes at New York State's Cancer Research Center, Dr. George E. Moore made it perfectly clear that no filter is effective in trapping harmful tars and nicotine. The only real protection against getting cancer or heart disease from cigarettes is to stop smoking.

But the tests he ran on nine brands did show that some filters are a bit better than others in catching the deadly ingredients. And this may have the useful side effect of spurring tobacco companies into more spirited competition in search of a safer cigarette, even if there is no such thing as a safe one.

Heretofore, cigarette makers had ducked the health problem by agreeing, through a trade organization called the Cigarette Advertising Code, not to use tar and nicotine statements in advertising. Publicly, they said this information was meaningless. Privately, they were relieved at not having to begin a competition which would necessarily parade their product's liabilities constantly before the public eye. They went breezily along talking about good taste sensations, advertising on children's television programs, and selling more cigarettes than ever.

Then, in the spring of 1966, P. Lorillard suddenly quit the Advertising Code organization and marketed a new brand called True, which it claimed was lower in tar and nicotine than other brands. Dr. Moore's study is a boost for True. It had less tar and nicotine than the nine other brands. (Some of the filter cigarettes he tested actually gave the smoker a bigger dose of tars and nicotine than regulars of the same brand. Filtered Pall Malls and Chesterfields are two examples.) P. Lorillard lost no time in tripling production of True cigarettes and hiring an advertising agency to put the study around.

Reprinted by permission of the New Republic, © *1966, Harrison-Blaine of New Jersey, Inc.*

In light of the Surgeon General's grim report on smoking and health, the government does shamefully little to warn the public about cigarettes. It ought, at the very least, to be insisting that the television networks, which carry a considerable amount of the cigarette advertising, carry a like amount of public service bulletins, urging people to stay away from cigarettes.

Time for the Truth

A NEW REPUBLIC EDITORIAL

Advertising is the most important news broadcast over television, because there's so much of it. In the case of cigarettes, the commercials are aimed at informing viewers, especially youngsters, that smoking is part of the socially acceptable, rich life and a good thing to do. This is inaccurate, for as the Public Health Service has demonstrated smoking can, and does, lead to cancer and heart disease.

In 1967 the Federal Communications Commission ruled that stations which carry cigarette commercials must give "fair time" for ads and programs telling of the dangers. The decision was unanimous and came in response to a letter from a New York citizen who complained that WCBS ran ads which portrayed cigarette smoking as desirable. He wanted equal time for the opposite view. The commission said:

> The advertisements in question clearly promote the use of a particular cigarette as attractive and enjoyable. Indeed, they understandably have no other purpose. We believe that a station which presents such advertisements has the duty of informing its audience of the other side of this controversial issue of public importance— that however enjoyable, such smoking may be a hazard to the smoker's health.

However, the FCC turned down the request for equal time, coming out for "fair time" which it vaguely defined as follows:

> A station might, for example, reasonably determine that the above noted responsibility would be discharged by presenting each week, in addition to appropriate news reports or other programming deal-

Reprinted by permission of the New Republic, © *1967, Harrison-Blaine of New Jersey, Inc.*

ing with the subject, a number of the public service announcements of the American Cancer Society or HEW in this field. We stress, however, that in this as in other areas under the fairness doctrine, the type of programming and the amount and nature of the time to be afforded is a matter for the good faith and reasonable judgment of the licensee, upon the particular facts of the situation.

Before making its decision, the FCC cleared it with Senator Warren Magnuson (D, Wash.), who heads the Commerce Committee, and his opposite in the House, Harley Staggers (D, W.Va.). Magnuson, whose comments on the industry have become increasingly harsh, said:

Frankly, until such time as a safe cigarette has been developed I firmly believe that the cigarette industry should withdraw all advertising from the mass media. Barring that, the cigarette industry, broadcasting, the advertising agencies should cooperate with such groups as the American Cancer Society in presenting the full known facts of the hazards of smoking in a way best calculated to get the message to our young people.

The American Cancer Society says it will open its own library to stations looking for spot commercials and programs. In the past HEW has done little to mount a general advertising campaign against smoking. It should now take the lead in putting together the ads and making sure they are used. The government also should push the FCC to rule that not only "fair time" but "equal time" be given to groups which seek to inform the public about the hazards of smoking. The tobacco growers and the ad agencies and the networks won't like it. But when the "public interest, convenience and necessity" is so clearly on the side of saving lives, their preferences and profits are a distinctly secondary consideration.

Columbia's Filter

by JAMES RIDGEWAY

Columbia University was in the midst of a $200-million fund-raising drive when it took on the Strickman cigarette filter to make a fast buck. It hoped to do this by playing on the public's justified fear of getting cancer from smoking. However, the venture backfired and all the university got was a bad press. As a consequence, Columbia has tried to wriggle out of the deal.

The whole business began in early July 1967 with rumors on Wall Street that Columbia would soon come up with a new filter. Tobacco stock prices began to climb. On July 12 around 3 p.m. the Columbia news office sent around word to newspapers that there would be a press conference the next day "to announce a development of far-reaching importance which promises to benefit mankind by reducing the health hazards of smoking." On July 13, it said it had got the rights to a "revolutionary new cigarette filter." Grayson Kirk, the president, declared: "Some time ago Columbia was offered an unusual opportunity to participate in an arrangement which our medical specialists here today believe may make a significant contribution to lessen the hazards of cigarette smoking."

The deal seemed odd, even then. Neither Kirk nor Robert Strickman, the filter's inventor, would disclose the terms of their agreement. The scientists who were brought out to answer questions did not disclose test data. They did say, however, that no animal tests had been made. This immediately aroused suspicions, since animal tests are usual in this sort of experiment. It was subsequently revealed that Mr. Strickman had tried unsuccessfully to sell the filter to tobacco companies, before going to Columbia.

Not long after the press conference, Senator Warren Magnuson, chairman of the Senate Commerce Committee and a critic of the tobacco com-

Reprinted by permission of the New Republic, © *1968, Harrison-Blaine of New Jersey, Inc.*

panies, asked the Department of Health, Education and Welfare to look into the filter claims. He then went ahead to schedule his own hearings. Shortly before they opened, members of the Commerce Committee staff met with three representatives from Columbia and told them that their own investigations suggested the Strickman filter was of dubious value, producing results little different from existing filters. The Columbia people were bluntly warned that President Kirk could expect some hard questions when he appeared before the committee, and that he had better be ready with straight answers. At this point, two of the three Columbia representatives said they thought Kirk should come clean, admit that the university had made a mistake, that it didn't in fact know very much about the filter, and cut loose from the Strickman agreement. But the third man, reportedly the university's counsel, argued for a middle course: Kirk would humbly promise to conduct further, more detailed tests. This would give Columbia a hedge. If the filter were not much good or public pressure got too strong, the university could back out a bit more tactfully and with less adverse publicity. On the other hand, if the filter worked and Congress got off the university's back, they could push on. Kirk adopted this line, and Congress let him alone.

In early fall, Columbia found out a bit more about Strickman. He had been widely described as a consulting chemist who had worked for eight years in his home laboratory before coming up with the new filter. Actually, in 1961 Strickman was an officer and director of a company called Casavan Industries Inc., which through its subsidiaries was in real estate and in the manufacture of packaging goods and building materials. In 1963, a federal grand jury in Newark indicted Paul R. Casavina, the president of the company, and certain other officers, charging them with stock fraud. The indictment charged that Casavan had defrauded investors by selling stock that was not registered, and by pyramiding the assets of the company in such a way as to give it an appearance of a growing and prosperous enterprise, which it was not. Casavina was tried, convicted and sent to prison for eight years.

The testimony in Casavina's trial gives a few hints about the company's business operation. Frank A. Cerruti, the controller and a twice-convicted forger, described to the court a lavish brochure which Casavina had made up for advertising purposes. Entitled, "This is Casavan Industries, 1961," it purported to show marble from Casavan's Italian quarries being carried to the United States on Casavan's ships. Cerruti testified that this gave a somewhat distorted picture, since Casavan owned neither ships nor quarries, and was unable to purchase any marble because it had no money.

Cerruti remembered the directors approving the acquisition of Casavan Carrara Marble Co., which was also owned by Casavina, and at book value was worth $3,710. Casavan Industries evidently considered this an unusual investment opportunity, for they gave Casavina 50,000 shares of stock worth $500,000 for it. Cerruti remembered that when he suggested to his employer that this was perhaps a bit steep, Casavina told him it was none of his business. The directors of Casavan Industries were so overcome by the brilliance displayed by Casavina in making these various acquisitions, almost all of which he or his immediate family owned, that they voted him in appreciation a special stock bonus of several thousand shares.

Strickman seems to have taken an active part in the company's affairs from its beginnings in 1959 until it went bankrupt three years later. He was variously listed as vice president and chief chemist at Casavan, and was vice president of Electro-Thermal Industries of New York, a predecessor company. A search of the company's bankruptcy proceedings showed that apart from whatever salary he made, he received separate payments from Casavina.

Columbia's enthusiasm for Strickman as a business partner is said to have cooled on receipt of this information. The university officials began in earnest to try to wriggle out of the deal. They had two problems: Columbia didn't want any more bum publicity in the middle of its fund-raising drive, and it was frightened lest Strickman sue them for breaking the agreement. (Strickman had a number of supporters in the medical school where he had first brought his inventions, and, indeed, some of these enthusiasts had been leaking highly complimentary information about the filter to the newspapers, which had dutifully printed it as coming from Columbia University spokesmen.) To win a suit brought by Strickman, the central university would have to turn on its medical school, indeed on the dean of the medical school, and show how it was his poor judgment and inadequate test data that had caused Columbia to take up the filter. This would be embarrassing.

One theory had it that the way to get away from Strickman was to take the filter and test it to death, two, three years if necessary, until people had forgotten the whole affair. But this must have seemed unnecessary when eventually the chemist made his own adroit move. He proposed to end Columbia's "anguish," take back all the rights to the filter, get on with the licensing, and put Columbia's share in a charitable trust. This arrangement would still have worked to Strickman's advantage, since he could continue to show some affiliation with the university. However, the Senate Commerce Committee insisted that Columbia make a clean breast of the matter. The possibility of more hearings was put to the university. Rather than that, Columbia finally agreed to send detailed test results on the filter to the committee which then could make them public. These test data were gathered by scientists believed to be loyal to the central university and not representing the Strickman clique in the medical school. They showed the filter to be little or no better than those on the market.

PART II

BIG BUSINESS
MALPRACTICES

Admen in Orbit

by DAVID SANFORD

Anyone who reads the ads knows all about the astronauts. The typical space hero wears an Omega ("the watch that orbited in outer space"), brushes his teeth with a Py-co-pay ("the toothbrush selected by NASA for use in the Gemini space flights"), washes up with PHisoHex, and drinks ersatz orange juice ("Tang has been aboard every space flight since Gemini IV"). He takes pictures with a Hasselblad on Kodak film. We don't yet know the "deodorant of the astronauts" only, it would seem, because no one has devised a product that can keep a man smelling fresh for 14 days in a Gemini capsule. That is one of the few commercial products which has not been tied in some way to the space program.

Astronauts have outdistanced baseball players as choice advertising symbols. When John Glenn retired he took a job with Royal Crown Cola —a company that has tie-in ads. Colonel John "Shorty" Powers found a home doing commercials for Oldsmobile when he was canned as "the voice of Mercury control."

This is big business; ask any of the 20,000 firms that are NASA suppliers. Even companies with no connection with NASA or the space effort try to cash in on the glamour. At the time of the Glenn orbital flight in 1962, Abraham & Straus, the Brooklyn retailer, published an ad showing a little boy kneeling by his bed: ". . . and thanks for Colonel Glenn too." Rambler ran a picture of a man sitting in his roomy car, with the caption "Man in Space." More recently AMSCO advertised that its toy rocket separates in flight "just like the Saturn V." A creative adman for Adler shoes thought up "walk weightless." General Mills has been marketing a new cereal called "Jets" which the company would like to tie in to future space exploits (pictures of US space achievements on cereal boxes).

Reprinted by permission of the New Republic, © *1966, Harrison-Blaine of New Jersey, Inc.*

I first became interested in NASA and the advertisers when a doctor sent me a copy of an ad placed in several medical and pharmaceutical publications by Hoechst Pharmaceuticals Inc. It was a 10-page color spread for Lasix (furosemide), a diuretic drug used in the treatment of edema (excess body fluids). Six pages of the ad, interspersed with advertising text, were full-color photographs of Major Ed White's 1965 space walk. The ad made no mention of the space program except in a picture credit: "Space photographs courtesy of the National Aeronautics and Space Administration." But the impression left was that Lasix either was used in the space program or was a medical advance comparable to the impressive space walk of Major White.

In late 1966, the Food and Drug Administration seized 10 bottles of Lasix because of alleged misrepresentations in the ad. The FDA said that it was not concerned with the safety and effectiveness of Lasix, when used according to approved label instructions, but rather that the ad did not show fairly the "effectiveness of the drug in conditions for which it is recommended" or prominently warn of its hazards. FDA's seizure was unrelated to the use of space photos, but FDA officials were nevertheless concerned about the misleading character of the promotion. Theodore Cron, acting Assistant Commissioner of FDA, told a group of advertisers the Hoechst ad was "very dramatic for a diuretic, but . . . somewhat misleading since the manufacturer is actually not interested primarily in the astronaut market." Senator Philip A. Hart (D, Mich.) extracted from NASA Assistant Administrator Richard L. Callaghan an admission that Hoechst had had NASA's blessing: "Our investigation . . . reveals that permission was indeed given by a NASA representative contrary to our policy. The individual who handled this request was in error. We have taken steps to see that this kind of mistake is not repeated." Hoechst agreed to stop the offensive ad campaign.

Advertising is a boon and a nuisance to NASA. When advertisers do them the courtesy of asking permission to exploit the program, the agency has to decide what is a permissible use and what is not. All NASA photographs, of which there are thousands available, bear a stamp warning that they are "released for noncommercial, noncopyrightable public information use. Written permission must be received from NASA if [they are] used in advertising, posters, books, etc., and layout must be submitted to NASA for approval prior to release." Since space photos are in the public domain and are available to interested individuals at "cost" from NASA and the wire services, the warning has little force. Advertising costs may not be billed to NASA contracts, and contractors are asked to submit advertising copy for a check on technical accuracy. NASA has a written policy dating to 1962 forbidding astronauts' endorsements of commercial products— direct or implied. (When Lucky Strike wanted to publish a photograph of

Colonel Glenn's blast-off, NASA asked them to disguise the rocket so it would not appear to be an Atlas and the nose cone so it would not be identifiable as a Mercury capsule.)

NASA goes through the motions of receiving requests for permission and passing on them as if it had the authority to bar unauthorized uses. Julian Scheer, Assistant Administrator for Public Affairs, is worried about advertising and NASA's image. "My concern," he says, "is with whether an ad reflects accurately what is going on and is in good taste." For example, an institutional ad for Boeing saying that the company built Lunar Orbiter is OK because its claim is true. The ad accurately states the company's participation, enhances its institutional prestige and gives NASA a welcome boost. If selling a commercial product is involved, the agency is less enthusiastic. If there is no true relationship, if the ad merely tries to create an atmosphere of association, NASA tries to be discouraging. It always refuses requests to do location filming at Cape Kennedy. When Saab, the Swedish automobile, asked NASA if it would be all right to quote a NASA official's appraisal of a braking system used in the car, it approved. When Adler shoes sought to publish space walk photos for its "walk weightless" promotion, NASA refused.

Last September, General Foods asked permission to shoot a TV commercial at Cape Kennedy for its orange-like breakfast drink, Tang. A General Foods official and a representative of the firm's ad agency had been given a tour of the Cape and got the idea for a commercial with two child models entitled "Kids at Cape Kennedy." "Naturally," he wrote a NASA official, "we would schedule any visit so as not to conflict with NASA operations at the sites." NASA turned Tang down but offered some launch footage and other material for use by General Foods.

The Block Drug Company wrote NASA of its plans to run a $99,999 Sweepstakes for which the first prize would be an expense-paid trip for a family of six to Cape Kennedy, $7,500 in cash and "front-row seats" at a Gemini launching. The proposed ad stated that "NASA selected Py-co-pay to make the toothbrushes used in the Gemini space flights." "The purpose of the sweepstakes," a Block official wrote NASA,

> is to encourage better oral hygiene—particularly among US youth. The astronauts are the "Jack Armstrongs" of today. We hope that by making youth aware of the importance of dental health for astronauts, they will also give it increased importance. . . . Through our dental contacts we will stress this aspect of the promotion. (Naturally we hope to get a fair share of the increased toothbrush business, too. This is only natural.)

The Py-co-pay ads ran in the August 5, 1966 *Life* and the August 1966 *Reader's Digest*. NASA officials were somewhat embarrassed, for the ads implied NASA endorsement, which was not the case. NASA had purchased a quantity of Py-co-pay toothbrushes *but never used them.* The astronauts, it seems, chew a special gum to clean their teeth. In an August 12 inter-office memo a NASA man wrote,

> I can find no correspondence to Py-co-pay or its representatives on the subject of the . . . promotion. However, Py-co-pay was told re-peatedly that NASA would not approve, and, in fact, objected to such a promotion. Py-co-pay toothbrushes have been carried in Gemini spacecraft but were never used. We advised Py-co-pay to restrict its advertisements to the fact that the toothbrushes were carried in the spacecraft. We also objected to any Py-co-pay ad-vertisement or promotion that indicated or gave the impression that a prize trip to Cape Kennedy included access to NASA sites for viewing of a launch.

NASA receives a "good number" of letters from people protesting such advertising and from others who wonder if NASA pays for the ads. Some letters come from companies who feel they have been put at a competitive disadvantage. The vice president of Longines-Wittnauer watch company, Leonard B. Sadow, wrote NASA complaining of an ad for Omega watches which had appeared in *The New York Times.* He wondered why Longines-Wittnauer had not been invited to submit a watch for possible use by the astronauts and whether NASA permits "trumped-up and puffed-up claims that ride on the reputation of NASA." NASA replied that 10 watch companies were asked to supply watches. Four of them (Hamilton, Rolex, Omega *and* Longines-Wittnauer) had replied. Of these Hamilton's was not a wristwatch as required. This left three. During the temperature, humidity and pressure tests to which the remaining watches were subjected, the crystal on the Longines-Wittnauer watch popped out. It was replaced and popped out again. NASA chose Omega. Its advertising claims, NASA concluded, were warranted.

Hear, Hear

A NEW REPUBLIC EDITORIAL

For several years the National Bureau of Standards has been making exhaustive comparative tests of hearing aids for the Veterans Administration to determine which aids are most effective. Consumers Union, Inc., which tests and publicly rates consumer products, would like to make the VA findings public.

Consumers Union made its initial request to the VA in August 1967, and then spent a year playing bureaucratic ping-pong; exchanging letters, memoranda and telephone calls, and holding conferences. At one point CU got a negative from, logically enough, the VA's Chief of the Paperwork Management Division. The final decision refusing disclosure of the data was made in a short, rather peremptory statement by William Driver, Administrator of Veteran Affairs. Because he failed to give reasons for the denial, and as the VA has been vague and evasive throughout, CU has filed suit under the Freedom of Information Act.

At various times, the VA *has* cited two basic reasons for not disclosing the information. An exemption under the Freedom of Information Act says an agency may not divulge "trade secrets and commercial or financial information obtained from a person and privileged or confidential." Second, the VA says there are contractual restrictions; that it fears legal action. The manufacturers simply supplied the VA with hearing-aid models for testing, no more than would be available to any consumer on the open market. This is hardly secret or confidential information, but John Manning of the VA's General Counsel says there are "other things" under the exemption. The Act itself makes no mention of "other things," and Manning feels it "wouldn't be appropriate at this time to say what they are."

The VA's second objection is equally unwarranted. Until passage of the Freedom of Information Act, the contracts had stated that the test information was primarily for VA use only, and that the data could be released to other government agencies identified by the manufacturer. This year, however, a new provision was added to the contracts, stating:

> Under existing law concerning the release of information by government agencies, the VA may be required to furnish such information to any other governmental agency for its official use, or to any other person considered by the VA to be entitled thereto, without the consent of the manufacturer.

Clearly, the decision about disclosure has been left to the discretion of the VA. In denying CU this information, and refusing to be explicit in its reasons for doing so, the VA appears to have decided that only deaf veterans shall benefit from VA's extensive testing. In hearings held before the Senate Special Committee on Aging, Senator Clifford Hansen (R, Wyo.) told Consumers Union: "I think you have made a good case . . . that the results of the VA testing of hearings aids ought to be made public." He went on to add, however, that

> . . . despite the fact that a consumer may be taken time and time again by a fast-talking salesman who makes his pitch most persuasively, sells, and then gets out and isn't seen again, I think there is something to be said for a system which permits anyone who believes he can make a product to get into the business and to try to compete against those who are in there.

Consumer legislation such as the Freedom of Information Act was passed to protect the public from low-quality products and fast-buck artists. The government thinks differently.

Selling Encyclopedias

by ERIC GELLER

Senator Warren Magnuson's consumer sales protection bill is designed to curb questionable tactics by the encyclopedia industry, dominated by four giants, Britannica, P. F. Collier's, Field Enterprises (World Book), and Grolier's (Americana). They account for 95 percent of all subscription sales in this country, and for nearly $450 million in sales a year. The companies mostly rely on well-disciplined teams of salesmen, operating so smoothly they make the Flim-Flam Man look like an amateur.

The FTC has repeatedly issued cease-and-desist orders against some companies' practices that nevertheless continue. Thus in February 1968 the Federal Trade Commission ordered American Marketing Associates Inc. (New Standard Encyclopedia) of Philadelphia to cease using deceptive means to recruit personnel. The company advertised that its "trainees" receive $89 a week, whereas "in reality, they are hired as door-to-door salesmen and receive no salary whatever but only a commission on sales." Encyclopedia Britannica is still "guaranteeing" prospective salesmen $500 per month; Collier's also is advertising lucrative rewards. However, one salesman recently reported in *Seattle* magazine that his total earnings in his first month were $64.

The salesmen have to memorize patter carefully devised to wear down most prospects within 30 minutes. Every statement, gesture, smile is carefully prescribed and designed to make the family feel inferior (Collier's instructs its salesmen to sit on a chair higher than the prospective buyer's), and also to play on young suburbanites' desire for status and recognition.

Like I said before, I'm not a salesman. My job is merely interviewing young families in different areas, and placing a few of these

Reprinted by permission of the New Republic, © *1968, Harrison-Blaine of New Jersey, Inc.*

encyclopedias in homes where they would be appreciated.... If a family we talk to honestly doesn't realize the importance of a major work of this type, then I'm sorry. I'm not a salesman, and I'm not trying to educate such a family. My job is merely to place these encyclopedias with people like yourselves who truly appreciate and respect education as it is in this fast-moving world of today.

(Although they are instructed not to seek out Negroes and Puerto Ricans —bad credit risks, one imaginative salesman recently sold a Puerto Rican couple a $400 encyclopedia set, by posing as a New York school official and threatening their children with expulsion from school if they did not buy. The couple could not read English.)

Like deceptive methods of recruiting personnel, the tactic of "selected families" has been ruled illegal by the FTC. As far back as 1949, the commission issued an order against Americana Encyclopedia (now published by Grolier's) to stop representing "that the publication is available only to selected individuals under special conditions when such is not the fact."

The Collier's salesman, after ingratiating himself with the family, offers to "place" the encyclopedia "free," in return only for a testimonial letter. But to receive the encyclopedia, the family must agree to purchase the company's yearbook and the use of its research service for the next 10 years. Total cost: over $400, payable within 24 months. This practice was ruled illegal by the FTC eight years ago; the commission charged that the publishers of Collier's Encyclopedia employed "lengthy and blatant use of deception to sell it.... Collier's misrepresented, among other things, that a set of Collier's Encyclopedia was to be given free if the yearly supplements are purchased, or in return for written comments and the right to use the writer's name." In 1961 Encyclopedia Britannica was the subject of an FTC cease-and-desist order involving unfair selling practices. And in 1965, Grolier's entered into a consent agreement in the Federal District Court of Maryland under which it agreed to pay a $100,000 civil penalty for violation of just such an FTC order. (Five years earlier it had been assessed a $16,000 penalty for a similar violation.)

The Magnuson bill, which the publishers oppose, would permit a buyer to abrogate any door-to-door sale involving more than $60, if he sends a certified letter to the seller within two business days after signing the contract. The bill would require that the companies conspicuously inform the buyer of his right on his contract. Also, the seller would have to present the buyer with a receipt stating the salesman's address and all details of the transaction.

Yet the bill does not adequately protect the low-income buyer, for whom the $60 exemption might be a week's earnings, and who might be unfamiliar with certified mail. It is entirely conceivable some companies would price many of their items at $59.95, and thus escape the bill's impact. The bill has fewer teeth in it than similar laws already enacted in England and Australia. In those two countries, before the new laws were passed, encyclopedia companies "were making money like it was going out of style." The publishers claim it is almost impossible for them to curb their salesmen. Yet Field Enterprises, the largest seller of encyclopedias, exercises firm control over its salesmen, and has never been cited in an FTC order.

Frederick Sherwood of Britannica told *Sales Management* magazine that "if the law is passed, marriage contracts would soon mean nothing, and the voters could go back to the polls and vote again." The publishers don't want the government interfering with them. With $45 billion being spent on education every year, a lot of encyclopedias are going to be sold.

Business Crime

by RALPH NADER

Tucked away in the ninth and final Task Force Report of President Johnson's National Crime Commission are a few words about business crime. Like the bank robber, business crime takes property away from those entitled to keep it and threatens or injures the physical security of persons. This double parallel is not ordinarily drawn. But the Task Force did not demur. It estimates, for example, that the annual cost to the public of securities frauds is in the $500 million to $1 billion range. Fraudulent practices in the drug, therapeutic device and home repair fields are said to drain the consumer of $1 billion to $1.5 billion a year. The report quotes Professor Sanford Kadish: "It is possible to reason convincingly that the harm done to the economic order by violations of many of these regulatory laws is of a magnitude that dwarfs in significance the lower-class property offenses."

The harm done to human health and safety by business crime should dispel the distinguishing characteristic of "white-collar crime" as being the absence of physical threat. Food and drug violations, lavish use of pesticides, defective automobiles, professional malpractice, building code violations, to name a few situations, are a much larger hazard to life and limb than crimes of violence on our streets. Other assaults on the human body, such as air and water pollution, are only now being brought under the rule of law.

What, then, is the explanation of the difference between our society's vastly greater preoccupation with street crime than with business crime? Why are there fantastic disparities in the penalties imposed on a car thief as contrasted with a corporate official who knowingly refused to report severe adverse drug effects to the FDA and to physicians, or on an unemployed $50 check-forger compared with company executives convicted

Reprinted by permission of the New Republic, © *1967, Harrison-Blaine of New Jersey, Inc.*

of conscious and systematic price-fixing on a massive scale in violation of the antitrust laws? Law schools simply avoid teaching students about the privileges and immunities granted business crime.

These privileges and immunities have served to split off much business misbehavior from meaningful sanctions. Yet both the Task Force Report and a highly useful memorandum by the antitrust division appended to it stress that criminal sanctions have their greatest deterrent effect in the area of business crime. Statutory maximums for business crime have been trivial (excepting penalties for tax violations). The maximum fine under the Sherman Antitrust Act was recently raised to $50,000. In June 1967 the Department of Transportation recommended criminal prosecution of the Greyhound Bus Company for knowing violation of the Motor Carrier Safety Act. The company was accused of employing regrooved, badly worn tires on a bus which skidded off a wet road, killing one and seriously injuring others. If convicted on two counts, Greyhound would have to pay no more than a maximum fine of $1,000. There is no imprisonment provision.

Knowing and willful violations of auto and aircraft safety regulations, even if they result in loss of life, incur no criminal penalties under the two statutes. Attorney Lloyd Cutler, representing the Automobile Manufacturers Association, succeeded in having the criminal sanction cut out of the auto safety legislation last year, even for willful violations. The statute provides only for civil fines, which scarcely deter large corporations in a concentrated industry.

Mr. Cutler's arguments against criminal penalties reflect the double standard that is rapidly being institutionalized for corporate and individual crime. He stated that a criminal penalty (for such acts as knowingly selling defective cars, adulterating brake fluid, etc.) would be punitive, difficult to enforce because of the difficulty of finding the violator, and unnecessary because the auto companies wouldn't violate the law.

Mr. Cutler's assertions point up the need for the law to pinpoint responsibility within the sprawling corporate structures by requiring the corporation to assign responsibility for compliance. This will avoid the common pleadings that top management didn't know about the violation and lower officials were simply following orders. Another suggestion, made by Professor Alan Dershowitz of Harvard Law School, is to impose a duty upon corporate executives, enforceable by criminal sanctions, of displaying reasonable care in preventing "acquisitive crime" under their business control. Finally, Mr. Cutler's stand points to the need for rigorous disclosure requirements and inspection procedures for early exposure of incipient illegal activity, or of outrageous practices not yet deemed illegal.

Another difference perpetuating a double standard is that corporate power is continually preempting the regulation of potential criminal behavior on its part, by merging with or controlling government regulatory agencies in a manner that jettisons the existence or applicability of legal sanctions. Here, corporate determination of the definition of criminal behavior is the quest. The *opus magnus* of many a corporate lawyer is his success in making antisocial behavior extralegal. Such a strategy reverses the path of legal history, in Maine's words, from "status to contract" to one of "contract to status."

Scratch the image of any industry and unsavory practices become visible. All was apparently proper with the leaders of the electrical equipment industry until the great decade-long, price-fixing conspiracy was disclosed. A similar situation obtained for six corporations selling hundreds of millions of dollars of pipe over the past 20 years according to rigged bids until the antitrusters caught up with them. But the Justice Department does not have the manpower to cope with the widespread prevalence of price fixing. (The combined annual budgets of the Federal Trade Commission and the antitrust division are under $30 million—less than 15 hours' gross revenue of General Motors.) A California highway patrol test of auto safety equipment found over 70 percent failing to meet state standards or the performance of the samples originally submitted (some years prior) to the state for approval by the manufacturers.

In a 1961 survey by the *Harvard Business Review* of its subscribing executives, four out of seven respondents believed that businessmen "would violate a code of ethics whenever they thought they could avoid detection." Detection is a major animus of prevention. But the task force, which took note of this survey, left no guidelines for preventing corporate crime.

The Money-Lenders

by JONATHAN KWITNY

A group of New Jersey borrowers stands to receive a windfall that could total well over $100 million from companies that for years have operated a second-mortgage loan business. The loan companies, based in Philadelphia and operating through agents in New Jersey, have given loans to thousands of homeowners. The loans are secured by second mortgages based on the equity the borrower has built up in his house, and have contained hidden charges that sent the effective interest rate soaring as high as 58 percent. The Appellate Division of the state Superior Court recently came down with a ruling that may free all the borrowers from their obligation to pay up.

This bonanza has fallen into the laps of some of the state's most financially strapped citizens—families who moved into their first homes in suburban developments several years ago and soon found themselves over their heads in debt, with monthly payments sometimes exceeding their incomes. Besieged by creditors, some of these inexperienced homeowners were ready to sign their lives away. They thought they saw a way out when they read newspaper advertisements advising them to "Wrap up all your financial headaches in one low-cost monthly package." All that was required was to call the local number listed in the ad. The number usually led to an answering service, which relayed names, addresses and phone numbers to the loan companies' New Jersey agents. The offices of these agents often were no bigger than the corner phone booth. An agent came calling, usually under a name different from the one used in the ad. The more devious the transaction, the more corporations it involved, the harder it would be to pin a complaint on the finance company that ultimately would collect the payments. The agent took information on the homeowner's financial needs and credit history, and departed with whatever he could get—perhaps $25 and the deed to the house.

The agent would call back a week or two later. The closing usually was over in a few minutes, with the borrower seldom knowing that out of the total principal of his loan, he was getting barely half. In deference to the state usury law (no more than six percent interest), the rest of the money was listed as payment for assorted fees—an appraisal, a credit check and "other disbursements." The companies would wind up charging as much as $1,500 for services whose actual cost was no more than $75, usually less. Since these fees were part of the principal of the loan, the companies were, in effect, lending the borrowers the money to pay them. Onto the entire package they tacked the six percent interest. The borrowers may have been unaware they had signed a second mortgage on their home to secure the loan.

The second mortgage usually passed through several more corporate hands within days, ending up at the master loan company in Philadelphia, which could claim rights as a "holder in due course" (someone who buys a negotiable debt in good faith and automatically obtains rights to collect on the debt, no matter what complaints the debtor may have against the original creditor).

•

Consider the case of a Edison, N.J., couple who received a direct mail advertisement signed Mortgage Financial Research. MFR was not registered as a corporation in New Jersey, although the couple didn't know that. They saw an offer of a $2,000 loan for payments of less than $30 a month and quickly mailed the business reply card. A week later they received a telephone call from a man identified as a representative of Consolidated Credit Corp. Consolidated Credit *was* registered, but the only office it listed was that of its attorney in Newark. The representative came to the couple's house and left with their request for a $1,800 loan—along with $50 cash for a credit investigation and their deed and payment book. These documents were not returned until after the couple signed the loan agreement. (Some companies hold the deeds for ransom; if the customer refuses the loan, he is charged another $15 or so to get his deed back.)

Two weeks later, the couple heard from Consolidated Credit: the loan had been approved for $1,700; they were to come to the attorney's office to sign the papers. There, they learned that in addition to the $1,700, they would have to borrow a "small amount" for appraisal, inspection, credit investigation and disbursement. But they would pay only 6 percent interest.

Unaware that the small amount was $1,560—almost as much as the original loan—the couple signed. With interest, they are paying $3,780—$63 a month for five years—for a loan of $1,700.

Then began the well-rehearsed process of creating a holder in due course. Consolidated Credit sold the second mortgages it took to Oxford Discount Co. in Newark, sometimes using an intermediary company called

Fiber-Lum Corp. of America. Oxford sold the mortgages to Atlas Subsidiaries of New Jersey, which transferred them to Atlas Credit Corp. of Philadelphia, which collected the payments.

Mortgage Financial Research and Consolidated Credit Corp. aren't doing business in central New Jersey anymore. Fiber-Lum, which had corporate ties to Consolidated Credit, is concentrating on the aluminum siding business these days. Oxford Discount, one of whose three incorporators is an officer of Fiber-Lum, handles financing for the siding deals and for the transactions of a backyard swimming pool company, Aqua-Rama. Fiber-Lum and Aqua-Rama were fined $1,500 for fraud by the New Jersey Office of Consumer Protection in October.

Under the name Sunasco, the result of a merger, Atlas Credit was listed by financial columnist Sylvia Porter as the most successful issue on the New York Stock Exchange in the six months following March 31, 1968. Atlas —or Sunasco—is controlled by the Wolgin family. Jack Wolgin is a close associate of Philadelphia Mayor James H. J. Tate, who sits with Wolgin on the board of directors of the Industrial Valley National Bank of Philadelphia. Walter E. Alessandroni, attorney general of Pennsylvania from 1963 to 1967, has been on Atlas' board of directors.

In an effort to drive the second mortgage shysters out of the state, the New Jersey legislature in the summer of 1965 passed a tough Secondary Mortgage Loan Act. It requires second-mortgage lenders to be licensed by the state Department of Banking and Insurance. It limits, under penalty of fines, the amount of interest that can be charged—including the deductions for appraisal, inspection, credit investigation and all other costs or fees. It forbids agents to take commissions from the borrower. It requires the lender to tell the borrower all important facts about the loan.

That law forced the mortgage-loan dealers to think up a new ruse. Unable to charge exorbitant fees for appraisals and the like, they proceeded to get the extra money by claiming they were running a furniture or appliance business on the side. Their advertisements continued to talk only about loans, and quoted the comparatively low repayment figures authorized by the new law. But borrowers unknowingly wound up buying merchandise from the agents. One agent sold a $10 radio for $500. Another sold a $65 television set for $519.50. A third sold a dinette set clearly priced in a catalog at $123 for $630.66.

Of course the borrowers either had no idea they were paying this extra money or else considered it an agent's fee. They usually were told about the merchandise after the rest of the deal was agreed upon. Then the agent mentioned that they had a free gift coming—a portable television set, a cheap lamp or a flimsy stereo. Among the papers they signed, usually without reading them, the borrowers agreed to "buy" the "free gift" at an outrageous price. In some instances, the loan companies arranged for signings to take place in Philadelphia, so they could claim the loans were made under Pennsylvania law, which permits higher interest charges. Borrowers drove to an agent's office in the Camden, N. J., area, then were hustled across the Delaware River into Philadelphia, often without knowing where they were going.

In September 1967, the *News Tribune* of Perth Amboy published a series of articles detailing the activities of the Philadelphia loan companies and their agents throughout New Jersey. Arthur Sills, a Perth Amboy area lawyer who is New Jersey's attorney general and who would like to be its governor, spoke of driving the money-lenders out of the state. He and former Congressman Charles R. Howell, the state Banking and Insurance Commissioner, charged four agencies and two loan companies with fraud, and have been investigating other companies. The state revoked the licenses of three agencies: Paul J. Truran, Patlind Inc., and Security National Fund Inc. Charges against three other companies—Crescent Investments Co., Mutual Home Dealers and First Mercantile of New Jersey—await disposition. Truran, Patlind, Security and Crescent, all with offices in the Camden area, all advertised to New Jersey borrowers and sent them or took them to Philadelphia to sign loans. Some of Crescent's customers excepted, the deals involved overpriced merchandise.

Mutual Home Dealers is a financing house that collects on mortgages negotiated by a number of agents, including Truran and Crescent Investments. Among its assets, Mutual Home Dealers has listed more than $7 million in collectable IOU's, many of which are secured by second mortgages on private homes. Hearings scheduled last winter on fraud charges against the company were postponed because Mutual's lawyer was busy elsewhere—as governor of New Jersey. (The lawyer, Sido Ridolfi, president of the State Senate, was acting chief executive of the state while Governor Richard Hughes was recuperating from an eye operation.)

First Mercantile of New Jersey is a subsidiary of First Mercantile Co., a multi-million-dollar Philadelphia second-mortgage lender. Persons who answered advertisements from Security National Fund often were led to First Mercantile of New Jersey if they wanted loans of less than $1,500. Persons who wanted bigger loans were taken to the parent company in Philadelphia.

•

The key enforcement section of New Jersey's Second Mortgage Loan Ace declares that if the law is violated in the making of a loan, the borrower does not have to pay back the money. It is on this section that both the state and the loan companies have trained their big legal guns. The battle began when one of the biggest second-mortgage lenders, Oxford Consumer Discount Co., Philadelphia, a subsidiary of Oxford Finance Co., whose stock on the American Stock Exchange more than doubled in value in

1968, filed what seemed to be a routine suit to collect a defaulted mortgage of $4,500 in Essex County Court, Newark. The defendants, Anthony and Theresa Stefanelli, apparently made their loan in the classic way—answering an advertisement from a New Jersey company, being referred to a Philadelphia agent who charged them several hundred dollars for a small appliance, then being sent to the loan company.

The Stefanellis were defended in the collection suit by a Newark lawyer, Bernard Bukarest, who raised the Secondary Mortgage Loan Act as a defense. Judge William J. Camarata ruled the law did not apply because the loan was signed in Philadelphia. Thereupon, Sills' office and Essex County Legal Services, a federal antipoverty agency, decided to appeal to the Appellate Division of the Superior Court. Mrs. Annamay T. Sheppard of Legal Services took over as the Stefanellis' lawyer, and Deputy Atty. Gen. Douglas Harper became *amicus*. Other court battles blossomed.

In August 1968, Superior Court Judge Herbert Horn of Atlantic County agreed to void the mortgage of a couple involved in a typical second-mortgage loan case, and said he would do the same for "the 'run-of-the-mill' case" under the act. Then, on September 11, a three-judge panel from the state's second highest court, the Appellate Division, decided the Stefanelli case. The Stefanellis did not have to pay.

As long as that decision stands, neither, it appears, do thousands of others have to pay. Of course there will be an appeal; more than $100 million is at stake.

Investing in Mutual Funds

by MORDECAI ROSENFELD

In 1965 Americans spent more than $4.25 billion—more than the entire foreign-aid program—for mutual fund shares. Yet most people who bought them know no more about their investment than they do about how aid money is spent in Upper Volta.

A mutual fund's only business is to invest in the stocks and bonds of *other* companies. There are now some 350 mutual funds competing for the investor's money, each with its own particular blend of several hundred different securities. All these funds have the same basic purpose: to enable small investors to diversify their holdings and to obtain professional supervision of their money. For instance, if a person has $1,000 to invest, he could afford to buy stock in only one or two of the several thousand companies whose shares are listed on the financial pages. But if he invests that $1,000 in shares of a mutual fund, his one stock certificate represents a proportionate interest in each of his mutual fund's several hundred portfolio securities. The idea has been made so attractive that there are now more than 3.5 million people who own mutual funds, with a total investment in excess of $36 billion.

In 1930, total mutual fund assets were less than $200 million; and they had just reached $1 billion in 1945. The multiplication of the industry's total assets by more than 36 times in 20 years has been gigantic, but it has raised ethical questions of equal magnitude.

Mutual funds grow in two ways. One way their assets increase is when (and if) the stocks they buy with the public's money go up in price. That aspect of their growth depends upon the vicissitudes of the stock market. Even when the prices of the stocks they owned have gone down, however, mutual fund assets have risen. This happens because mutual funds have

Reprinted by permission of the New Republic, © *1966, Harrison-Blaine of New Jersey, Inc.*

always been able to attract vast new sums of money by their determined sales campaigns.

It is almost an axiom that mutual funds are not bought, but sold. Fund salesmen are ubiquitous—they are your accountant, real estate broker, notary public or third cousin. These salesmen, who sold over $4 billion worth of mutual fund shares in 1965 alone, collected, in the process, sales commissions that totaled approximately $200 million. The only reason these salesmen have for selling mutual funds is the fact that they earn a large commission. Typically, when a buyer purchases a mutual fund, more than eight percent of his purchase price is paid as a sales commission. This means that the instant you "invest" $100, your investment is worth $92. In order for the purchaser to recoup that $8 and at least break even, the stock market must rise by eight percent, a very substantial increase.

With commissions being such a prize, it is not surprising that the industry and its salesmen push hard to earn them. In 1963, the Securities and Exchange Commission, after an exhaustive study, reported: "Mutual fund sales organizations are constantly engaged in extensive programs of recruiting. . . . Recruits are overwhelmingly drawn from persons totally inexperienced in the securities business, often by deliberate choice. . . ."

One mutual fund distributing company recently advised its selling staff to hire persons who had experience as "cosmetic, brush, roof and siding, real estate, storm window and food freezer salesmen." The SEC, in analyzing present requirements for mutual fund salesmen, sadly concluded that "a lack of securities experience may even be preferred."

The problem of the hard sell used by mutual funds is doubly important because most mutual fund sales are made to small investors who have little sophistication about finance. A 1966 survey showed that 60 percent of mutual fund shareholders had incomes of less than $10,000 per year. It is, therefore, largely the small investor who has been paying the sales fee of $8 for the privilege of investing $92.

But this $8 deficit is modest when compared to what is paid by those who are persuaded to buy mutual funds on the easy installment plan. As with all installment contracts, the sales commissions are exorbitant and the sales pressures relentless. In the mutual fund industry, the installment plan is known as the "front-end load." It exacts from the purchaser's first year's $100 investment a commission of $40. The unhappy arithmetic is this: You sign a contract which commits you to buy a fixed amount of a mutual fund each and every month for the next 10 years. If you agree to buy $100 worth a year (which would cost $1,000 over 10 years), the normal commission of eight percent would amount to $8 per year (or $80 over 10 years). But the mutual fund industry knows from experience that installment buyers of mutual funds, like installment buyers of furniture or vacuum cleaners, often cannot complete their contracts. There may be illness, or a new baby or a new house. But since the mutual fund encourages its salesmen to enroll long-term purchasers, it guarantees that their commissions will not be lost if the buyers cannot continue to pay. So, as part of the easy-to-pay 10-year plan, the buyer "agrees" to pre-pay five years' worth of commissions (or $40) in the first year. And if he cannot continue his payments, his first year's investment of $100 is worth, at the end of the year, a shriveled $60.

There are, it should be noted, a few mutual funds which employ no salesmen and use no pressures to sell their shares. Called "no-load funds," they sell their shares to the public with no sales commission added. A person who buys such a mutual fund saves eight percent at the outset. Since they are not advertised, their names are not well known and they are relatively small. These funds, like the funds that charge an admission fee, vary in their aims and in their performance. But the important fact is that the no-load funds, as a group, have performed at least as well as their more flamboyant rivals. Although the no-load funds charge no sales commissions, their sponsors are in business for profit; they receive that profit by being paid for giving investment advice to their fund. But high as the 8 percent and 40 percent sales fees collected by the typical mutual funds are, their managers have made most of their money from the investment advisory fees that they charge their funds and the funds' investors.

•

Having collected more than $36 billion from over 3.5 million people through the efforts of tens of thousands of inexperienced, moonlighting salesmen, mutual funds must invest their moneys in stocks and bonds. In order to determine what securities to buy, the typical mutual fund "hires" an outside company, called the investment adviser. The typical investment advisory company formerly charged the fund and its investors for its advice at the rate of one-half of one percent of the fund's assets. Thus when a mutual fund had assets of $200 million (a modest-sized fund), the investment advisory company charged it $1 million a year for investment advice. As more shares of the fund were sold, the fund grew and its advisory fee increased. When a fund was a toddler of $200 million and paid $1 million a year for investment advice, the advisory company made a good deal of money for its services. And when that fund reached $400 million, its investors were then charged $2 million a year for the very same advice. Since the adviser was already making a handsome profit on the $1 million fee, the second million was pure chocolate mousse.

The reason that the one-half of one percent fee survived so long is that to most people it sounded insignificant. But that was only because the advisory fee was stated in terms of a mutual fund's total assets. A much more meaningful yardstick would have been to measure the fee in terms of a fund's income. A one-half-of-one-percent advisory fee amounted to between 15 and 20 percent of a fund's total income. That means that for every dollar the fund earned, it paid between 15 and 20 cents to those who decided which stocks to buy and which to sell. When the advisory fees grew to be so large, mutual fund shareholders sued to reduce them. As a result of those lawsuits, almost all of the investment advisers to the large funds were forced to adopt a sliding fee scale; that is, the advisory fee, instead of just rolling merrily along at a flat rate of one-half of one percent, was reduced in stages as the fund's assets increased. Consequently, most of the advisory fees now reflect the economic fact that the adviser's work does not increase *pari passu* with the increase in a fund's size.

Before the fees were reduced, the question was asked: How good is the advice for which mutual fund investors pay millions of dollars each year? Several faculty members of the University of Pennsylvania's Wharton School made a study of this for the Securities and Exchange Commission, and reported in 1962 that: "The average performance by the funds did not differ appreciably from what would have been achieved by an unmanaged portfolio with the same division among asset types."

Translated, that means that an investor who was blindfolded and picked his stocks with a pin and a donkey's tail would do as well as the high-priced investment advisers. The funds' mediocre performances have been caused, in part, by their own successful sales campaigns. Some have such huge and unwieldy holdings that it takes several months for them to get out of a situation gone sour. And, too, when you've $36 billion to invest you can't limit your purchases to "good buys." Most of the money must be invested in the most common of the common stocks. There is just no reason to pay the *sommelier* several million dollars per year for *vin ordinaire*.

If outside investment advisers charged so much for advice that was so undistinguished, why were they hired by the mutual funds in the first place? Simple. The people who have run the mutual funds have also owned the "outside" investment advisory companies that service them. Those who managed the mutual funds had those funds pay out lavish investment advisory fees because those fees were paid, in large part, to themselves. Congress, when it enacted the Investment Company Act, tried to protect mutual fund investors against the foreseeable evil of this duality. The Act requires mutual funds to have a certain number of directors who are in no way associated with the investment advisory company. These directors—called "unaffiliated" directors by the statute—have the solemn responsibility of keeping the investment advisory fee as reasonable as is possible. But this careful congressional plan has not always been successful because the "unaffiliated" directors have included few Patrick Henrys. It was the shareholders and their lawsuits, not the "unaffiliated" directors, who brought about the fee reductions.

Despite the fees and charges, most of the people who invested in mutual funds have made money. Although they might have made more had they

149

invested on their own, most mutual fund shareholders would probably have left their money in the bank and missed entirely the benefits of the great bull market. Indeed, the bringing of the public into the stock market has probably been the industry's most significant accomplishment. But the great market rise has not only made the funds successful; it has also masked their faults because few people care to complain as long as times are prosperous and they are ahead.

It is unrealistic to expect that Congress will pass a law that limits the profits of mutual fund advisers. "How much is too much?" The answer could be and would be debated forever. Furthermore, the courts, responding to shareholders' suits, have been able to reduce management charges by approving separate formulas suited to each case. But there is at least one abuse that the SEC and Congress can eliminate—the front-end load. Although the industry has had many spokesmen over the years, not one has advanced a convincing reason for charging small investors a 40 percent commission for mutual fund shares they may never buy.

Eastern's Shuttle Service

by JAMES RIDGEWAY

Why does it cost $18 to fly 215 miles between New York and Washington, but only $12 to fly 340 miles from San Francisco to Los Angeles?

Senator Edward Kennedy asked the Civil Aeronautics Board this question in 1965. He never got an answer. The CAB is meant to control interstate air fares in the public interest. Yet it has granted Eastern Airlines four rate increases since the Washington-New York-Boston shuttle began and has never completed and made public an independent analysis of the operation's costs. Instead the CAB took Eastern's word for it that the East Coast service with guaranteed seats for all passengers was more expensive to run than the West Coast system of densely scheduled flights with no guarantees. Until late 1965 Eastern used antiquated Constellations; Electras and jets fly the Western route.

Since 1961, prices in the Los Angeles to San Francisco market, with four competing airlines, have declined; those on the East Coast, where Eastern enjoys a virtual monopoly, have steadily gone up.

Fares rose along the East Coast shuttle run as Eastern increased its take of total business. In 1960 Eastern and American each held about one-third of the market; Northeast had about 20 percent. In the spring of 1961, when Eastern's shuttle service started, the fare between Washington and New York was $12.73 without tax. In eight months, Eastern's share of this market increased by 35 percent; the price went to $13.64. By the end of 1962, Eastern had 50 percent of the traffic, and the fare was $14.29. By January 1964, Eastern had captured 77 percent of the market and sought and was granted another hike—to $15.24. Eastern is said to have made its first shuttle profit in 1964. The CAB's reaction to the airline's improved position was to let it go ahead in January 1965 with a $2 in-

Reprinted by permission of the New Republic, © *1966, Harrison-Blaine of New Jersey, Inc.*

crease, setting the price of $18 with tax. In a dissent to this CAB order, Robert T. Murphy and G. Joseph Minetti declared:

> It is singularly incongruous that at the close of a record-breaking year for airlines and on the threshold of what promises to be an even better year—the greatest in aviation history—additional tolls should be exacted from air travelers in short-haul markets without any meaningful investigation to determine the compelling justification for them.

Eastern's price hike, they forewarned, would mean $6 million in additional cost to users of the shuttle system during 1965.

It is cheaper to go to New York on American's Electras: the coach fare is $16.12 and one can have a bite to eat. However, there has never been any real competition here, since American's Electras have few coach seats; most are first class at $18.85 with tax.

By contrast, the commuter fare for the San Francisco-Los Angeles run, 125 miles longer than between Washington and New York and with more traffic than any other intercity market in the world, is $12 with tax for jet prop Electras and $14.18 for jets. In 1961, this same Electra service had cost $14.85—jets $25.25. West Coast fares declined under the competitive pressure of Pacific Southwest Airlines, which operates only in California and whose rates therefore do not fall within the purview of the CAB. PSA, once called the "Poor Sailor's Airline," started out in 1949 with a single, rented DC-3 and now is the leader among four major carriers.

Eastern believes it is unfair to compare its shuttle with the West Coast flights, since Eastern guarantees a seat to all passengers; in the West there is no such assurance, but flights are scheduled with high frequency. Because of the guarantee, Eastern says, it must maintain more aircraft in service and keep more flight and ground crews on duty. Also, airport landing fees are higher in the East: $36 on average per landing as compared with $18 in the West. Flying time often is longer along the East Coast because of congestion; traffic is routed round about. And there are more numerous delays and cancellations because of weather which add to the cost of ground operations in the winter.

Although Eastern has been showing a loss for its system as a whole since 1958, in 1965 it was in the black. The airline does not make public the costs of its shuttle.

One may get a very rough idea, however, of the sort of expense Eastern incurs in its shuttle service. Studies by the Federal Aviation Agency show it costs about $1.90 a mile to operate the four-engine piston planes Eastern used for shuttling during 1964. (This figure takes into account crew, fuel, insurance, maintenance, and depreciation.) That year the shuttles flew a total of 11.3 million miles for a base cost of $21.6 million. Add to this airport landing fees of $2 million and another $500,000 for standby crews. (Based on Eastern's own figures, that would cover the cost of one crew on a standby basis all day long all year long at each of three main shuttle airports.) When these figures are put together, the cost comes out around $24 million. Various administrative costs may boost this figure. In 1964, Eastern's shuttle had revenues of $40.5 million.

The shuttle's financial position for 1965 might well show further improvement, since it got the $2 fare boost at the beginning of the year, and because it is turning in piston planes for turboprop Electras which are less costly to operate. Costs will go down further when Eastern puts jets on the shuttle route.

It has been suggested that when Edward Kennedy took up the shuttle business he may have been less interested in the way Eastern was running it, than he was in trying to help Northeast Airlines, headquartered in Massachusetts, cling to markets along the East Coast. At any rate, Eastern *is* improving its equipment, and it is about to put into effect cut-rate family and weekend shuttle rates ($25.71 per person round trip Washington to New York between 7:45 p.m. Friday and 2:45 p.m. Sunday). These changes may mollify Mr. Kennedy and the CAB, as well as the Senate antitrust subcommittee which briefly toyed with the idea of an investigation. Eastern will be off the hook, without disclosing its shuttle costs.

High Flying Fares

by GILBERT B. FRIEDMAN

In June 1960 I flew round trip from Los Angeles to New York for $170 on Trans-Continental, a ticket agency for several airlines. Trans-Continental's license was not renewed by the Civil Aeronautics Board. In January 1964, I flew round trip from San Francisco to New York for $188 on US Overseas Airlines. Sometime in the fall of 1964, the CAB refused to renew US Overseas' license. As of February 17, 1967, the cheapest price for the flight from Los Angeles or San Francisco to New York was $152.36–$304.72 round trip.

My trip on Trans-Continental in 1960 was on a DC-6 which made one stop in Chicago. The plane was supposed to leave at 11 p.m., but left at 12:15 a.m., arriving in New York one hour and fifteen minutes late. No movies, no free magazines. But I did get from Los Angeles to New York in approximately 11 hours' flying time. The Greyhound Bus would have taken me 72 hours, and cost $143.50 round trip, besides bending me into a human pretzel.

Trans-Continental did not represent nonscheduled airlines, but was an agent for several supplemental airlines. It made only a few flights a week at non-busy hours at the airports and between heavily populated centers. Trans-Continental was always booked solid, and why not.

After Trans-Continental's commercial license expired, the airline that provided those of us who could not stand buses with a cheap means to get across the country was US Overseas Airlines. Its main flights were to Hawaii and the islands in the South Pacific, but it was allowed two runs a week between New York and San Francisco and Los Angeles, as connecting links to the Pacific. These flights were also booked up solid, and reservations had to be made well in advance. The planes were DC-6s and service was about equal with Trans-Continental's. The only major airline which tried to compete with either Trans-Continental or US Overseas Airlines was Trans World Airlines, which ran a few flights from San Francisco or Los Angeles to New York City for $118 on a DC-6. But the plane made six stops along the way. A few months after US Overseas Airlines' last commercial flight on September 24, 1964, TWA dropped its flight.

In 1967 the price all airlines charged for crossing the country from San Francisco or Los Angeles to New York was exactly the same: $152.36 one way, $304.72 round trip. But don't think that competition is dead. It is keener than ever. Now that the petty issue of price has been eliminated, airlines compete on the more subtle level of a "product differentiation." Which airline shows the best movies, which shows only movies in technicolor, which has 10 channels of entertainment on a five-hour trip? Who prepares, or should I say, inspires the meals of the passengers—Maxim's of Paris, or the Four Seasons of New York? Which airline's silver comes from Tiffany's, which from International Sterling? Which stewardesses have their wardrobes designed by Dior, which by Oleg Cassini? Is this any way to run an airline? You bet it's not!

I have yet to meet anyone who wanted to see a first-run movie or eat a first-class meal for $152 while he travels 2,587 miles. A person flies because it is the fastest way of getting from here to there. The frills are incidental. If each passenger was offered a $15 reduction in his fare if he were not allowed to view the movies or TV or to eat a fancy meal, the vast majority of passengers would take the refund. Perhaps you feel that most people really like the frills and prefer to pay for them. I point to the Trans-Atlantic flight to Europe as an example that people do care about price.

All the jet airlines charge the same fare from the US to Europe, because they all are members of the International Air Transport Association (IATA). The cheapest flight from New York to Europe on a member of IATA is to Shannon, Ireland, a bit out of the way, but a lot less to pay. Any of the major US or international airlines will fly you there in the off-season for $362.90 round trip, or $437 round trip in the summer season. All IATA airlines fly only jets. The flight takes approximately six hours. (An inclusive-tour-group fare—$205 round trip—is now offered if one stays more than two weeks but less than three, and is willing to book, in advance, $70 worth of ground services—hotel rooms, car rental, etc. It was instituted unilaterally—without IATA approval. Restrictions apply to certain "peak" periods during the summer.)

There is one airline, however, that is not a member of this organization. Icelandic Airlines flies CL-44 prop jet planes and makes one stop in Iceland. The fare from New York to Luxembourg—centrally located between France and Belgium and just a few hours by train to Paris or Amsterdam —is $319 round trip in the off season and $389 round trip during summer months. This flight is approximately 3,600 air miles and takes about 10 hours. IATA members charge $456.40 round trip in the off season, and $541.90 in the summer, for the same trip. Icelandic Airlines is always heavily booked. You must make reservations well in advance for the summer months.

•

Realizing that price might have some bearing on travel habits, the airlines have begun to offer all types of bargains. The first plan offered reductions to families flying Monday noon to Friday noon who were going for at least six days and not more than 30. Daddy paid full fare, mommy half fare, the children one-third fare, and children under two got free passage. But the very ground rules of its operations were the problem. With a week's vacation, for example, a man would probably prefer to leave Friday night and return Sunday, stretching his five-day vacation to nine. Unless his trip was cross-country he probably could reach his destination earlier by driving on Friday than flying on Monday. He would also save money. The problem on the return trip was even worse, since by coming back before Friday noon he would shorten his vacation to four days. If he waited and returned after Monday noon, his employer might not like it.

This is the very same problem with the airlines' excursion fare innovation, the one which went into effect March 27, 1966. Under this plan, if you go for not less than six or more than 30 days, you receive a 25 percent discount; a $304.72 round trip ticket from Los Angeles to New York is reduced to $228.54. But again, you can't fly on weekends and are still not able to stretch your vacation. And if this isn't enough of a discouragement, the airlines disallow "excursion fares" during "peak periods"! "Peak periods" are: June 12 to June 30, the first week of July, the entire month of August, the days immediately preceding and after Christmas and Thanksgiving, New Year's Day, Labor Day, Easter, etc., etc.—in short, during the time you might be taking a vacation in the summer or anytime you might be visiting a relative on a holiday. The plan does help some, many do use it, but it does not help those who would appreciate the savings most, working people who cannot arrange their lives to take advantage of the current bargains.

Probably the most effective innovation allows persons between 12 and 22 to purchase a ticket for $3 and fly for one-half the regular fare on a standby basis. A ticket from New York to San Francisco would be $76.18. The Christmas, New Year's and Thanksgiving rush days are excluded as the regulations now stand. Initiated by American Airlines, this policy has been adopted by almost all major airlines on nearly all flights. These youth fares enabled airlines to increase by 71 percent the number of people in the 18–24-year-old group taking their first commercial air trip. And there are 3.7 million persons entering the 18–24 age group each year. Perhaps if the airlines gave a large flat discount on certain flights (for example from 11 p.m. to 6 a.m.), regardless of the day, to the general public on a standby basis, they would increase the number of persons who take their first commercial flight in other age groups and increase other persons' frequency of taking flights.

One reason the airlines may have initiated this program is that the college students, although unorganized in most respects of "commerce," are becoming highly organized in one specialty: chartering planes. Since a large number of students will be leaving campuses or returning at the same time, it becomes quite easy for a student organization or some outside commercial company to charter a plane. These charters usually charge quite reasonable rates. For example, at the University of California at Berkeley over Christmas 1965, there were two chartered planes to New York, through the Trans-Continental Agency, one at a cost of $179 round trip, the other by jet for $208 round trip. Both charters were arranged by agencies outside the university.

On foreign flights, incidentally, the charters have become unbelievably popular. They go from Los Angeles or San Francisco to Europe for approximately $380 round trip; a saving of approximately $300 over commercial flights. This may account in part for an almost 35 percent reduction in average fares (non-charter) across the Atlantic during the period 1960–66. Harold Gray, president of Pan Am, predicts that the trend will continue through new promotional fares—that is, if you can find a computer complex enough to unscramble all the available "excursions."

•

The newest form of travel is the air clubs, which make charter flight prices seem high. A group of people, about 750, get together and buy a plane, say a DC-7. You buy a membership in the club for about $100, which is refundable upon termination of membership, and you pay annual dues of about $70 a year. The savings are incredible. Last summer, the Magellan Club of Oakland, California, scheduled two four-week flights to London from San Francisco for $220 round trip.

It is my opinion that the price for a ticket from New York to Los Angeles or San Francisco should cost a flat $100, if not less, rather than $152, regardless of the time or day of the flight. It should be pointed out that whereas in 1960, Greyhound and Trailways charged $143.50 for a round-trip ticket from New York to San Francisco, they now charge $99 for a ticket good for 99 days.

Perhaps you think that $100 is ridiculously low, that no airline could possibly make money at that price. Then consider the following facts. The distance from Los Angeles to New York is 2,474 air miles, whereas the air miles from Los Angeles to Honolulu, Hawaii, are 2,400. While the cheapest non-excursion jet from Los Angeles to New York is $152.36, you can fly to Hawaii from Los Angeles on a jet for $100.06 (with movie, no less, but no meal) on either Pan American or United Air Lines. It is five hours' flying time from Los Angeles to New York, or to Hawaii, but this varies with wind conditions. It is only fair to say you can spend more money to go to Hawaii—it's $110.06 one way if you want a meal with your movie, and it's $142.54 one way if you want to go first class, and God only knows what you get then, but the point is you can go for $100.06 if you don't want any frills. I assume the airlines are making money on the $100.06 ticket. So, United Air Lines will take you from Los Angeles to Hawaii on a DC-8 jet with a movie, for $52.30 less than the same airline will fly you from Los Angeles to New York (also on a DC-8). In short, you are paying an extra $52.30 for 74 air miles. Well, perhaps it's cheaper to fly over water.

San Francisco to Los Angeles is only 59 air miles less than the distance from Boston, Massachusetts, to Washington, D.C., but one can make the former trip for as little as $12 one way on a Pacific Southwest Airlines (PSA) prop jet, and $14.17 coach on TWA, United, and Western; the least expensive ticket from Boston to Washington, D.C. is $25.88. Los Angeles to San Francisco is the more heavily traveled route, but air traffic and weather only partly explain the contrast in price. It is better explained by the fact that PSA is an intrastate airline, operating only in the state of California, and is therefore not controlled by the CAB. Pacific Southwest Airlines' prices are controlled by the Public Utilities Commission of the state of California. Needless to say, PSA has profited from these low fares and takes passengers away from United, TWA, and the other interstate lines. The only way United, TWA, etc., could stay in business on this particular route was to cut prices to be competitive.

Look around your region and you will find huge price discrepancies where the routes have almost identical air miles and approximately the same amount of passengers. Check where both cities are in the same state and therefore not subject to CAB regulations. You will be startled by the discrepancies. What is needed in the airline industry is competition in fares and competition to fill all those empty seats, rather than competition over who designed the stewardesses' wardrobes.

Well, aren't the airlines doing a good job today? Aren't the planes full now? They may be during the big vacations, and sometimes on Friday or Sunday, but have you ever boarded a plane on a Tuesday afternoon from San Francisco to New York? More often than not, it is a third, or at best half full. The average passenger load of all flights for 1965 was 55 percent of capacity. One wonders what it will be when the 450-seat "stretch-out" jet appears in 1970.

There are millions of Americans who cannot afford present jet air fares, but who would much prefer to go by plane, even a prop plane, rather than take a bus. There are still other millions who would rather take six hours longer each way on a DC-6 for $170 round trip from New York to Los Angeles, than pay $304.72 for the jet. Half the fun to many would be saving the $134.72 to spend when they get to their destination, or just the chance to go more often, or to go at all.

The Trans-Pacific
Air Route Tangle

by DAVID SANFORD

In commercial air route cases every Civil Aeronautics Board decision is controversial. The airlines that get the routes are pleased; those that don't, feel aggrieved. The current trans-Pacific case, the biggest in CAB history, is the latest and bloodiest example.

The route structure in the Pacific has been essentially the same for 20 years. In the fifties the CAB recommended to President Eisenhower, whose approval was required, that competitive routes be established in the Pacific, ending the near monopoly of Pan American, Northwest and United Air Lines. Two days before his term ended, Eisenhower decided, on foreign policy grounds, to reject Board proposals and leave the matter to the incoming Democrats. Similarly, at the end of his term, President Johnson had the opportunity to act. He agreed with his Board's recommendations, except notably with its plan to allow service to Tokyo by American Airlines. The Japanese, whose own Japan Air Lines resented the competitive intrusion, objected, and the State Department advised that the President should not permit another US line to fly into Japan. Johnson accordingly rejected American's application, while approving the remainder of the CAB decision. The President's action was controversial because he and the CAB, whose members are Presidential appointees, had come to quite different conclusions from those of the Board's independent examiner, Robert L. Parks. Parks had held hearings and recommended that the plums be allocated otherwise. Now President Nixon, heeding the pleas of airlines that lost out, has, possibly illegally, intervened by rescinding the awards and for the moment putting things back where they were 20 years ago. When the conflict is resolved, if it ever is, Nixon may wish he had never got involved.

For years, air business in the Pacific has been divided between Northwest, which flies the polar route from New York and other US cities to Tokyo; Pan American, which flies the Pacific to Honolulu and Tokyo; and United, which has the major share of traffic from West Coast points to Hawaii. Trans World Airlines flies around the world, except for a stretch between Hong Kong and the western United States. (TWA, unlike Pan Am, has an extensive domestic route system as well.)

President Eisenhower asked the CAB in 1958 to consider revising and modernizing this route structure, opening the area to competition and thus improving service and reducing fares, which were and are disproportionately high. The adequacy of service was considered and projections were made of future traffic. The Board in late 1960 recommended certain new routes. However, the President, who has jurisdiction in international cases, rejected the recommendations in toto, on the grounds that foreign relations would be adversely affected. The United States generates more than half of all airline traffic in the world, but is reluctant to pit more than one or two of its privately owned airlines against foreign lines, often state-owned. Triplication of service abroad is considered bad international relations.

In the fifties case Pan American, which stood to lose from any change, argued that the routes could not withstand additional carriers, especially since jets, with their increased seating capacity, were about to go into service. (Pan Am is now arguing that the big 747's are on the way and that they can handle the load, and the profit, themselves.) However, in rejecting any change, Eisenhower was primarily concerned about Japanese fears of declining revenues for Japan Air. The can of worms was not opened again until 1966, when President Johnson asked the CAB to take another look.

So instructed, the Board follows a complicated procedure of hearings, briefs, and studies, and also submits the issues to an independent examiner who conducts his own quasi-judicial hearings. His final opinion, submitted to the CAB, is considered in the Board's decision, reached by a vote of the five members. The examiner is generally more isolated than the Board; he considers fewer cases; he is perhaps not as familiar with the overall industry situation as is the Board, whose members do a good deal of fraternizing with airlines and their representatives. In the current case, examiner Parks proposed new routes for Eastern, Northwest, Pan American, TWA, United, Western and Flying Tiger. He rejected routes for Braniff, American and Continental. The CAB disagreed and granted routes to Braniff, American and Continental, as well as to Northwest, TWA, Western, Flying Tiger, and United. The CAB, unlike its examiner, gave no new service to Eastern.

The discrepancies between the recommendations of the Board and those of its examiner made the Board's final recommendations more controversial than they would have been had there been a consensus. The President was sent the Board's findings and he approved them, but as noted, he refused, on advice from the State Department, to allow American to fly to Tokyo. This left American unable to fly to Hawaii *or* Tokyo since the CAB's original recommendation gave American permission to fly to Hawaii only if the planes and passengers were going on to Tokyo or elsewhere west. A tangential flap arose when Johnson wrote the Board recommending that since American would not be allowed Tokyo, then it ought to be considered for Hawaii alone. Presidents have international jurisdiction but are not to meddle in domestic routing. The whole question is now up in the air, and at least insofar as American's service to Hawaii is concerned the planes are grounded.

•

Naturally, carrier representatives on both sides are spreading rumors they hope will establish that Johnson's decision was, or was not, tainted by cronyism and special interest. Both cases can be made.

When Johnson approved the trans-Pacific case in December he thought the matter was closed. Petitions for reconsideration were invited by the CAB, as is customary, but the airlines that had won routes felt so certain they had their bequests secured that they began spending money. Continental's President Robert Six took planes out of his Southeast Asia fleet (a service solicited by the CIA when its own Air America was about to lose its cover in 1964). He rented counter space in Honolulu, ordered new planes.

But four days before the Nixon Inaugural, newspapers began to run stories implying that improper influence had been exerted to gain routes for airlines run by or employing pals of Lyndon Johnson. Senator Robert Griffin (R, Mich.) gave a speech about Johnson cronies, and the campaign to sway Nixon began.

Thomas Finney, Jr., a law partner of Clark Clifford, the recent Secretary of Defense and Johnson friend, represents Continental Airlines. He believes that the flurry of news stories was not coincidental but had been planted by Eastern Air Lines to get Nixon to intervene. Had the Johnson action been questioned in December, Finney contends, there would be no suspicion of manipulation, but beginning as they did in mid-January, the stories were clearly part of "an enormous campaign by Pan American and Eastern, supported ineptly by United, to get Nixon to interfere."

Finney charges that Eastern, whose largest stockholder is Laurence Rockefeller, was represented by the Rockefeller brothers in the New York financial community, on Capitol Hill and to the President directly, and was ultimately successful in getting Nixon on January 24 to rescind the Johnson approval.

It is unclear whether Nixon acted in response to a letter-writing campaign by congressmen and senators, as he says he did, or whether he had decided some time before, after talking with Nelson Rockefeller, that the case should be reopened. But between the press and the pressures, enough serious questions had been raised to give Nixon an excuse to step in.

Those who support the Nixon intervention argue that the CAB examiner, not the Board itself, should have been listened to. Board members are appointed politically (Johnson named the present chairman, John Crooker, a Houston attorney and Johnson fund-raising friend). Senator Griffin was impressed by a column by Rowland Evans and Robert Novak that listed the Johnson friends in the airline industry: Troy Post, James Ling, Walter Jenkins and Cliff Carter (Braniff); Warren Woodward, Horace Busby and Jake Jacobsen (American); Continental was represented by Clark Clifford et al; Lloyd Hand is "closely connected" with Continental. Johnson's last Secretary of Commerce, C. R. Smith, was once president of American. Johnson's assistant, Joseph Califano, is now a lawyer with the firm representing Braniff. Another assistant, Harry McPherson, will join a firm representing Northwest.

In fairness, the President did not make the awards; he approved the Board's. His defenders say he had set ground rules which included his intention to approve whatever the Board recommended, limited only by considerations of US international relations, and not to attempt to modify the awards in any way. In the case of American Airlines, the company of which the President was said to be most enamored, the three Democrats who make up the majority of the five-man CAB voted for American's routes to Tokyo. The President, in some pain, rejected American. That does not look like cronyism. Secretary C. R. Smith, the former chief executive of American, took himself and his department out of deliberations on the case to avoid any appearance of conflict of interest. The award of routes to Hawaii and the South Pacific to Continental won out over Eastern by a four-to-one bipartisan majority of the Board—G. Joseph Minetti, a Democrat appointed by Eisenhower; Robert T. Murphy, a Democrat appointed by Kennedy; John G. Adams, a Republican appointed by Johnson, and John H. Crooker, a Johnson Democrat. Only Whitney Gillilland, a Republican placed on the Board by Eisenhower, dissented.

Continental seemed preferable to Eastern in part because it could provide point-to-point competition with United from California points to Hawaii, whereas the Eastern application was for routes that would bypass California and the West. Its planes would have taken off from the East and flown to Hawaii and the South Pacific either directly or with intervening stops in Mexico. It would be stretching a point to suggest that Eastern could have competed with Pan Am and United, which fly the California-to-Hawaii route. The necessity for competition was the reason for the case in the first place.

According to press reports both Eastern and American have attempted, albeit unsuccessfully, to hire lawyers from Nixon Administration law firms.

American tried to co-opt the law firm of Secretary of State William P. Rogers. Eastern tried to cozy up to Nixon, Mudge, Rose, Guthrie, Alexander & Mitchell. Pan American contributed to the Nixon campaign. And Nelson Rockefeller reportedly approached Nixon in behalf of Eastern.

Aside from whether the decision has any political taint, Nixon's recision of the Johnson approval may not be legal. The law provides for CAB decisions in international route cases to be submitted to the President for approval prior to their publication in the Federal Register. President Truman once approved such a board order, then changed his mind and called it back for a veto. TWA, the airline involved, went to federal court. The court refused to upset Truman's action on the grounds that he had changed his mind *before the order had been published*. "We see no good reason," wrote the court, "why delivery of an order to the President's adviser [the CAB] should put beyond his control prompt reconsideration of it while the order still remains unpublished and unknown to the parties, and no one can have acted in reliance on it." In the current case Johnson signed the order, it *was* published, and the airlines have already sunk money in their new routes (Continental has 5,000 reservations for flights to Hawaii which cannot now take to the air). Continental's attorneys view Nixon's reconsideration as Indian-giving but say they do not plan to sue. "You don't get an injunction against a President who's been in office for four days, then spend years in court if you want your planes in the air next month," says Continental's Thomas Finney. The most that can be hoped for is that Nixon will now act with dispatch and allow some answer to the need for airline competition in the Pacific.

Togetherness in the Air

A NEW REPUBLIC EDITORIAL

Ten little airlines that do 58 percent of their business shuttling troops back and forth to Vietnam and on other errands for the government are trying to cash in on the commercial traffic and thus justify their independent existence. To do this they have gone into the "packaged tour" business, chartering their planes to travel agents who plan itineraries, book passengers and charge little more for it all than commercial airlines do for their cheapest round-trip air fare. The "inclusive" tour supposedly benefits the tourist (because it's cheaper), detracts little from the business of the giant airlines, and keeps the small, supplemental airlines in the black. But the courts have ruled, at least insofar as international flights are concerned, that the Civil Aeronautics Board may not have had authority to sanction the practice.

The little airlines (including Capital International Airways, Modern Air Transport, Overseas National, Purdue, Saturn, Southern, Standard, Trans International, Universal, and World) are asking Congress to amend the law slightly to clearly authorize the CAB to bless their commercial activities. They have the support of the chairman of the CAB, congressmen from Hawaii (to which a majority of the charter flights go) and Betty Furness, President Johnson's consumer affairs adviser, among others. The arguments raised in behalf of the charter airlines are largely negative and ignore the central problem of the air industry from the consumer's point of view —competition.

CAB Chairman John H. Crooker told Congress that the services of the little airlines are so modest that he couldn't understand why anyone would oppose them. By law, the full tour price they charge must be no less than 110 percent of the lowest available individual travel fare offered by a scheduled carrier. The price must include all hotel accommodations and air and surface transportation. Each tour must be on a round-trip basis, last at least a week, and have at least three overnight stops at least 50 miles apart. Therefore, according to Crooker's defense,

> The charter tour passenger would be subjected to the rigidities of the group itinerary, would have to be willing to travel and share facilities with strangers, and would have to agree to the necessary regimentation entailed in group travel. Moreover, the tour passenger would . . . be confined to predetermined departure and arrival times selected by the tour operator. Under these circumstances, tours could not be used as an inducement to substitute travel on them for point-to-point transportation offered by the scheduled carriers.

The "inclusive" tour may seem a horror to some, but it has its appeal for low-income, inexperienced travelers who are wary of going to faraway places except in packs, who enjoy eating together, sleeping together, and going on guided tours. The scheme would never have been devised in the first place save for the argument that it would not lose business for the established airlines with their exclusive, identical fares. Only six percent of Americans have ever been out of the country, by one estimate, and under half have ever been in the air. It was reasoned that this great untapped market might be interested in inclusive tours, thus giving the small airlines something to do when they are not carrying troops.

Federal law requires that the supplemental airlines have enough civilian business to sustain them in peacetime or when the government can't keep them in the air. To get military contracts the supplementals have to get 30 percent of their revenues from commercial sources. To have commercial revenues they have to be permitted to fly commercially. It was to avoid the complaints of the big airlines that they were given a niche in the packaged tour business.

What bothers the commercial airlines is the thought of competition. Those in international commerce who are members of the International Air Transport Association collude every so often in classy resorts to fix prices. The air traveler is thereby deprived of a real choice. He may like the steaks better on TWA or the jokes about Alitalia or the stewardesses on SAS. But the fares are all the same. Only a few airlines like Icelandic remain aloof from IATA and offer lower prices. And some countries, with national airlines that are IATA members, deny them permission to land. The industry similarly resents the puny incursions of the small supplemental airlines.

The quasi-monopoly in the airline industry is the best justification for giving the supplementals a share of the business. And Congress might think also about freeing the little fellows to engage in more domestic and international business, at lower fares.

Come Right in "Colonel," "Admiral," or Whoever

by DAVID SANFORD

In 1962 the Civil Aeronautics Board decided to look into private clubs maintained by major airlines for their special customers—the plush "members only" lounges at airports across the country that provide everything from free liquor to color TV, free phones and secretarial service.

The clubs, of which most air travelers are unaware, date from 1938 when flying still had a trace of adventure and members of American Airlines' "Admirals of the Flagship Fleet" felt a kinship. An admiral's hat on the club's front door was identification for the initiated. The occasional non-member who wandered in by mistake learned from the pretty "skipper" at the door that he did not belong.

One doesn't become an "Admiral" simply by flying American. One must make "an outstanding contribution to the promotion of aviation." Admirals include businessmen, frequent travelers, celebrities, journalists and the chairman of the Senate aviation subcommittee. One cannot apply for the membership (there are no forms); one is nominated by the airline's district sales office and sent a membership card signifying his "meritorious service to air transportation." The card gets him past the skipper and into any of the ten Admirals Clubs at US airports.

Until about 1960 TWA's Ambassadors Club at Washington National Airport was open to everyone who flew. But it became so crowded with people waiting for the Eastern Airlines shuttle that it had to be restricted to TWA passengers. And only to a few of them. A typical club, according to Rosemary Aurichio, a TWA official, is a comfortable lounge set away from the hurly-burly of the public waiting areas of a terminal. It is equipped

Reprinted by permission of the New Republic, © *1966, Harrison-Blaine of New Jersey, Inc.*

with a stereo or TV, writing tables, a conference table for small meetings, and a bar. Customers pay for their drinks, except in states where, to get around liquor laws, the lounges operate as bottle clubs. Members store their bottles in lockers provided by the club and are served by waiters who charge only for "setups." Ambassadors are nominated by TWA district sales staffs, "who generally know the individual and what amount of travel he gives us." For flying often on TWA a customer gets a card identifying him as "one of a select group of patrons of air transportation and one who is thus contributing by travel and trade to better understanding, amity and unity throughout the world." Ambassadors are life members unless they pass bad checks at the TWA ticket counter (cashing checks is another "members only" privilege).

Members of Continental Airlines' Presidents Club (including Senator Peter H. Dominick of Colorado and Senator George Murphy of California, who represent states in Continental's service area) may, if they wish, sip free drinks in any of five airports and admire the private art collection of Continental's president Robert Six. Delta has a Colonels Club; Pan American a Clipper Club; Braniff an International Council Club; Northwest a Top Flight Club. United, the extra-care airline, takes extra care of members of its 100,000 Mile Club (one star on the membership plaque for every 100,000 miles in the friendly skies of United, or any other airline). Services differ from club to club and airport to airport, but all the clubs are not advertised, charge no dues, and are exclusive.

The airlines make a practice of offering memberships to public officials. For example, Senator Norris Cotton of New Hampshire, the ranking Republican on both the Senate Commerce Committee and its aviation subcommittee, holds memberships in three of the airline clubs. Senator Mike Monroney (D, Oklahoma), chairman of the aviation subcommittee, is an Admiral of the Flagship Fleet and a former "Ambassador." Senator E. L. Bartlett of Alaska, also of the aviation subcommittee, is a member of the Admirals and Northwest's Top Flight Club. He believes the clubs are discriminatory, but only in the sense that they favor heavy travelers. He tells of having once walked into a club of which he was not a member, announcing himself as a United States Senator and being turned away like a man of no distinction.

Passengers who pay the same fare as an "Admiral" or a "Colonel" may see no reason why they should subsidize a service which they are denied. A provision of the Federal Aviation Act of 1958 seems to justify their sense of grievance: "No air carrier . . . shall make, give, or cause any undue or unreasonable preference or advantage to any particular person."

In March 1962, after receiving several complaints from passengers, the Civil Aeronautics Board instituted an investigation of clubs maintained by American, Continental, Pan Am and TWA, each of which has restricted waiting rooms at various airports. The investigation was to determine whether the carriers' practices of maintaining "members only" facilities constituted unjust discrimination, preference, prejudice, rebates, or unfair competition. A year later, in March 1963, the Board concluded that "continuance of the matter to hearing would not serve the public interest" and dismissed the investigation without prejudice. Two members of the five-man board, Robert T. Murphy and G. Joseph Minetti, dissented:

> This proceeding has not moved forward and is now being dismissed. . . . In our view, insuring that consumers are not subjected to possible discriminatory practices is certainly in the overall public interest, and we believe the proceeding would resolve the matter.
>
> While there are no accurate and complete figures available to us, we understand the operation of these clubs may cost the carriers an almost one million dollar loss annually. If this is the case, the practice may well be questionable in respects beyond the bare discrimination.

The CAB has continued to receive complaints from passengers bounced from airline clubs. In December 1965, Herbert A. Goldberger, a Rhode Island businessman, found himself between planes at New York's Kennedy Airport. Inside American's terminal he noticed several passengers disappear behind the door with the admiral's hat on it. He followed them inside, was told he was not welcome, protested, but was refused admittance.

On his return to Providence, he spoke with American's district sales manager, John C. Ryan, who told him membership could be obtained only through appointment of the applicant by American. Then Goldberger asked an "Admiral" friend of his to write him a letter of recommendation to the club, which was done. The Airlines replied, "We have had to limit the number of new Admirals that we commission so as not to overcrowd the club's facilities. However, you can be assured that as this request comes from one who is an Admiral, it will receive our consideration as soon as this situation eases."

In a formal complaint to the CAB, filed January 21, 1966, Goldberger charged that "to the extent that American Airlines, Inc. has arbitrarily selected a segment of the traveling public to which they choose to extend additional and superior terminal facilities and service, it is engaging in a discriminatory practice."

170

Henry Fonda's Steak

A NEW REPUBLIC EDITORIAL

"We prepared a steak dinner for Henry Fonda and this kid ate it," begins a current magazine ad for American Airlines. "A travel agent put him on the airline we built for Henry Fonda." The point of the pitch is that service tailored for the professional traveler ("a Henry Fonda buys up to 50 tickets a year") is available to everybody with the price of admission, including little boys in patched Levis and dirty sneakers. However, there are some services American and eight other commercial airlines provide which are subsidized by all passengers but available only to the Henry Fondas—services the airlines don't advertise.

The nine carriers maintain sumptuous private "clubs" at major airports across the country for the convenience of favored customers. The clubs dispense gratuities—free drinks, phones, secretarial service and special stand-by privileges—to designated "frequent travellers," celebrities, senators, and Civil Aeronautics Board members. This month the Enforcements Bureau of the CAB informed the airlines that it considered the VIP treatment illegal and was asking the Board to investigate. The division's rationale is a clause in the Federal Aviation Act of 1958: "No carrier . . . shall . . . give any undue or unreasonable preference or advantage to any particular person . . . in air transportation."

The notification, which will require Board action to have any force, was spurred by a Rhode Island businessman's complaint. He said he had been bounced from American's "Admirals" club at Detroit's Metropolitan Airport and again at New York's John F. Kennedy International Airport because he was not a member. Continental, Pan American, United, Braniff,

Reprinted by permission of the New Republic, © *1966, Harrison-Blaine of New Jersey, Inc.*

TWA, National, Trans Caribbean, and Northwest have similar clubs, and have also been called upon by the CAB to justify their exclusivity.

American, which in 1965 counted 11 million fares, has explained its 90,000-member "Admirals of the Flagship Fleet" as legitimate promotion not covered by the Federal Aviation Act. If the club is discriminatory, said the airline, it is not unduly, unjustly or unreasonably so. Since the clubs are located on the ground, they can hardly be covered by a law governing "air transportation." And "membership in the Club is generally available to the public." The only hitch is not everybody can get in. An American official said the waiting list is "probably just as long" as the roster of members. "A limitation on the number of new members in the Admirals Club," the airline stated, "is required to prevent overcrowding of the existing facilities. In this respect the Admirals Club is no different than public housing projects or state universities." Besides, "if we opened up the Admirals Club and people came in, with children aged one-and-a-half and two, wheeling baby carriages, it would kind of lose its meaning."

The airlines do everything they can to appeal to all classes of travelers and get the edge on the competition. If you don't like Braniff's true fruit-colored planes, perhaps you'll go for the steak prepared for, but not eaten by, Mr. Fonda or for the private art collection of Continental Airlines President Robert Six that decorates that company's Presidents club lounges. American has gone to the length of setting up youth lounges to give teen-age passengers a place to frug and drink Cokes while waiting to use their half-fare tickets, and a "fair ladies club" for the "very important secretaries who make reservations for the fellows who are the frequent travelers." "By being nice to them and making them know we feel they are important, it helps our business," a spokesman said. American takes the ladies out for an occasional drink and to the theatre in hopes that next time the boss wants a plane reservation they'll know whom to call.

PART III

YOUR SAFETY
IS AT STAKE

Safety on the Job

by RALPH NADER
and JEROME GORDON

Imagine yourself sitting in your office a few months from today. A young man barges in. You recognize him as a man you once refused to hire. He had no education and no potential you could use. His main experience consisted of cashing welfare checks. But he shows you he's now a representative of the federal government —an inspector with the Department of Labor. And he threatens to padlock your gates and have you fined $1,000 a day if you don't do as he says.

With minor historic adjustments, the foregoing remarks could have issued from the business barons of the McKinley era. Actually, they were written in April 1968 by the US Chamber of Commerce as a call to obstruction by US business of the Johnson Administration's worker health and security bill. With a lobbying effort, in conjunction with such other major trade associations as the National Association of Manufacturers, that has led the Chamber to unfurl its true colors, there is a growing probability that Congress will not act to institute a comprehensive federal program designed to end colossal inaction and penury by our society in dealing with the following conditions:

Every working day 55 workers die, 8,500 are disabled and 27,200 are injured (a case can be made that these data are under-enumerated by at least 25 percent annually.)

Unlike traumatic injuries which are relatively visible, the longer-range injuries causing insidious deterioration of the human body

Reprinted by permission of the New Republic, © *1968, Harrison-Blaine of New Jersey, Inc.*

come from exposure to coal dust, asbestos, lead, cadmium, beryllium, cotton dust, carbon monoxide, chemicals, dyes, radiation, pesticides, benzene and thousands of other toxic materials. Industrial uses of chemicals are growing so rapidly that voluntary exposure limits have been set for only 400 of the 6,000 chemicals in substantial use.

The federal government has no authority to issue mandatory safety standards for various private occupations, with few exceptions including longshoremen, stevedores, maritime workers and to a smaller extent, coal miners and uranium miners. Adverse health and safety conditions have been worsening in the past decade, while workmen's compensation benefits have not kept up with living costs. (One third of the labor force is not covered by any workmen's compensation.)

Paralleling this deterioration is the pathetic and industry-indentured performance of the states, which traditionally have had exclusive jurisdiction over worker health and safety. Only 1,600 state safety inspectors are around, some tied by ambition, laziness or lucre to winking at violations. By contrast, the states retain at least double that number of fish and game wardens. Overall, the states' worker safety programs spend an average of 40 cents a year per non-agricultural worker, with Texas and Oklahoma, for example, spending about two cents per non-agricultural worker. Further, of the 1,600 state inspectors, about 700 inspect boilers, elevators and mines, leaving the remainder for general safety inspection, construction, safety promotion and education, health and industrial hygiene. Four states have no inspection staff at all; 17 states have fewer than 11 safety inspectors. More dismaying, only three states have staff specializing in the area of occupational health and industrial hygiene.

•

Over, underneath, and around this fragile state framework are the representatives of industry and commerce making certain that there are no applied sanctions to even the meek laws, and controlling the process of developing standards through their so-called United States of America Standards Institute (until 1966 the American Standards Association), whose promulgations are hurried into state statutes or regulations. Even data collection reflects the omnipresence of business: in 1966, less than half the states required employers to report all accidents, and less than two-thirds of the states required employers to keep accident records. Just what constitutes work injury is defined for states by industry through the USA Standards Institute (USASI). The present standard 216.1 vests considerable authority in plant medical personnel in determining whether an injury constitutes an "injury," and does not count third-party fatalities in an industrial catastrophe as "industrial fatalities," even if they were employees in nearby establishments.

176

The factory climate surrounding data collection makes deep skepticism the minimal response to the Chamber of Commerce's claims of progress and superiority over other industrial nations. Accident and injury reporting in many industries, such as steel and autos, is deliberately aborted in numerous cases. Testimony before the House Education and Labor Subcommittee earlier this year by Public Health Service employees and medical professors cited cases such as a man bodily carried from his hospital and given a bed at the work place in order to eliminate lost-time accidents. Less extraordinary but far more frequent are "make-work" activities after injuries or "no work," such as sitting the worker at a table doing nothing. Data on occupational diseases such as respiratory and liver ailments from toxic exposures are woefully incomplete, according to a report by the Department of Health, Education and Welfare.

One of the major canons of medical science—free communication—is severely undermined by the subordination of professional dictates to corporate expediencies. Dr. Hawley A. Wells, a pathologist and professor at the University of West Virginia Medical School, offers two illustrations of little-known corporate censorship:

> A Dr. John Zalinsky told us about 30 cases of a chronic lung disease caused by exposure to "safe" levels of beryllium dust. He was told by his company's management that if he published these cases in the medical literature he would have to look for another job. He was torn between professional honesty and personal security—he had had one heart attack and would have difficulty in finding another job. Before he was able to resolve this dilemma, he died from another heart attack. His material has never been published.
>
> I have personal knowledge of a plant which uses manganese, long known to be a toxic metal. Through bitter experience, management recently found that it poisoned the nervous system, causing permanent brain damage in exposed workers. They are now using a simple test, no more complicated than a prick on the finger, to detect exposure to manganese long before permanent nerve injury occurs. Hundreds of other companies who now use manganese do not have the advantage of knowing about this simple test because it has not been published in this country.
>
> Unless each physician, each industrial hygienist and safety engineer has available to him the research experience of all of those who preceded him in his profession, he must duplicate the research in every case, often at the cost of human life.

Under-reporting of occupational diseases is also related to the lack in some states of laws permitting health officials to have a right of entry into the plants. One plant in Pennsylvania (a right-of-entry state) was using

177

the chemical beta naphthylamine, which a health specialist learned was causing carcinoma of the bladder. The plant promptly moved to Georgia (not a right-of-entry state) and resumed operations unhindered.

Under-reporting has other harmful consequences. Not knowing the patient's occupational exposure, a physician can produce a mistaken diagnosis. For instance, in 1966 the Public Health Service reported three "pneumonia" deaths that were later traced to the use of silver solder containing deadly cadmium.

Definitional absurdities have resulted in these abuses uncovered by the N.Y. State Department of Labor:

A plant employing over 2,000 persons did not consider reportable any injuries that did not entail lost time, nor did it report any temporary injuries that fell within the seven-day workmen's compensation waiting period. The corrected injury frequency rate was almost triple that originally reported by the firm.

Another firm, employing over 10,000, was reporting a low rate of injury by comparison with the rest of the large companies in the same industry, until it was discovered that it was reporting only compensable cases. This practice may require revising our notion that big plants are safer than small plants.

With both industry and the states grievously deficient in defining new hazards and in collecting adequate data, the cumulative toll annually of 500,000 disabled by occupational diseases, over two million disabled by occupational accidents and over seven million injured must be considered a substantial understatement. And we haven't begun to measure the deleterious effects of noise, artificial light, vibration and other assaults on man's physiological integrity.

The insurance industry, taking in $2.3 billion in workmen's compensation premiums in 1967, spent an unspecified $35 million on industrial safety and inspection. This relatively tiny sum has resulted in little loss-prevention work and no significant contributions to data collection and retrieval. Contrary to popular impression, workmen's compensation insurance is enormously profitable to most companies, with a range of between 10 and 35 percent gross margin profits in the past 20 years. Their public relations to the contrary, such insurance carriers have not been eager to publicize new worker hazards in any forum and have not shared their knowledge with governmental authorities as befits good corporate citizenship. The highly touted safety record adjustment or "merit rating experience" applies for only 20 percent of all insurance risks. The underwriters have shown almost no interest in plugging loopholes in state laws—for example, only 18 state laws cover all employment. Others have exemptions of varying scope, such as all work activity *except* mining and construction.

•

Against such a background, it is not surprising that the Chamber and the National Association of Manufacturers are moving to block a federal bill by delaying it or proposing a study commission as an alternative. Failing that, they will strive to strip it of meaningful penalties, surround it with advisory committees and demand usage of industry standards via USASI. Big business benefits from the do-little symbolic state laws with their financially starved administrators, and from the lower costs of insuring against risks of industrial injury that are possible with incomplete reporting of accidents, injuries and disease.

As proposed by the Administration, the worker safety and health bill would provide for setting mandatory standards applicable to employers affecting interstate commerce (roughly 50 million employees). The bill authorizes the Secretary of Labor to inspect the premises, issue cease-and-desist orders, and invoke other civil and criminal sanctions where necessary. Compliance with such standards can be made a condition of continuing federal contracts with the firm. The bill would provide for grants of up to 90 percent of the cost to the states to upgrade their role in data, inspection, enforcement and general administration. The Department of Health, Education and Welfare is given a mission in research, training of personnel and developing safety criteria. The projected total cost over the next five years (1969–1974) is estimated at $300 million, or approximately $30 million a year beyond 1968 levels. Compare this sum with the cost in 1966 of work accidents and illnesses—$6.8 billion.

Americans far from the blue-collar world have absorbed a decisive image of industry as gleaming, one-story, antiseptic space-age firms where frequency rates of injuries and disease are not far from zero. Unfortunately, work is getting more complex and dangerous all the time, not just for the blue-collar worker but for the white-coated scientist or laboratory technician handling exotic materials. Dr. Miriam Sachs told the House Subcommittee something of this trend when she described the "shift from a mechanical to a broadly diversified array of new hazards," including many new agricultural hazards flowing from the use of synthetic chemicals as fertilizers or as pesticides.

Secretary of Labor Wirtz, in perhaps the most feeling testimony of his career, told the Senate subcommittee on Labor what the grisly evidence points to as the central issue:

> It is whether the Congress is going to act to stop a carnage which continues for one reason, and one reason only, and that is because the people in this country don't realize what is involved, and they can't see the blood on the food that they eat, and on the things that they buy, and on the services they get.

Secretary Wirtz has the facts, enough in themselves for action, but pointing to a larger dimension of industrial neglect than was thought possible previously. One datum in his testimony: half of the nation's 137,000 coal miners suffer from the cruel dust disease, pneumoconiosis of the lungs; they breathe with difficulty and spit black sputum daily. Not many Americans know of this human depletion when they receive the benefits of coal energy. That's what Secretary Wirtz is talking about and that is what the Chamber of Commerce doesn't want us to hear.

—

They're Still Breathing

by RALPH NADER

It starts with breathlessness and ends with death. Along the way, the victim can experience bronchitis, emphysema, an enlarged heart and progressive massive fibrosis leading to severe respiratory disability. The disease is coal pneumoconiosis. In 1963, a US Public Health Service study concluded that, at the very least, about one of every 10 active bituminous coal miners and one in five inactive miners have it.

It was a little late to discover this widespread prevalence of the disease. Coal miners have been depleting themselves for an energy-hungry society for over a century. However, even more unsettling has been the inaction during the years after the PHS study.

Far more attention and expense is being devoted to the aesthetic costs of strip coal mining than to preventing the human wreckage which continues to stumble out of the mines after years of working in quietly miserable conditions. These are the coal mines which are bringing their owners record profits. This is the industry which is subject to coal mine safety laws that have been deprived of both their nourishment and inspiration by inert administrators who are surrounded by indifference.

Reports on coal mine safety emanating from the Department of the Interior have never fully reflected the health hazards endemic to this occupation. Recommendations for action, particularly those not dealing with mine operating safety, have been cut out of final revisions so as not to discomfort coal operators. Both the operators and the officials of the United Mine Workers are more concerned about the problems of competing energy sources and anti-air pollution drives than the slow death in the mines. UMW hospitals are available for the sick worker but the UMW seems far less interested in the toxic environment of the mines.

If the dimensions of this occupational hazard are not revealed by the Interior Department, which is responsible for coal mine safety, then most certainly the resources to develop methods of disease recognition and treatment, engineering techniques for dust control and safer working standards will not be forthcoming. And, despite the very vague rhetoric, they have not been forthcoming.

In 1952, there were 335,217 coal miners employed. A little over a decade later, the number of miners dropped to 128,698. These figures give some indication of the number of inactive and active miners exposed to coal dust. Coal is far from a dying industry, however. Its star has been rising since 1961, and now coal accounts for about 27 percent of US energy output, with a dollar value at the mines exceeding $2.3 billion. The larger coal companies are so profitable that they have become prime acquisition targets of oil, copper and other industrial giants. But growing concentration, efficiency and profit have not brought a more healthful mine environment. On the contrary, government specialists believe that mechanization may have increased the miner's exposure to coal dust.

Workmen's compensation costs run $27 million annually in Pennsylvania alone—a state which accounts for just 20 percent of total coal mining employment. Yet when Congress finally appropriated $100,000 in 1963 for a PHS study of the incidence of coal workers' pneumoconiosis, the European Coal and Steel Community was spending $9 million annually researching this disease from coal mine to laboratory. Environmental controls in the mines, such as water spraying for dust suppression during blasting and on automatic equipment, have resulted from the findings.

The PHS study concluded that death rates for coal miners were twice that of the general working male population, while death rates for diseases of the respiratory system were about five times that for the general working male population. British soft coal miners were reported to have a considerably longer life expectancy than American coal miners.

Danger: Death at Work

by J. V. REISTRUP

Eola Garner can see Charley Steen's big house on the hill from the front door of her trailer home in Moab, Utah, although it is about a mile away. Charley Steen, who once described himself as a petroleum geologist turned uranium prospector, struck it rich in the early 1950's and was one of the few who made millions out of finding uranium for nuclear bombs. Eola Garner's husband, Douglas, was one of the hundreds who contracted, or will contract, fatal lung cancer after mining the same newly precious element. His widow now supports their two teen-age children on Social Security payments, for Mrs. Garner failed even to collect workmen's compensation after her husband's death. As the landmark case in Utah, her claim went all the way to the state Supreme Court, which said in a 4-to-1 ruling that evidence of high incidence of lung cancer among uranium miners "is indeed impressive and may well be regarded as calling attention to the question whether lung cancer of uranium miners should be included in the occupational disease listed by statute as compensable. However," the court added in upholding the state's rejection of Mrs. Garner's claim, "that is a legislative, not a judicial problem."

Lung cancer among the uranium miners has been somebody else's problem for a long time. Presumably few of the miners read the medical and scientific literature that, over four decades, has built up evidence that theirs is a dangerous occupation not only because of the hazards ordinarily associated with mining but also because of the colorless, odorless, tasteless—and deadly—substances known as radon daughters. These radioactive products of the decay of uranium and its offshoot, radon gas, appear to be the culprits which, inhaled by the miner, can cause cancer.

Reprinted by permission of the New Republic, © *1968, Harrison-Blaine of New Jersey, Inc.*

But it usually takes about 20 years after initial exposure for lung cancer to develop and US uranium mining began in 1948, so the theory was a long time being proved. By early 1967, the number of uranium miners already dead of lung cancer was reported at about 50. Within a few months, the total being given was 115. Before projections of future deaths—from radiation already received—were written off as unscientific, numbers ranging to over 1,000 were mentioned.

The news was embarrassing to several federal agencies. The Atomic Energy Commission, which regulates uranium products from the mill onward, had never sought to extend its jurisdiction to the mines. The Department of the Interior, given authority by the Federal Metal and Non-metallic Mine Safety Act of 1966 to set safety standards in the mines, had dallied about appointing the advisory group that was to recommend these standards. The Department of Labor, which under the depression-era Walsh-Healey Act had authority to set standards in mines whose production was bought by the federal government, had also waited. Everybody was waiting for a recommendation from the interagency Federal Radiation Council, which had been studying the problem for two years. In the absence of federal standards, rules among the states varied—a couple closed down mines only if their level of radiation was measured at 10 times the maximum recommended, without the force of law, by the US Public Health Service a decade earlier.

•

With this background, the Joint Committee on Atomic Energy announced hearings on the uranium miners in April 1967. But, as all students of Congress know, standing committees of Congress often develop strongly protective relationships with their client agencies. The Joint Committee on Atomic Energy shows a strong preference for witnesses whose view of the Atomic Energy Commission is largely favorable. Further, the committee is charged by law with overseeing the growth of the atomic energy industry.

"I don't think that this problem should be confused as human life against dollars," Chairman John O. Pastore (D, R.I.) said as the hearings opened. That theme faded away as the sessions droned on into summer, however, and the leitmotiv became the economic cost of imposing radiation standards in the mines. Uranium mining in this country, which is concentrated on the western slope of the Rockies, is in the midst of a "stretch-out" period right now, a period in which the federal government has, in the words of Senator Pastore, "enough uranium coming out of our ears" but continues to buy the stuff to tide the mining industry over until the big market of the 1970's develops: electrical utilities using nuclear reactors as power plants. By 1980, the AEC and the Federal Radiation Council figures indicate, there should be demand for more than $700 million worth

184

of uranium a year—a major source of income for sparsely populated states.

Also in common with other committees, the joint committee tends to fall into the hands of the man most interested in the subject under review. In this case, it is Representative Chet Holifield, a California Democrat who has been on the committee since its founding and who alternates the chairmanship with Pastore. Another dedicated member is Representative Wayne Aspinall, a Democrat from the major uranium mining area of Colorado, who sides with Holifield. Representative Melvin Price, the malleable Democrat from Illinois who chairs the radiation subcommittee nominally charged with the hearings on miners, gradually fell into line as the hearings went on.

Angry at a newspaper editorial which had accused the joint committee of being unconcerned about the miners, Holifield said on that first day of the hearings: "Maybe we have not moved fast enough. But maybe we didn't know how to move fast. . . . I want the record to show the uncertainties of knowledge which have existed during the past 15 or 20 years that we have been mining uranium in this country."

Actually, the 1,373 pages of record tell a great deal more about bureaucratic buckpassing and wheelspinning in the name of research than they do about scientific uncertainty, but the joint committee staff took its cue from Holifield. The staff released a 58-page "summary analysis" of the hearings. Presumably published to save anybody interested the time needed to examine the full record, the summary is weighted heavily toward citations showing that the problem isn't so bad after all: "Dr. Robley Evans presented a mathematical formulation. . . . In the words of Dr. Robley Evans. . . . Dr. R. D. Evans believes. . . . Dr. Robley D. Evans, MIT, has conducted studies. . . ."

A one-man consensus, Dr. Robley D. Evans, professor of physics at Massachusetts Institute of Technology, noted in a biography filling more than half a page that he has served as a consultant to the Office of Scientific Research and Development, the Army, the Air Force, the Navy, the US Public Health Service, the State Department, the Secretary of Defense, the Research and Development Board of the National Military Establishment, the Federal Radiation Council and the Division of Biology and Medicine of the Atomic Energy Commission. He neglected to note that he is also a consultant to Kerr-McGee Corp., the largest producer of uranium in the United States.

When Senator Pastore pointed that out, Dr. Evans said that his professional judgment was unaffected by money. "Intellectual honesty is the only thing I know, sir," he said.

In a recent telephone interview, Dr. Evans said that none of the organizations he serves has been billed for his extensive work on the case of the uranium miners. "It's part of my academic life," he explained. But at the end of the 1967 hearings the Atomic Energy Commission decided to up its grant to Dr. Evans' project at MIT to $173,919 for the year. Dr. Evans' arrangements with Kerr-McGee are not on public record.

•

In his testimony before the joint committee, Dr. Evans concentrated his attack on an order issued in May 1967 by Secretary of Labor Willard Wirtz. Under the impression that the joint committee really did want prompt federal action, Wirtz had moved before the hearings opened to set stringent limits on uranium mines that sell their production to the federal government, still the major buyer. (Wirtz's opening statement to the joint committee was a remarkable one. "The record reflects continuing attention by a variety of state and federal agencies—including the Department of Labor—to both the standards and the inspection problems in connection with uranium mining," he said. "It is a record, nevertheless, of literally hundreds of efforts, studies, meetings, conferences and telephone calls— each of them leading only to another—most of them containing a sufficient reason for not doing anything then—but adding up over a period of years to totally unjustifiable lack of needed consummative action.") Along with other companies, Kerr-McGee submitted statements that it could not meet the Wirtz standard for radiation in the mines.

Dr. Evans attacked the standard as unscientific. He concentrated his fire on the lower levels of radiation, just above the limit set by Wirtz, where Public Health Service studies so far have failed to turn up enough corpses of miners to provide statistical proof of hazard. Evans argued that there appears to be a "practical threshold" of radiation damage, that there would be "only negligible risk" of lung cancer for a miner exposed to radiation between three and 10 times the limit Wirtz specified in his order. (Kerr-McGee officials said they could comply with a limit in this range.)

Oddly enough, Dr. Evans based his conclusion not on studies of uranium miners but of people who had high body burdens of radium, mostly from painting radium dials. The cancers involved were not lung cancers but bone and sinus cancers.

The staff's "summary analysis" of the hearings calls Dr. Evans' finding "one of the most important contributions to the hearings in terms of scientific basis for a standard. . . . Enthusiastic response and constructive criticism from experts throughout the United States and other parts of the world have been received subsequent to publication of the hearing record."

It's a pity all that documentation couldn't be printed; perhaps it would have provided balance. For the reaction that did beat the deadline could be more accurately characterized as enthusiastic criticism.

"I think Dr. Evans has produced either one of the most ingenious propositions or one of the most ingenious red herrings that we have either respectively seen or smelled for a long time," Herbert M. Parker said at one session. A specialist in the radiation-safety field known as health physics from the Pacific Northwest Laboratory of Battelle Memorial Institute, Parker later submitted a written critique of the dial painter/uranium miner analogy. "We submit that the alleged relationships are tenuous and superficial," he wrote. "Collectively, they do not provide an adequate basis for relating the lung exposure in any quantitative way to the existing experience with bone tumors."

Dr. Victor E. Archer, a US Public Health Service physician involved for more than a decade in the study that proved a relationship between mine exposure and lung cancer, allowed that "there are enough similarities between the cancers of paranasal sinuses of radium cases and the bronchiogenic cancers of uranium miners so that it might be possible to derive some meaningful relationships between the two." Then he disposed of Dr. Evans: "However, that has not yet been done."

The third printed comment on Dr. Evans' study came from W. S. Snyder of the health physics division of Oak Ridge National Laboratory. Snyder addressed himself to a defense of the "linear" concept of radiation protection, which in contrast to the threshold theory holds that ill effects extend to very low dose ranges—and, in effect, that radiation damage is cumulative and no amount, however small, can be considered absolutely safe. From this it follows that the risk of each exposure (such as having a medical X-ray) must be weighed against the benefits (such as diagnosis of a serious disease). Snyder pointed out that the International Commission on Radiological Protection, the National Council on Radiation Protection and Measurements and the Federal Radiation Council all use the linear theory rather than Dr. Evans' threshold. Snyder said:

> Those who prefer to base radiation protection on a threshold hypothesis, which is just as unproven and just as uncertain and unsupported by data as is the linear hypothesis, often charge that the linear hypothesis is too conservative. There is no evidence ... that it is conservative at all. However, one may wonder why it is considered so undesirable to use a conservative criterion where human life is in question. Surely if the linear hypothesis is conservative and is not in conflict with the data that are available, this is a point in its favor. When human life is in the balance, it would seem that conservatism in safeguarding these lives has much to commend it.

"Black Lung":
Mining as a Way of Death

by ROBERT COLES
and HARRY HUGE

Towns like Farmington, West Virginia or cities like Harlan and Hazard, Kentucky struggle with enough ironies to make even children a little sociological as they size up the world: "Some daddys here, they make good money, but a lot of them, they get killed in the mines; and if they don't, they have to stop working after awhile, because they can't breathe very good. Then they're as bad off as the rest of us in the hollows. That's what my uncle says." The boy's father was killed in a mine accident in 1963. The boy's uncle has "black lung" and coughs and wheezes and spits up black phlegm and feels short of breath a lot of the time and has chest pains:

> I've had it. I'm an old man at 31. I started in the mines when I was 16, and no one asked any questions. My daddy, he started when he was 11. I was lucky to have a job. Hereabouts if you have a job, you feel like you're lucky and you give the foreman every ounce of energy you've got. Some of our kinfolk, they never went to the mines, and they near starve to death and freeze to death, come every winter. But you know, as bad as it is for them, I'm beginning to think they're better off than me and my brother. They don't see the money we do—if we live and don't get sick—and they can't have the things we buy. But I'd rather have it real, real terrible up in the hollows than end up like my brother—he got killed, in a second, just like that. The roof fell in on him down in the mine.

And me, well you can hear me trying to catch enough air to stay alive. I never know when my lungs will just stop working altogether, and that will be the end. It's no way to die, let me tell you. It's no kind of reward for those years down in the mine. I wonder if a lot of people, they know that the coal they use to run the factories, it's all done at the expense of our lives. We get killed down there, or our lungs go and get killed. And then a lot of us, we don't get hardly anything to live on.

●

The fate of thousands like him doesn't seem to bother us. Yes, we become upset when a particularly severe disaster takes place, like the explosion in November 1968 that claimed 78 lives in Consolidated Coal Company's No. 9 mine near Farmington, West Virginia. In a matter of weeks, though, Farmington's tragedy was forgotten; it was just one more in an apparently endless succession, all recorded carefully by the Interior Department's Bureau of Mines. In this century about 100,000 men have been crushed to death, burnt to death, choked to death in the coal mines, and since 1930 approximately 1.5 million serious injuries have been recorded. Over 40,000 men have been permanently or partially disabled—and for every miner officially declared disabled, more than one has tried and failed to have his hurt, ailing body so recognized. In 1907, 3,242 miners were killed. In 1952, the year President Truman signed a Coal Mine Safety Act which he insisted was inadequate, 548 miners died in accidents. In 1962 another 220 men died underground; and lest anyone suppose that things are getting better, the accident rate per thousand miners has increased since 1952 from 1.37 to 1.50. All in all, then, mining has become more hazardous for the 150,000 or so men who work in about 5,500 deep mines and 2,200 surface ones. Since Harry Truman severely criticized Congress for failing to enact even half-satisfactory legislation to protect the safety of miners, over 200,000 miners have been injured, and today the coal companies continue to confront their workers with awful risks and dangers, more of them than any other major industry in America dares allow. Each month the journal put out by the United Mine Workers spells out the result: 29 killed in August, 1968; 24 in September; and on and on. Even before November more men were killed in 1968 (182) than in 1967 (173).

None of those statistics measures the incidence of "black lung," an insidious disease which gradually destroys the lung's ability to function normally. Every year hundreds of miners die of the various complications that come with the disease—called by today's doctors "pneumoconiosis," and by others long ago (going back to 1862) "miner's asthma." The Surgeon General of the United States has said that "conservatively speaking" over 100,000 miners suffer from "black lung disease," which means that most if not all miners have it, suffer every day from it, and in significant numbers

189

die from it; die because, literally, the lungs become increasingly scarred, lifeless, useless—and eventually the time comes for the last breath to be taken. Anyone who has seen a miner waging that battle, fighting for breath as a drowning man does for air, can never forget it.

Because 78 miners died all at once, the Department of the Interior held a conference on December 11, 1968, and those of us there heard speeches and outbursts and accusations and denials and resolutions and confessions and promises of change—but one can only wonder at something else, as a miner did who sat with us in that large, federal amphitheatre:

> That doctor [the Surgeon General] said over 100,000 of us have the damn disease and everyone knows that if you stay down there long enough, you get it, you get it worse and worse. And you heard him, Corcoran [President of the Consolidated Coal Company], say they had to do something to reduce the dust. But they didn't tell people what it *is*, what the disease we get *is*. How is someone here in Washington or in California or in New York supposed to know what they're talking about—that the mines are full of coal dust, and it gets into your lungs and eats them up, and then you die? Of course, when I first asked the company doctor if anything was wrong, because I was having trouble breathing, he didn't even want to listen to my chest. He just came over to me from across the room and he said: "Look, if you want to stay working, you'd better not complain, you'd better not mention this." I looked at him as though he was a crook or something. Then I guess he just got mad, because he raised his voice at me: "Every miner has trouble with his breathing one time or another. So why should you start complaining. Don't you talk to your buddies? Haven't they all got the same troubles?" And he was right there—we all do. And he was right with the last thing he told me, before I left: "Look, you're better off working than complaining. You'll die faster from not eating than from some coal dust in your lungs." You know what I said? I said, "You're right, doctor." You know why he's right? I could be on my deathbed—from not eating or from "black lung," either of them—and between the doctors like him, and all those lawyers they've got, and the bosses and the county courthouse people, I'd still not get a cent from the company or the welfare people or Washington or anyplace. And every miner knows that.

●

In 1966 in Perry County, Kentucky, one of us carefully examined a 37-year-old man who had been digging coal out of nearby land for 20 years. He was of medium height, blue-eyed and with thinning brown hair. Unlike some of his kin, who do what textbooks rather generously call "subsistence farming," he went to the mines: "You either get a job there, or you don't work at all. It's up to you to decide. All I want to do is work, keep working until my kids are grown up. I don't care what happens after that, but I can't stop working now. We'd starve to death."

The stethoscope picked up telltale sounds in his chest, evidence that the lungs were in trouble. He had twice been hurt in the back by cave-ins, which he dismissed as "nothing," though he never can really forget that miners die each year from just that—a landslide that happens because proper roofs have not been built to cover men who are probing and cutting away at earth and coal. His back gave him constant pain, for all his brave denial that anything was wrong, and even a cursory neurological examination, done in his home, demonstrated that he had sustained an injury to his back, and to the nerves which enter and leave his spinal column all along the back's length. He had something to say about that difficulty, too: "Look, every miner worth anything gets his back hurt, and his legs and his arms also; all he has to do is stay down there long enough. I'd as soon live in pain and have the money, than have my back in shape and an empty stomach."

We saw him recently and he was less defiant. He no longer has a job. His "lung problem" made him a "risk" in the mines. For six months he looked elsewhere for work, but found none. His savings diminished. Now he has nothing except some good furniture and a good but aging car, which he cannot afford to drive. His kinfolk bring over food and a little money. He can "always go up a hollow and live with them," which means, in the true spirit of what a "community" is, he will not starve to death so long as the entire Appalachian region doesn't—in some cases, *barely* doesn't. We asked him why he hadn't applied for Social Security payments which are supposed to go to those with "permanent and total disability." He told us he'd tried, tried everything—and anyway don't we know about things like that, in his words, "about the way they operate, the welfare people and their lawyers and the doctors they send you to."

If we didn't know "the way they operate," we eventually found out, thanks to miners like him—and to a whole series of welfare hearings and legal proceedings that the one of us who is a lawyer has attended and studied. Unlike Europe's major industrial nations, the United States has no overall program to support injured, seriously injured, workers. In county after county of Appalachia, and all over the country, men like this miner are excluded from welfare. Unless they have some high-priced form of private insurance, they get nothing. Some states provide money for a few months, even a year, to men suddenly unemployed; but eventually that stops, and in a region like Appalachia, where unemployment can be a way of life, nothing goes to men who want to work and can't find jobs—and to sick men, badly sick men, many of whom desperately try to find something to do, even though by rights they deserve a pension and good medical care, neither of which they get.

Congress has made sure that disabled workers don't get Medicare. Congress has made sure the language in the public assistance schemes that are federally supported (for the aged, the blind and children) is extremely restrictive and vague, which means local welfare officials do all the interpreting. In each case a doctor must decide whether a man is "permanently and totally disabled." In most cases the doctor is a "state doctor," appointed and paid by the welfare department. In Kentucky, as in many other states, even if a private doctor makes a particular claim for his patient, a Medical Review Team goes over the forms and has the final say in the matter—and the doctor on that team does *not* examine the patient, but simply evaluates the citizen's claim. Again and again miners —and of course others, too—go to those county courthouses and get the following kind of treatment:

I went there and told them I couldn't work no more in the mines, that it was my lungs, they were giving away and I couldn't catch my breath, and the company doctor, he said it was time for me to go. I had some money saved up, and I thought that maybe in a while my lungs would get better and I could go back to work; but they didn't—instead they've become worse. I tried to get a job in a store, and a gas station, too—that my brother-in-law runs. But he says he can't keep going except by himself and with his son at his side, and he doesn't make the money to hire anyone else— and a lot of men, miners like me, fallen sick, come and ask him if he knows of any work around, and he has to say that the answer is no, sorry, he doesn't.

The welfare lady, she let me apply and it's the same old story, over and over again. They sent me to their doctor and he looked me over and listened to my chest and asked me to walk and bend and like that, and said, "o.k., you can go." As I was leaving I asked him if he thought I could qualify, and he said that wasn't my business, to ask him that, but he'd say this much: "You can walk in here and sit and stand and bend and get up, and you can work—not in the mines, but in a store, you could do that, or an office." Then I tried to tell him that a man like me, he can't overnight become an office man, and besides there aren't those kinds of jobs around here. But he cut me off, in the middle of a sentence. "I know, I know. You all say that." That's what he said.

Well it wasn't long before the news came back that I wasn't "permanently disabled," and so I couldn't get a cent; and that means I can just go and starve to death so far as everyone's concerned—

the coal company and the county courthouse people and the Washington people. Of course, if I can get to be 60 or so—that's over 20 years off—I can get Social Security and after that Medicare. But with this "black lung" inside of me and no money, I'll be lucky to hit 40. Yes sir.

Again and again we have heard miners like him and others in Appalachia, too, say that only a "man about to die" will be found eligible for any kind of financial help, all of which has been substantiated by a statistical analysis of the federally supported welfare programs: "The death rates for disabled workers under 50 finally declared eligible for support approximate those of the United States population 70 to 74 years of age. . . . Disabled beneficiaries 50 to 64 years of age had death rates higher than persons 75 to 84 years of age."

•

Just in case its civilized and humanitarian purposes might be misunderstood, Congress took up the issue of eligibility for Social Security disability payments in 1967 and spelled out exactly what the world's first nation intends for its citizens. The courts—so often these days susceptible to fits of soft-headed compassion—had decided that the Social Security Act requires a claimant to be unable to do the kind of work that is available in his hometown. No, said a coalition of Republicans and Southern Democrats: the claimant must be unable to do any work at all, and if a disabled miner is found medically suitable for a job, say, on the Stock Exchange on Wall Street—well, then, too bad for him and his devious effort to milk Washington of money. In addition, the courts had ruled pain to be evidence of physical or mental impairment; no, said the Congress—because, after all, people in bad pain can still work. What is more, the courts had foolishly defined disability as a man's "practical inability to be hired by an employer," a definition Congress flatly refused to sanction. Applicants—perhaps supplicants is the better word—are either flat on their backs, virtually at death's door, or else they can expect nothing; and lest anyone slip through that tightly woven net, the Congress thoughtfully made its new restrictions apply retroactively to all cases in any state of appeal before the Social Security Administration or the courts.

In the counties of eastern Kentucky and all over the country, welfare departments do nothing to encourage thorough medical examinations. The forms are brief, the doctors are not given standards or even instructions to use as guides. To many miners we have interviewed, the doctors and their examinations are in fact something worse: "It isn't that they're not thorough, the checkups the doctors give. It's that they're used to disqualify us. The one who saw me, he said 'Sure you're sick, but you're not dying.' And if

I was dying, he'd probably have said there's no point for the government to be giving money to a dying man."

That is a harsh judgment for a miner to make about a doctor. In nearby West Virginia we found a little more goodwill and charity for doctors, some of whom are now becoming "agitators"—which means they are demanding that adequate compensation be payed to men who suffer from "black lung." (In recent years exactly four men with the disease have been compensated.) We visited Farmington, talked with miners who worked in Consolidated No. 9. We went through the miles of property that adjoin the particular section of the enormous mine that exploded this last November. We talked with company officials, and a number of doctors, both in northern West Virginia, where Consolidated No. 9 is, and in the southern part of the state, where a first-rate team of specialists is studying the nature of "black lung disease" at the Appalachian Regional Hospital in Beckley. One of us went to Charleston and watched a meeting of the Silicosis Medical Board, assembled to consider the case of a 50-year-old miner who had worked in the mines for 31 years, was now obviously sick with "black lung" and had been denied assistance by the Social Security Administration. The man's doctor was prodded by a coal company's lawyer. Couldn't all sorts of things cause the miner's distress? Were specific tests done to determine the cause of his illness? Might not cigarette smoking cause the same kind of damage to the lungs? No, insisted the doctor: "A man could smoke four packs a day and not begin to show this particular kind of abnormality." For all his effort—trips here and there, examinations and more examinations—the miner had received a flat award of $1,000; he was appealing for more. In one miner's words:

> You go there, they treat you like you're some kind of animal in a zoo; they tell you it could be cigarettes and polluted air and well—maybe the dust that falls down from the moon or something. Then, if you keep after them long enough, they give you maybe a thousand dollars, or maybe if you're real lucky, double or triple that, and then you've had it, brother, for keeps. That's how it is with us. Then you ask if we mind it, doing the work down there.

After the disaster in Consolidated No. 9, we read that the miners frequently endanger themselves by their recklessness, their bravado, their seeming reluctance to heed various rules or regulations. We had been talking to miners in various parts of Appalachia well before that terrible accident in West Virginia and had, on the contrary, been struck with something quite else: the resignation, the stubborn fatalism, the anything-but-casual manner of the men we watched going down those shafts. So we asked survivors of Consolidated No. 9 about their "attitudes":

194

Yes, we do a lot of laughing. What else can you do when you go into a gassy mine, a dusty old one like that one? If you start talking about the danger, they'll fine you as a troublemaker. All I want is for my kids to grow up. I don't care if I die then, in an accident or an explosion or from "black lung." One way or the other I'll die from one of those causes anyway. It's just that if I can last long enough, my kids will get some good schooling—and *they'll* never go into the mines.

Down there, the fans didn't work right. The whole ventilation system wasn't good enough, and they knew it. You bet they did. Now they all say we could have done more and we should have. Well, they knew that a long time ago. You hear it said that mining is dangerous, and there's not much you can do. Well, if they worried about us the way they do about men who go under water to explore, or in submarines, or up to the moon, they could do a lot. If they did what they're *supposed* to do—keep pushing those gases out with the fans and keep the coal dust down, we'd be safer. The fact is that in some mines—like with Bethlehem—where the company uses the coal itself, and doesn't sell it, the mines are much safer. Everyone knows that. There's something wrong with the whole business, if you ask me. You read that it's Gulf Oil and Mobil Oil and Humble Oil that are buying up these mines. Our Consolidated No. 9, did you know who owns it? The foreman, he told us that the Consolidated people, the Consolidated Coal Company, they're one of the biggest owners of the Chrysler Car Company, and that actually it's the Continental Oil Company—I don't know where they come from—that owns our Consolidated Coal mines. Even the foreman—and he's a company man—he said if they can give huge tax favors to the oil companies they can do it for us, to the coal people, and they could make it a million times safer—because they know how to. They just don't want to dig into their profits.

•

Ironically, poorer coal-producing countries like England and Germany and Czechoslovakia spend much more money studying ways to make mines safe—and *do* something about what is discovered. In those nations miners are regularly given X-rays, and immediately withdrawn from such work when evidence of lung disease begins to appear. They are given jobs elsewhere; or if injured or disabled, given decent and honorable pensions as a right. In those countries the mines are ventilated far more efficiently than are ours, and in some instances miners are given safe and comfortable masks, and even whole uniforms that preclude any inhalation whatsoever of coal dust. One very fine physician, Dr. Donald Rasmussen, whose recent

195

paper in *The American Review of Respiratory Disease*, "Pulmonary Impairment in Southern West Virginia Coal Miners," is already a classic in the medical literature that has to do with "black lung," told us he finds himself ashamed when he talks with British or German doctors:

> They are doing so much more there, preventatively—it's embarrassing to compare notes with them. If we really wanted to do something about "black lung" we could. Each mine goes on as before; the men fall sick, but stay at work because they have no choice—and we see them suffering here, every day. True, a bad disaster brings us some attention; but not for long, and pretty soon things are back to normal around here, which means thousands of miners are slowly getting sicker and sicker and eventually they die, of course—many of them still young men.

In 1917, Upton Sinclair's novel *King Coal* aroused the conscience of many. Today miners get much better pay, but what one of the characters in *King Coal* says still holds true:

> ... The frequency of accidents in this district was not due to any special difficulty in operating their mines, the explosiveness of the gasses or the dryness of the atmosphere. It was merely the carelessness of those in charge, their disregard of the laws for the protection of men. There ought to be a law with "teeth" in it. . . .

President Johnson also thought "there ought to be a law," but to no avail as far as the Congress was concerned. What will President Nixon do? Will these thousands of coal miners qualify in his Administration as "forgotten Americans"?

X-ray Exposures

by RALPH NADER

In the pre-World War II generation, some physicians treated acne with X-rays, irradiated children's tonsils instead of removing them and generally employed X-ray machines for a variety of serious and trivial ailments without knowing the long-term effects of such exposure. A few months ago, a research group at the University of California Medical Center analyzed the records of patients over the past 45 years and found the incidence of thyroid cancer to have increased at "an unprecedented rate." During the twenties, 2 percent of patients suspected of having nodular goiter were found to have cancer. That proportion rose to 15 percent in such patients for the decade 1955–1965. Similar findings have come from the New York State Department of Health. The evidence shows a strong connection with profligate use of X-radiation a generation ago.

Knowledge of the physical and genetic effects of X-radiation has advanced significantly in the postwar era. So has the use of X-rays, with over 150 million pictures taken last year. So has the technology to get better pictures with lower dosage. Nevertheless, while the benefits of X-rays are immediate and well publicized, the costs are long-range and largely covered up—to the extent they are known. (September 1967) Institutionalized silence over X-radiation exposure is about to give way to the first, comprehensive scrutiny in a public forum. The Senate Commerce Committee is beginning a series of hearings, chaired by Senator E. L. Bartlett (D, Alaska), on ionizing radiation hazards of electronic products. Attention will be directed to the condition of over 200,000 medical and dental X-ray machines. Various professional groups have been reluctant to recognize candidly the real dangers and to go about reducing them.

Reprinted by permission of the New Republic, © *1967, Harrison-Blaine of New Jersey, Inc.*

A key expert witness before the committee is Dr. Karl Morgan, director of health physics at the Oak Ridge National Laboratory. Dr. Morgan's data and findings pose a serious challenge to the posture and policies of the dental, medical and radiological professions and their influence on the US Public Health Service. His studies conclude that:

Medical and dental exposure accounts for about 90 percent of all exposure of the American population from man-made sources of ionizing radiation.

The average dose to the gonads in the US today from medical radiation is as much as 100 times the average dose from radioactive fallout.

Diagnostic radiation (medical and dental X-rays) doses in the US are much higher than those obtaining in other modern, industrialized societies. The average dose in the US is 10 times higher than in the United Kingdom, four times higher than Japan and 15 times higher than Norway.

Dr. Morgan notes that "no matter how great the medical benefits derived from X-rays, this is no justification of the fact that because of the use of poor techniques with obsolete and improperly operated equipment, many X-ray exposures are 10 or more times that needed for the best diagnostic results." He emphasizes that readily available technology, skills and practices could "prevent hundreds and perhaps thousands of children being born each year with mental and physical handicaps of varying degrees, the vast majority of which go undetected." He is mindful of the lifesaving contributions of X-ray diagnosis, but estimates a possible range of 3,600 to 11,000 deaths per year from such radiation, and "probably thousands of injuries for every death."

The style of violence unleashed by X-radiation is shown in this summary by Dr. Morgan:

> The geneticist H. J. Muller has pointed out that there may be as many as 10,000 nonvisible mutations for each of the visible variety. It is my firm belief that these more subtle forms of damage, many of which are never recognized, may in the long run do greater damage and place a greater burden on our society than those forms of radiation damage which result in the death of the individual. Also, I believe that this same thing applies to somatic [bodily] forms of damage as well as to genetic injury.

Dr. Morgan is considered an interloper by many in the dental, medical and radiological professions. They see his studies as a threat to exercise of professional judgment in the use of X-rays as diagnostic and therapeutic tools. No profession likes to be told that its machinery needs modernizing or that its training is inadequate. But though 40 states have legislation and regulations governing X-ray machines, the reality of state and local regulation is dismal.

New York City probably has the strictest inspection program in the country. In 1961, over 3,600 X-ray units in that city were inspected and 92 percent were found defective. In 1965, the states reported that of a total number of 113,806 medical X-ray units in use, only 25,174 were inspected, and nearly half were found defective; but corrections were reported in only 7,713. California has not finished its first round of inspections yet. Connecticut has only two inspectors for the entire state, Indiana one.

A Connecticut dentist says that in 20 years he has never had an inspector come to his office. His use of lead aprons is self-imposed. The American Dental Association does not recommend such protective covering, though the US Public Health Service does. Most dentists do not bother with any protective covering to shield against spraying. In many offices, a patient sitting in a dental chair can be exposed to radiation from eyeball to abdomen, including his gonads.

In 1965 there were only 143 full-time men working in X-ray and control programs in the entire nation. Professor Hanson Blatz, director of the New York City Office of Radiation Control, cites X-ray machines with inadequate shielding that spray daily doses on unknowing workers in other rooms of the building. Many mobile X-ray units in hospitals that cater to the poor use hand-me-down equipment.

Professor Blatz has pointed out that relatively simple changes can reduce much of the excess dosage. Aiming and timing devices and new, high-speed films are inexpensive measures which reduce sharply the dosage from X-rays and also improve the amount of radiological information obtained.

Training of operators of X-ray machines is inadequate. This lack of training includes members of the dental and medical professions. The deficiency affects both patient and operator. A Johns Hopkins University study concludes that X-ray technicians have a statistically significant greater-than-average chance of producing mongoloid children.

Most students receive very little training in radiology at US medical schools. At Yale Medical School, an institution with high standards, most students take one short course in radiology which deals primarily with the reading of X-rays. With the exception of New York in 1966, no state requires the licensing of X-ray machine operators after a proficiency examination. Dr. Granville Larimore of the New York State Department of Health described the situation in his state:

We knew that a large number of these other people taking X-rays were not really X-ray technicians. They were nurses, secretaries, receptionists, medical assistants, and others working in the offices of private physicians.... For the most part their "training" was limited to a few hours of instruction by a representative of the equipment manufacturers.

199

Dr. Larimore says unskilled operators "often can expose the gonads of patients to as much as 100 to 200 times the amount of radiation necessary from a purely medical point of view." Public Health Service surveys indicate that a large number of dentists and their assistants are overexposing and underdeveloping the films.

The Dick

by JAMES RIGEWAY

Ralph Nader is a lanky Washington attorney who went after the automobile makers for not designing safer cars. He wrote a book, *Unsafe at Any Speed*, which told what was wrong with cars, and he was a major witness before Senator Abraham Ribicoff's subcommittee on traffic safety.

The auto makers, who first ignored Nader, finally turned on their most vigorous critic. This is precisely the sort of knockdown public fight Nader was hoping for, but instead of open battle, he found himself suddenly distracted from the task at hand and locked in a subterranean struggle against an uncertain enemy.

Nader first felt someone was watching him in January 1966 in the Kirkwood Hotel at Des Moines, where he had gone to testify before the state attorney general's inquiry into traffic safety. He remembers seeing a man two or perhaps three times in the hotel, once on his floor; for reasons Nader can't explain, the man made him feel uneasy.

Nader was to testify before the Ribicoff subcommittee February 10. In the days before he was to appear, he received several odd phone calls that increased in their frequency until on the evening of February 9, when he was trying to put the finishing touches on a prepared statement, Nader got half-a-dozen phone calls. A voice would say, "Mr. Nader, this is Pan American," and then hang up. Or, "Mr. Nader, please pick up the parcel at Railway Express." And finally, "Why don't you go back to Connecticut, buddy-boy." (Nader's home is at Winsted, Conn.) Nader's appearance before the committee was marked by a sharp clash between Senator Carl Curtis of Nebraska and Senator Robert Kennedy of New York. Curtis kept pretending he could not understand what Nader was saying and finally Kennedy, in short temper, said this was a deliberate attempt to keep Nader from completing his statement, and to let him alone. The next day, a Friday, Nader went to the New Senate Office Building for a television interview. As he was coming out, one of the building guards told him two men had been tailing him. The men asked the guard which room Nader had gone into, and then volunteered they had been following Nader around the country. The guard reported the incident to his superior, who asked the men to leave the building.

•

During the next week, Nader's landlady got a call from a man checking to see whether her tenant paid his bills on time. Nader's stockbroker received a visit from a man who said he worked for "Arundel Investigations." His client wanted to hire Nader. He wanted to know about Nader's credit and his habits. In Cambridge, Massachusetts, Harold Berman, a professor at Harvard Law School who taught Nader, got a call from a man who as Berman remembers it, said he worked for a research organization. He said Nader had given Berman as a reference for a job. In Boston, Thomas Lambert Jr., the editor-in-chief of the American Trial Lawyers Association *Journal*, a publication that had carried a number of articles by Nader, was visited by a man who looked very Ivy League. He said his name was "Mr. Dwyer" and he worked for a "Management Consultants" or "Management Associates" at 53 State Street in Boston. He also represented a client who wanted to hire Nader. He asked about his drinking habits and his technical capabilities. Lambert was pleased to recommend Nader; he sent Nader off a note telling of the visitor and wishing the young attorney well in whatever the new job might be. But Nader had not applied for any job.

Sunday evening, February 20, 1966, Nader left his room in northwest Washington and went up the street a couple of blocks to a drugstore. He was standing at the magazine rack when a young, attractive brunette he had never seen before approached and said, "Pardon me. I know this sounds a little forward. I hope you don't mind, but can I talk to you?" She said a few of her friends often got together to discuss various problems of foreign affairs. They wanted to get all viewpoints. Would he join them? Nader was dumbfounded. Trying to get rid of her politely, he said he was from out of town. But the girl persisted. Oh, she said, that's all right; there was a meeting that night. Nader said he wasn't interested and turned his back. The girl left.

Monday morning Nader took a plane to Philadelphia, where he was to appear on ABC's Mike Douglas Show.

That same day at a little after noon, Frederick Hughes Condon, a lawyer for a life insurance company in Concord, New Hampshire, to whom Nader had dedicated his book, got a call from a "Mr. Warren," who said he wanted to come by the office and ask Condon a few questions about his friend, Ralph Nader. He said he had a client who wanted to hire Nader to do some research and writing, and in this connection he was looking into Nader's background, partly to make sure he led a normal sex life and was not involved in leftwing politics, and also because he needed to know whether Nader was capable of doing work in fields other than car design. Condon asked Warren who the client was, but Warren said he could not disclose that. So Condon asked him who he was. Warren said he worked with an attorney, a Mr. Gillen of New York City, who specialized in investigations. His suspicions already aroused, Condon told Warren to come by the office later that afternoon.

Nader had finished the Mike Douglas Show in Philadelphia; he was late for a 3:30 United Air Lines flight back to Washington. The other passengers had boarded when he hurried up to the gate at 3:25. Suddenly, he was aware that two men who had been sitting on a bench nearby had risen and boarded the plane after him. They took seats near his. They seemed to be especially interested in Nader.

It was mid-afternoon that day when the telephone rang in the New York City apartment of Dexter Masters. Masters had written a complimentary review of the Nader book that had appeared a few weeks before as the lead article in *Book Week*. Masters remembers picking up the phone,

> A smooth-talking fellow said he understood I had reviewed the book for *Book Week* and could I tell him anything about Nader. I said I didn't know him and what did he want to know for. The man said he represented the "Gillian" Agency or something that sounded like that. He said one of the operators was a former FBI agent. They were investigating for a client who was interested in hiring Nader to write some articles. Did I think it really was a good book? I said I thought it was an excellent book and so had written.

The man thanked Masters and hung up. Masters, thinking this one of the silliest pieces of detective work he ever had encountered, called Nader's publisher, Richard Grossman, to tell him the story.

At about 4:15 the United flight with Nader aboard was in its landing approach at Washington's National Airport; the two men seated near him looked like small-time salesmen. The plane came to a stop, and Nader went down the ramp, then ducked in and out of a number of doors at the airport to shake the men. He got into a cab, and as it headed for downtown Washington, Nader looked through the back window for the men. They had disappeared.

Condon, meanwhile, was closeted with a vice president of his company for much of the afternoon and it wasn't until 4:30 that he got free to see Mr. Warren, who now was calling himself Mr. Gillen. As the secretary ushered Mr. Gillen into Condon's office, the lawyer remembered he wore heavy black-rimmed glasses, was of medium height with a barrel chest and gray hair combed straight back. Gillen had a nervous manner when he asked leading questions and he insisted on holding an attaché case in his lap. By now Condon was sure the man was a detective, and he was ready to believe the attaché case held recording equipment. But Condon was playing dumb.

Gillen came right to the point. He asked repeatedly whether Nader had a driver's license and from what state. Had he owned a car at Harvard? Had Condon ever seen him drive a car? What make car did he own? Had he ever had any automobile accidents? Condon could not remember Nader driving and didn't know whether he had a license or not. (Actually Nader has a Connecticut driver's license.)

Gillen said he heard Nader traveled a lot. Did Condon know where he had gone? Why wasn't Nader married? Did he get financial help with his book? Did he have any left-wing political affiliations? Gillen said Nader was of Syrian ancestry. Was he anti-Semitic? Condon assured Gillen that Nader's personal life was normal; that he didn't to Condon's knowledge belong to any political groups on one side or the other, that he had traveled to Mexico, and perhaps he had gone to see relatives in Lebanon, where his parents came from (not Syria), and that he was decidedly not anti-Semitic. Then Gillen sought to discover when Nader had met Senator Ribicoff and what his connections with the Senator were. Condon said he didn't know, and wasn't at all sure that Nader even knew Ribicoff.

•

Finally, Gillen asked Condon a few questions about himself. Condon is a paraplegic. Some years ago he fell asleep at the wheel of his car, which went off the road and crashed. The doors opened as it rolled over, and Condon, half in and half out, had his spine twisted. Gillen wanted to know if Nader had dedicated his book to Condon because of this accident. Did Condon think his injury was caused by unsafe design? What was the make of the car he was driving? Where had the accident taken place?

Having in this manner discovered the depths of Nader's intellectual abilities from his friend, Gillen said he really didn't know what job his client had in mind for Nader but he was sure it would be a good one, and picking up his attaché case, he bid Condon goodbye. Condon immediately wrote up the conversation, sent Nader a wire, and later that evening phoned him in Washington.

Now Nader was sure he was being investigated and probably followed. The girl in the drugstore had been a lure; he reasoned that the auto companies would like to get anything they could to discredit him as a future witness before congressional committees considering auto safety legislation. His suspicions were further aroused two days later, on Wednesday, February 23, when on the way to meet a friend in the afternoon, he stopped off to buy a package of cookies at a Safeway store near his boarding house. There were perhaps 30 people in the store, the usual raft of children, some women and a few single men. As he was looking about for the cookies, a girl, blonde and wearing slacks, came up to him and said, "Excuse me, but I need some help. I've got to move something heavy into my apartment. There's no one to help me. I wonder if I can get you to give me a hand. It won't take much time. Will you help?" Nader said he was sorry but he had a meeting and was late already. The girl persisted. "Please," she said. "It won't take long." Nader refused. Then, although there were a number of other people in the store who might have helped her, the girl turned around and left the store.

Management Consultants, a private detective firm in Boston, didn't care to discuss this matter. John Dwyer of Management Consultants at 53 State Street said, "I am not at liberty to discuss any of these matters." But a reporter was successful when he reached Vincent Gillen, of Vincent Gillen Associates, the detective firm in Garden City, New York. Mr. Gillen seemed flustered. "We've made inquiries about Nader," he said. "I spoke with Condon myself; another of our men contacted Masters." Gillen said he could not disclose the name of his client, but he said, "A lot of people were mentioned adversely in that book." Recovering his composure, he told the reporter:

> I am a private investigator. We have hundreds of clients; we write thousands of reports, primarily on employment matters. I was asked by a client to make an investigation of Ralph Nader. I understand that he is an intelligent, articulate fellow. And my client told me he was considering him for an important job, to do research on something, I don't know what. I knew Nader was a writer, and I went out and bought *Unsafe at Any Speed.*

Gillen read the book and "felt like staying in bed. I was afraid to drive a car," he said. "I thought at the time, he'd better know what he's talking about or somebody might yell."

"Is somebody yelling?" the reporter asked. There was a pause before Gillen said once more that Nader was being considered for a job. The investigation was not yet complete, the detective said, and then added, "All I can say is, it is good for Nader."

GM Hired the Dick

A NEW REPUBLIC EDITORIAL

General Motors has admitted it had been investigating Ralph Nader, the auto-safety author. But the company denied it was trying to harass or intimidate Nader. Ford and Chrysler disclaim any knowledge of the snooping.

GM said the investigation was "routine" and undertaken because of Nader's "extreme criticism" of the Corvair, the company's compact. Nader has written technical papers lambasting the car's design; a chapter in his book, *Unsafe at Any Speed*, is devoted to the subject. More than 100 different damage suits have been brought against GM. They allege that engineering defects in the Corvair brought on accidents. (Five earlier cases have been disposed of in the courts: in two instances, juries found in favor of the company; in one California case, the company settled a few days after the trial began; in Chicago, GM's failure to produce technical data on the car's design resulted in a default judgment against it; and in New Orleans a trial judge found against the company.) GM said it was investigating Nader to determine whether he was acting on behalf of the litigants or their attorneys in any of these cases.

In reply, Nader said, "There is absolutely nothing wrong with representing clients in cases against Corvair. But I am not representing any clients in Corvair cases and never have done so."

GM made its admission the day after Senators Nelson and Ribicoff asked the Justice Department to find out who was tailing the author. Nader had been a witness before Ribicoff's Government Operations subcommittee, which had been looking into the government's role in traffic safety. It is a federal crime to impede, harass or intimidate a congressional witness. Maximum penalties are $5,000 fine and five years in prison. Senator

Reprinted by permission of the New Republic, © *1966, Harrison-Blaine of New Jersey, Inc.*

Ribicoff asked the president of GM, representatives of the detective agencies and Mr. Nader all to appear before his subcommittee.

Nader had suspected GM had hired detectives to investigate him. The tip-off came at a state legislative hearing at Lansing, Michigan, the first time GM officials spoke out against the Nader book. Frank Winchell, chief of research at Chevrolet, said Nader neither owns a car nor has a driver's license. Private detectives had repeatedly asked Nader's friends whether they had seen him drive, and what kind of an automobile he owned. Any cursory check of licenses in Connecticut would have shown he had one.

There is nothing whatever "routine" about GM's Gangbusters stuff. The dicks didn't ask any questions about the Corvair cases. They sought to discover the details of Nader's sex life, whether he was left-wing, or anti-Semitic, where he traveled. It was calculated intimidation and they were caught red-handed. The Justice Department ought also to look into what other "routine" investigations GM may have under way. And Senator Edward Long's committee on snooping might profitably spend time on this interesting aspect of automobile manufacturing.

GM Comes Clean

by JAMES RIDGEWAY

The enormous, ornate Senate caucus room was tightly packed with spectators as executives of General Motors told Senator Abraham Ribicoff's committee how they plotted to spy on Ralph Nader.

Mr. Aloysius Power, the general counsel, ran the show for GM. He said he got the idea Nader might be "the mystery man" behind 106 lawsuits involving $40 million in claims against GM by reading magazines and papers that carried excerpts from Nader's book, *Unsafe at Any Speed*. A chapter in the book is devoted to the Corvair. Power ordered a background investigation in Nader's home town of Winsted, Connecticut, in November 1965, but it didn't turn up much. In early January Miss Eileen Murphy, who keeps the law library at GM, was dispatched to Washington where she met Richard Danner, a former FBI agent and now an attorney with Alvord & Alvord. Miss Murphy knew Danner from her days in the library of the Justice Department. Miss Murphy said GM needed a background investigation done on Nader, and Danner agreed to get the detectives. He then called up Vincent Gillen, another former FBI agent working as a private investigator in New York. Gillen took the job, and subcontracted parts of it to Management Consultants, Boston, and Arundel Investigative Agency, Saverna Park, Maryland. Both agencies are run by ex-FBI men. In making their inquiries, the detectives agreed to use the pretext of a pre-employment investigation. Gillen put out the following instructions to his net on Nader:

> The above mentioned is a free-lance writer and attorney. Recently he published a book, *Unsafe at Any Speed*, highly critical of the automotive industry's interest in safety. Since then our client's

Reprinted by permission of the New Republic, © *1966, Harrison-Blaine of New Jersey, Inc.*

client made some cursory inquiries into Nader to ascertain his expertise, his interests, his background, etc. They have found out relatively little about him. . . . Our job is to check his life and current activities, to determine "what makes him tick," such as his real interest in safety, his supporters, if any, his politics, his marital status, his friends, his women, boys, etc., drinking, dope, jobs—in fact, all facets of his life. This may entail surveillance which will be undertaken only upon OK of Vince Gillen.

On January 13, 1966, the Ribicoff committee announced Nader would be a witness. None of Gillen's inquiries was turning up much information, and on January 26, in a meeting, Danner and Gillen decided to put Nader under surveillance. He was picked up and tailed beginning February 4. Detectives followed him about the city, into banks, restaurants where they watched whom he dined with, what he ate and drank. They got the license plate numbers of taxicabs he took. The surveillance was discontinued at 4:30 p.m. February 9, because Nader had not appeared since 3:30 when he entered the offices of the *New Republic*. The detectives called Danner and he told them to tail Nader on a spot basis. Nader testified before the Ribicoff committee the next day, February 10. On February 11, Gillen's detectives were discovered in the New Senate Office Building where they had gone to pick up Nader, and were tossed out by the guards. (It is a federal crime to harass, impede or intimidate a congressional witness. The maximum penalty is five years in prison.)

Gillen denied his men made harassing phone calls to Nader, that they followed him in Philadelphia or in Des Moines, and he said women were not used as lures to trap him. Gillen said he did use a fictitious name to get the interview with Frederick Hughes Condon, a lawyer in Concord, New Hampshire, to whom Nader dedicated his book. When he got to Condon's office, Gillen correctly identified himself. Gillen told the committee about parts of that interview:

I asked if at Harvard where they had been law school classmates, they had "double-dated." Condon said no, and explained that he, Condon, was married and living with his wife off campus. He believed that Nader lived in a rooming house. I asked if he had ever met any of Nader's girl friends or had seen him with a girl. Condon said, "Oh, if you are concerned about that don't worry about Ralph. He's all right," or words to that effect. We then had a casual discussion regarding the difficulty such an intelligent fellow with a wide range of interests has to find a suitable girl to marry. It certainly was not my intent in that casual talk to pry further into that aspect. . . .

Please keep in mind the pretext. Any investigator conducting a pre-employment background investigation of a mature, healthy, intelligent unmarried man who apparently has sufficient income to support a wife, must ask questions of this nature. . . .

Gillen's men asked whether Nader was anti-Semitic:

Virtually everyone we talked with in Winsted cautioned us not to attribute to Ralph the attitude and obvious feelings of some members of his family. In fairness to Ralph, we had to ask that question of all those with whom he associated during his adult life. I am happy to state that none of the people we interviewed believes Ralph Nader is anti-Semitic. . . .

Gillen's reports were filed on an almost weekly basis beginning February 7 and ending March 4 to Danner, who relayed them, unedited, to Miss Murphy in the general counsel's office at GM. There they were scrutinized by men working on the Corvair cases, as well as by both Louis Bridenstine, the assistant general counsel, and Power himself. The reports contained in a thick, blue volume turned over to the committee cost GM $6,700, and according to the senators who read them contained little if anything about Nader's relations to clients or attorneys in the Corvair cases. Most of the investigatory reports concerned his personal life.

Mr. James Roche, president of GM, said he first learned of the investigation March 8, 1966, when, ironically, he was preparing to issue a denial. He apologized to the committee and to Mr. Nader, and said it would not happen again. Roche was accompanied to the witness table by Theodore Sorensen, who had been hastily retained as counsel. This apparently was an effort to blunt the expected attack from Robert Kennedy, who had been eager for the hearing; to enhance the statesmanlike pose Roche was assuming; and to snatch a bit of good publicity. Kennedy was sharp nonetheless; if anything, Sorensen looked foolish when first Roche and then Power misquoted a Supreme Court decision to make it seem the reverse of what it actually said. Sorensen sat like a Buddha most of the time, and joined only with Roche in laughing at Gillen, who was meant to serve as fall guy for the company. But if that were the intent, it was lost on Gillen. He was clearly fascinated by the whole show, every so often pulling out of his pocket a miniature camera and clicking off pictures of the senators in action. As for his role in the case he said, "I attempted to do a job for my client and frankly I think we did a darn good one."

210

The Nader Affair

by JAMES RIGDEWAY
and DAVID SANFORD

In 1966 Vincent Gillen, a Long Island detective, was caught off guard by an editor of the *New Republic* and admitted he had investigated Ralph Nader, the auto safety critic. This touched off a series of startling disclosures that led to a Senate hearing and a public apology to Nader from the president of General Motors. But it now appears that this was only the opening to a fantastic tale of industrial spying. Gillen has now heightened the drama with sworn statements that the General Motors officials who hired him hid the truth from the Senate committee. These allegations have in turn led to embarrassing political questions.

At the special hearing before Senator Abraham Ribicoff's (D, Conn.) subcommittee in March 1966, James Roche, president of GM, said the Nader investigation was undertaken without his knowledge or approval by Aloysius Power, the general counsel, who believed it necessary to hire detectives to find out whether Nader, who had criticized GM's Corvair, was connected with attorneys representing disgruntled Corvair owners. Power didn't find substantive ties, and Roche apologized to Nader. At the time, he said the Nader investigation was unusual, and to his knowledge was the "first one of this kind that has ever been undertaken." Roche said, "There has been no attempt by, and it has at no time been the intention of General Motors Corp. or any of its officers or employees to annoy, harass, embarrass, threaten, injure or intimidate Mr. Nader. . . ."

The senators commended Roche for his forthright stand before the committee and reserved their scorn for Gillen. He was pictured as a bumbling, unscrupulous detective who had taken it upon himself in tracking Nader to direct his men to find out "what makes him tick . . . his politics, his

Reprinted by permission of the New Republic, © *1967, Harrison-Blaine of New Jersey, Inc.*

marital status, his friends, his women, boys, etc., drinking, dope, jobs. . . ." Gillen was outraged. "I attempted to do a job for my client," he said, "and frankly I think we did a darn good one."

Since the hearings, Nader has filed two suits: in one against both GM and Gillen he accuses them of invasion of privacy and asks $26 million. In another against Gillen, Nader accuses him of defamation. Gillen cross-claimed against GM and Nader in the first suit, and has counter-sued Nader in the second. Spokesmen for GM have said the company is not legally responsible to Nader.

In documents filed in Nader's invasion of privacy suit, Gillen swears executives of GM made false statements about the Nader case to the Ribicoff subcommittee. (Roche maintains what he said at the hearings was true.) Gillen swears that company officials sought to go back and destroy copies of a damaging letter from Eileen Murphy, a GM employee, to Richard Danner, a former FBI agent who is now a Washington lawyer and who had been hired by the company in connection with the Nader investigation. Gillen claims he received oral instructions from Danner to "get something somewhere on this guy . . . get him out of their hair . . . shut him up." In addition, Gillen says there was a seven-page memorandum from Miss Murphy to Danner which was passed on to him (Gillen) as a "guide" in conducting the investigation. This memo didn't mention the Corvair cases but, Gillen said, instead suggested he investigate Nader's tax records, his possible anti-Semitism, suggested he might be on dope and asked, "Does he drink?" Gillen also swears the front page of a detective report given the committee was altered to change its meaning.

Gillen further swore in these court documents that he had conducted more than 25 investigations for GM since 1959. These included investigations of a well-known entertainer (later identified by the *New York Times* as Danny Kaye), a Harlem antipoverty group that had charged GM discriminated against Negroes in its hiring practices, and officials of the United Auto Workers.

The letter dated in February 1966 from Miss Murphy to Danner says, "Dear Dick . . . everyone is going overboard to impress us with what a great, charming intellectual this human being is—Eagle Scout type. There are too many variances for this to be accurate. . . . What is his Army record? What did he do for six months in the Army? . . . He mentions an accident which happened a decade ago. *He saw* a child decapitated. See if this gem can be uncovered as to where, when or how he was involved. . . . Well, friend, have fun. . . ." Gillen swears that when he went to Detroit shortly before the March 22, 1966, Senate hearing, GM officials asked him to return this letter so copies might not fall into Ribicoff's hands.

Because of these new allegations by Gillen, Ribicoff asked the Justice Department to begin an investigation to determine whether federal criminal statutes had been violated. He said, "Perjury by witnesses under oath before congressional committees cannot and should not be tolerated."

When it was first revealed that detectives had been following Nader, Senators Gaylord Nelson (D, Wisc.) and Ribicoff had been particularly concerned that the detectives might have been used to intimidate or harass the auto critic who had been a witness before congressional committees. (To harass or intimidate a witness before the Congress, is a federal crime, punishable by a five-year prison term.) Both Nelson and Ribicoff asked the Justice Department to investigate, and then Ribicoff called his own hearings.

On March 10, 1966, after GM had admitted hiring the detectives to follow Nader, Ribicoff said in the Senate he would invite the president of the company to testify before his subcommittee. Senator Robert Kennedy said, "Could we also request that he bring all of his records in connection with this agency?"

Mr. Ribicoff: That request will be made concerning the records of the agency and the investigation.

Mr. Kennedy: Could we also have the detective agency bring all its records. . . .?

Mr. Ribicoff: I think the request is a proper one, and that request will be made of the detective agency.

Mr. Kennedy: Could we also ask General Motors Corp. to have available in the room any individuals from General Motors who have detailed knowledge about these transactions with the detective agency?

Mr. Ribicoff: The request will be relayed to the president of General Motors.

•

But Jerome Sonosky, the subcommittee counsel, who later resigned to take a job with a law firm representing Mercedes-Benz, indicated the subcommittee may never have asked for *all* the company's records in connection with this case. Sonosky said there is no written record of such a request. He said an original telegram was sent inviting Roche to appear. Later on, Sonosky says, he called the company and as he remembers it, asked them to bring the reports filed by the detective agencies and to come prepared to answer all questions. Sonosky said that before the hearings he met in his office with GM officials, including the chief counsel, Mr. Power. Of this interview Sonosky said, "I just asked them to be prepared to answer all relevant questions."

At the hearing, the senators did not ask Roche if he had brought his records with him. Nor were the detective reports formally introduced into the records.

The one person in the company who had "detailed knowledge" of dealings between GM and Danner, the go-between with the detectives, was Eileen Murphy, a former employee of the Justice Department, who now works in the company's law library. It was Miss Murphy who flew to Washington to discuss hiring the detectives with Richard Danner. It was Miss Murphy who supposedly gave Danner the seven-page memorandum which was passed on to Gillen as a guide for his work. And it was Miss Murphy who Gillen now swears wrote the "Dear Dick" letter. But Miss Murphy was not asked to testify at the hearing. She sat in the audience and listened to the other witnesses discuss her role in the case.

As for the mysterious seven-page memorandum, which Gillen says never mentioned the Corvair cases, page seven appears in the subcommittee's hearing transcript. Asked what happened to the other six pages, Sonosky said the complete document had been sent with other materials to the National Archives where it is held in confidence. Asked whether the subcommittee got the memorandum before or after the hearing, Sonosky paused for a long moment and then said, "I'd rather not say." If the committee had this memorandum at the time of the hearing, then why wasn't it used to show that GM wasn't interested in the Corvair cases as much as it was in getting something on Nader? If the subcommittee got the memorandum after the hearing, why didn't it reopen the case?

Sonosky said GM gave the Ribicoff subcommittee two detective reports. He won't say where he got the seven-page memorandum. After the hearing, Nader asked the committee to see the reports the detectives had filed on him, but he was refused permission. However, after Theodore Sorensen, the GM lawyer in the case, made persistent requests that the detective reports be returned to GM, Sonosky sent them back to him. It later developed that Sonosky had made copies of the materials. When Sorensen found this out, he wrote asking Sonosky to send back the copies. Finally in October Sonosky stuck all the documents in an envelope and sent them over to the National Archives where nobody can see them without explicit permission of the committee chairman. Ribicoff has never permitted Nader to see the documents.

All of the documents turned over to the subcommittee, of course, are available to the Justice Department, which was asked to make an investigation to determine whether there had been harassment of a congressional witness. On June 1, 1966, Fred M. Vinson, an assistant attorney general, wrote Ribicoff,

... we have concluded that criminal prosecution is not warranted in this matter and that additional investigation by the department would provide no useful function. The extensive investigation by the Federal Bureau of Investigation pursued every logical and relevant lead suggested by the reported facts and allegations.

As it now appears, this seems to have been a perfunctory investigation. Nader said he was interviewed on one occasion by two agents in March 1966 who asked him to describe what he knew about the detectives. Nader's brother briefly discussed the matter with an FBI agent over the phone in Connecticut. Sonosky said he discussed the matter twice with Justice Department representatives, once when they came to read the transcript of the hearing and later when they returned to say the investigation was finished.

We have found no other principals in this case who ever talked to the FBI. Gillen says he never talked with the FBI; neither did Ribicoff, even though it was suggested that Gillen was gathering dirt on him; Sorensen says he didn't talk with the FBI. Larry Scalise, then the attorney general of Iowa, who was so sure Nader was being followed that he ordered his own statewide investigation, was never approached by the FBI. Neither was Frederick Hughes Condon, a lawyer in Concord, New Hampshire, whom Gillen had interviewed using a fictitious name. Richard Danner, the man who hired Gillen and ran the investigation for GM, said he had never talked to the FBI, and it was his impression that the Justice Department had not made an investigation. Nor did the agency interview 11 other people who had talked with the detectives investigating Nader. This looks embarrassing for the Justice Department and the FBI as well. The detectives who followed Nader are all former FBI men. It would be ironic should the FBI find it necessary to expose its alumni as unscrupulous hacks.

Had not Nader filed his private suit, he never would have seen what was in the detective reports or known about the seven-page memorandum. There never would have been any questions raised about the committee's dealings with GM. Very probably nobody would have asked whether Justice made a real investigation. The senators, the press, and the public would have been satisfied with Roche's forthright apology.

Bureaucracy and Highway Safety

by DANIEL POSIN, JR.

The National Highway Safety Bureau is letting dozens of contracts to find methods to improve highway safety. Bureau officials complain about the lack of engineering developments in this field. But the Highway Safety Hearings of 1967 showed that the obstacles to improving safety on the road are often not technical at all, that there is much highway safety hardware already around that has never been used.

The story of the Isle-Guard Median Highway Barrier is an example of how vested interests, personality conflicts, and bureaucratic torpor block effective inventions. Invented by Henry Such Smith of Bayonne, New Jersey, the Isle-Guard is used to separate traffic on narrow roadways and bridges. Its smooth steel surface, and encasing concrete, coupled with the particular angle it makes with the roadbed, guide the tires of a side-swiping vehicle back into the flow of traffic without any spin-out, slow-down, or damage to the vehicle. The barriers which state highway departments use to separate traffic on narrow roadways have a high-friction concrete surface which causes accidents or increases their severity—vehicles either crack up on the barrier itself or spin back out into a collision. The Isle-Guard, however, has virtually eliminated accidents at the one place it's been used: the narrow and heavily travelled Willis Avenue Bridge in New York City.

After the Isle-Guard had been in place there seven years, Royal Riley, public information director of New York City's Department of Public Works, wrote in 1965:

> ... Concerning the effectiveness of the Isle-Guard ... since its installation on the Willis Avenue Bridge no accidents have been reported, whereas theretofore a number of collisions of varying

Reprinted by permission of the New Republic, © *1968, Harrison-Blaine of New Jersey, Inc.*

degrees of seriousness were recorded annually. . . . It has been the observation of our bridge tenders that the barrier is equally effective in deflecting every type, size and weight of vehicle in general use today.

Smith demonstrated the Isle-Guard on the Willis Avenue Bridge to Fletcher Platt, manager, Traffic Safety and Highway Improvement Department of the Ford Motor Company. Platt later wrote,

I was extremely impressed by the dynamic demonstration given by Mr. Smith as he drove the car into the barrier at approximately 20 degrees at 30 mph. Not only was Mr. Smith able to remove his hands from the steering wheel before impact, but the car was directed by the barrier parallel to the line of traffic. . . . This demonstration was probably more impressive to me because of my experience in witnessing many crash tests at our Ford Motor Company track, where a 30 mph crash at right angles against a barrier can result in decelerations of 25 to 30 g's. I have described my Isle-Guard demonstration to a number of people and have said, "You have to see it to believe it."

Similar praise came from Kenneth A. Stonex, chief safety engineer for General Motors, and Robert A. Wolf, head of the Transportation Research Department of the Cornell Aeronautical Laboratory.

After Senator Harrison A. Williams of New Jersey underwent a test crash into the barrier, he decided to try to help Smith in his continuing efforts to get the Isle-Guard installed in New Jersey. Rep. Richard Ottinger (D, N.Y.) also became an enthusiastic supporter after a test crash.

Smith has been negotiating with the New Jersey State Highway Department to put the barrier on the narrow Route 22 viaduct over Frelinghuysen Avenue in Newark. Though the price is right ($.82 cheaper per linear foot than the New Jersey Department's own barrier), as of March 1968 negotiations with the New Jersey Department had been stalled for three years. The nub of the problem is that Smith wants to retain complete control over his invention by being the prime contractor on the job. The New Jersey Department says that in order for Smith to be the prime contractor he must meet state standards with respect to financial security, equipment, and experience. Smith probably cannot meet these requirements, and the New Jersey Department refuses to exercise its discretionary power to waive them. Neither side will give in, and the motorists who pile into each other on the Route 22 viaduct and similar new and old roadways around the country are the losers.

Smith's demands may be unreasonable, but the relevant policy question is whether New Jersey has done everything it can to bring the barrier into use. Idiosyncratic inventors come and go, but agencies like the New Jersey State Highway Department remain, clothed with a public responsibility. Their procedures should be flexible enough to bring life-saving inventions into public use, if at all possible, despite any difficult demands of inventors.

New Jersey State highway officials have made no efforts to break the impasse. As negotiations with Smith bogged down, department officials reversed themselves and began to deny the Isle-Guard's usefulness. In response to an inquiring letter, Dwight R. G. Palmer, commissioner of the New Jersey State Highway Department, wrote in the fall of 1965, ". . . The Route 22 overpass is too narrow for any divider so we are, until a duplicate structure is erected, devoting ourselves to other reliefs for this route."

•

This statement is amazing, because at that time Palmer had been negotiating with Smith for over a year to put the Isle-Guard on the Route 22 viaduct. Moreover, it's well established in traffic safety literature that parabolic-shaped dividers such as the Isle-Guard *increase* effective driving space. Drivers shy away less from them than from a simple paint line, which provides no protection from oncoming traffic.

Nor have appeals to New Jersey Governor Richard Hughes helped. In response to a letter from a man whose wife was killed on the Route 22 viaduct, Hughes simply reiterated the department's position that Smith would not comply with regulations. Hughes further noted that the Stevens Institute of Technology in Hoboken was studying the problem of center barriers. The Stevens study completely ignored Smith's barrier. Though the same New Jersey Highway Department officials who had dealt with Smith, Dwight R. G. Palmer and Russell H. Mullen, had also let the contract to Stevens, Stevens Institute researchers never got in touch with Smith to include the Isle-Guard in the study. The fact that Smith and the department cannot come to terms hardly seems reason to ignore Smith's barrier, since the purpose of the research is to study the state of the art in highway barrier design. The three-year Stevens study was an admitted flop. Mullen said upon its completion that New Jersey was no closer than before to the development of a "safe, effective barrier." For purposes of the study, Mullen and Palmer had simply denied the existence of Henry Such Smith.

Smith met this same resistance to an inventor who's outside the highway safety establishment from the New York State Department. Smith demonstrated the Willis Avenue Bridge (which is under city rather than state jurisdiction) to Malcolm D. Graham, director, Bureau of Physical Research, New York State Department of Public Works. Graham later wrote to a friend of Smith's that the Isle-Guard was "very effective at redirecting the vehicle under the conditions at which it was tested." When Graham was later asked whether the New York Department knew of any barrier

218

superior to the Isle-Guard, George W. McAlpin, deputy chief engineer, replied for him in May of 1964, "... The barrier designs that *we* are currently using are good designs; *we* have actively pursued a program of barrier research that has been productive; and, *we* will continue to modify *our* designs to take advantage of significant research findings and objective observations by *our* field forces" (emphasis supplied).

A year later the New York Department commenced a series of crash tests on highway barriers. Graham, in charge of them, said the purpose was to develop a barrier that would reduce injury to passengers and decrease damage to vehicles when they collide with barriers. Graham said, "The barriers are designed to yield sufficiently to temper impact and to deflect the striking vehicle back into its driving lane." Smith was never asked to include the Isle-Guard in the tests.

Other states and the American Association of State Highway Officials have ignored the ready protection offered by Smith's barrier. States have traditionally set safety standards for highways, even those overwhelmingly funded by the federal government. The Bureau of Public Roads has known about the Isle-Guard for nearly a decade but has not used its close relationships and leverage with states to prod them toward such highway designs. In response to a question by Senator Robert Kennedy about the Isle-Guard, Dr. William Haddon, head of the National Highway Safety Bureau, said that the Isle-Guard has the approval of the Bureau of Public Roads and would be favorably considered as part of a state's proposed safety improvement program. Thus the initiative is passed back to the states.

People are killed every week all over the country by death-dealing highway guardrails and barriers. Smith's invention, like many others in the highway safety field, has been cast aside by a state administrative structure that cannot or will not respond to outside innovation.

Highway Murder

by JOSEPH KELNER

Fifty thousand Americans die on our highways each year. Their deaths are not accidental, but caused by recklessness. The auto makers think they are the whipping boy of the highway accident problem and they are partly right. They brought federal regulation on their own heads by their procrastination, but the apathy of the auto industry is shared by every segment of our society.

Our psychology is that the serious injury, the "bad one," always happens to the other guy. We lawyers handle human wreckage—the man whose leg is cut off by a speeding car, the woman who is decapitated. Most of us believe it never can happen to us.

Travel by automobile is the most dangerous. For every 10 billion miles of travel, five train passengers die, 13 bus passengers die, 14 airplane passengers die, but by automobile there are 570 fatalities for the same number of miles of travel. The federal government requires periodic examinations and strict licensing standards for airplane pilots, but automobile drivers have a field day. I strongly disagree with Ralph Nader and others who seem to think the safety automobile will greatly reduce the annual toll of highway deaths. The safety automobile, when it comes, will hardly make a noticeable dent on the death and injury statistics for another 10 years. Ninety-five million autos now crowd our highways and over nine million new autos are produced annually. Autos now in use will take at least 10 years to wear out and be replaced. Highway fatalities are likely to reach 100,000 annually by 1977.

Perhaps 90 percent of all deaths and injuries can be blamed on the American driver. With our population nearing 200 million, and three-car

Reprinted by permission of the New Republic, © *1967, Harrison-Blaine of New Jersey, Inc.*

families becoming commonplace, it is time to set proper standards for our 130 million drivers, many of whom not only drive while drunk or nearly so, but speed, tailgate, bob and weave in traffic, fall asleep at the wheel, fail to use belts or to insist that passengers use seat belts, fail to drive defensively, jump traffic signs and traffic lights, fail to yield the right of way, ignore the other fellow's rights.

To compound the problem, we allow every Tom, Dick and Harry to drive. Dr. F. H. Mayfield, Cincinnati neurosurgeon, estimates that more than six million of the country's drivers are subject to convulsive diseases. How many of our millions of older citizens have lost their reflexes, their ability to react to highway traffic emergencies? How many of our millions of persons with defective eyesight still have licenses to drive? In most states the only vision test ever given is when the driver's license is first granted. Human vision is presumed never to deteriorate with the passing years.

In Pennsylvania, a motorist was killed when he crashed into a tree. He was totally blind. An eight-year-old boy beside him directed his driving. In Florida, a highway patrolman stopped a man who was traveling 26 mph down the middle lane of a highway with a posted minimum speed of 40. The driver admitted his eyesight was too poor to read the signs. He could see where he was going only by looking down to watch the dividing line.

In 30 states licenses are renewed by mail—a lucrative mail-order business.

About half of all auto fatalities are caused by drinking drivers. In most states intoxication is presumed shown by a percentage of 0.15 alcohol in the blood. North Dakota is the one state in which 0.10 percent is presumptive evidence of intoxication. Drinker-drivers with blood-alcohol levels between 0.5 and 0.15 percent are the bulk of the problem; the extremely intoxicated driver, as a rule, is taken off the road by either himself, his friends, or the police. The drinking driver does not recognize that his judgment, reflexes and vision have been impaired.

Among other things, we should:

1. drop the permissible blood-alcohol rate for driving to .05 percent in every state (no more than one drink for the average drinker).

2. adopt "implied consent laws" in every state. Under these, a driver's license is automatically revoked if he refuses to submit to chemical tests when arrested on a drunken driving charge.

Today, our 50 states present a spectacle of chaos, with laxity and no uniformity in licensing of drivers. Congress should enact legislation requiring every driver crossing a state line to obtain a license from a Federal Bureau of Drivers' Licenses, under the newly created Federal Department of Transportation. The system of licensing would require written certification by a licensed physician that a driver

1. has minimum prescribed visual capacities;

2. does not have specified physical ailments such as epilepsy, diabetes, palsy or other disorders which make his driving hazardous;

3. can respond with reasonable alacrity to highway emergencies under modern high-speed highway conditions;

4. is free from prescribed mental and personality aberrations resulting from designated mental diseases and disabilities;

5. is certified by his physician not to be a chronic alcoholic, or dependent on or addicted to tranquillizers, narcotics or drugs.

New physical and eye examinations and doctor's certification should be needed for license renewal.

The Infernal, Eternal,
Internal Combustion Engine

by RALPH NADER

Since 1951, when Professor Arie Haagen-Smit of Cal Tech discovered the bond between smog and autos, the car manufacturers, by act and inaction, have been telling Southern Californians that there is something eternal about the internal combustion engine (ICE). For years, the industry's assertion was that only the ICE could give Americans what they were deemed to want in vehicle performance. Californians and the rest of the nation believed it and began to strain over how fast to clean up the ICE, rather than how fast to displace it entirely with far superior systems.

Now the advanced, virtually pollution-free steam engine—a far cry from the Stanley Steamer of yore—is making an enduring debut. Far more than with the electric vehicle proposals, the auto industry will have a difficult time obfuscating the issues, suppressing innovation and dismissing steam's advocates as atavistic eccentrics.

In an authoritative analysis by Resources for the Future Inc., physicist Robert Ayres concludes that recent innovation and advances in new materials have solved many of the nagging problems that plagued steam engines early in the century. These solved problems included slow start-up, weight and exorbitant water consumption. The modern reciprocating steam engine belches less than 1 percent of the various kinds of pollution given off by the ICE; it performs with very little noise and can be fully competitive in price and performance.

One such steam-engine car has been designed and built by the Williams

223

Brothers, inventors in Ambler, Pa. Using kerosene as its fuel, the Williams car has attracted serious attention among specialists and visits from domestic auto companies. The interest is obvious: here is a steam engine that provides extremely high torque, low maintenance, very high combustion efficiency and low fuel consumption even under repetitive start-stop conditions. Such a steam engine eliminates the transmission, clutch, starter motor, distributors, spark plugs (except one), muffler and carburetor. The engine would be cheaper to build and easier to maintain.

Ford Motor Co. has shown the most overt interest in steam engines. It has done unrevealed work at its own facilities and recently moved to establish a strong relationship with Thermo Electron Inc., a small science-based plant in Waltham, Mass. A two-year joint development venture was launched ostensibly to develop low-power steam engines for use as outboard boat motors or golf-cart power plants. An application to motor vehicles was not officially contemplated in the agreement. Ford was also given the right to buy 100,000 shares of Thermo Electron at a stated price (20 percent of their shares outstanding). What made Thermo Electron a natural candidate for such an acquisitive move issued from work that company did for the Pentagon on steam generators that could not be easily heard by the Viet Cong. When the company began looking for opportunities to use this know-how for civilian application, Ford decided that a footloose innovator could cause trouble or, alternatively, could bring into the Ford stable a bit of self-insurance for a rainy day, should steam become a focal point for antipollutionists in and out of government.

Ford's concern is not misplaced; though one would have liked to sense something more positive in attitude. Clear signs point to a serious revival of the steam principle for vehicle propulsion. The Commerce Department's Technical Advisory Panel on auto pollution has reported that the reciprocating steam engine power plant is a reasonable alternative to the ICE "in terms of performance and emission requirements." The chairman of the panel, Professor Richard Morse of Massachusetts Institute of Technology, has become such a believer in steam engines' licking pollution that his company, Energy Systems, is seeking to interest government departments in funding the development of demonstration vehicles.

Steam engines have other advantages over competing displacements such as electric vehicles—even assuming the latter's range, speed, and recharging problems are overcome. Steam engines burn fuel which would keep the petroleum industry busy, though the elimination of the need for tetraethyl lead (itself a major pollutor) would upset Ethyl Corp., jointly owned by General Motors and Standard Oil of New Jersey, and DuPont. Service stations and repair and maintenance industries would not suffer as much disruption as would be the case with electric vehicles. And because steam is less economically disruptive to existing capital commitments, the level of non-technical obstacles to such an innovation is lower.

The next step is to awaken the federal government to steam's potential for drastically curbing pollution. In a carefully conceived government strategy lies the main hope for a breakthrough. Certainly, the industry cannot be relied upon to lead the way. No domestic auto maker has published any research findings on the steam engine. All are mum; but behind the corporate curtain, engineers are plainly following managerial directives to prepare the case against.

There is some stirring in the executive branch. The Department of Health, Education and Welfare is trying to obtain more funds for demonstration vehicle-propulsion contracts; the Department of Housing and Urban Development is interested in applying steam propulsion to city buses. Government weakness in standards-setting emphasizes the need for more fundamental solutions. Many exhaust devices on California cars are failing to meet the state standard after an average 8,000 miles. It's too easy for drivers to disconnect the anti-smog devices (in contrast to systems inherent in the car, like steam engines).

So it's time for the federal government to invoke its procurement power to encourage steam engine producers. The government created the private nuclear power industry, spending enormous sums aimed at cheaper power. Now it is human health that's at stake. HUD, HEW and the Department of Transportation should reconsider their coolness to Senators Magnuson and Muskie's 1967 proposal to launch a research and development program for alternative vehicle-propulsion systems.

The auto industry has been unprogressive about propulsion systems because of its capital investment in building and servicing the gas-gluttonous ICE. Professor Morse excoriated the industry at the annual meeting of the Society of Automotive Engineers as "not really moving with the mainstream of many other technically based progressive industrial groups." He added that "the time is ripe for automotive innovation in *other* industries" (his emphasis). As auto pollution problems worsen in our cities, the trail to alternative power sources for motor vehicles can be blazed by new pioneers. Antitrust enforcement, government procurement and government-sponsored demonstration projects can give critical help.

PART IV

INSURANCE—
ASSET OR LIABILITY?

Underground War
on Auto Insurance

by JAMES RIDGEWAY

The automobile insurance business is a giant which appears to have gone out of control. In the years 1962–1966, companies that write $8.5 billion in annual premiums pleaded they would go broke without rate increases, and languid state insurance commissioners, who are meant to regulate the industry, usually acceded to this demand with the result that insurance in 1966 cost nearly 25 percent more than it did in 1960.

However, once having received a rate increase which the commissioners authorized in the general public interest, the insurance companies turned around and narrowed the market of people they want to insure. This is because the big companies are locked in ruinous competition to insure preferred risk drivers—people between 30 and 50 who don't drive their cars around much and haven't had any accidents. At best, the preferred risk group may include 30 percent of the 100 million drivers in the country.

Those not included in the prime risk category are paying more and more for insurance, and in some cases find it hard to get policies from reputable companies. The squeeze is especially severe on people between 16 and 25, or over 65, or anyone owning a car and living in a metropolitan center. Some companies simply will not write any business in poor Negro neighborhoods. There have been complaints that amputee and paraplegic veterans have had policies canceled. These veterans, who drive especially equipped cars, often have excellent driving records. By concentrating on prime risks, the industry has opened the way for a booming business by the "high risk" bucket-shop operators—companies which specialize in insuring drivers with bad accident records. They charge usurious rates.

Senator Thomas Dodd's (D, Conn.) insurance subcommittee looked into the high risk business in 1965 and discovered that since 1960 65 companies had become insolvent, leaving 300,000 people, many of them badly injured in car accidents, with $100 million in unpaid claims. To remedy this Dodd wants to establish a federal Motor Vehicle Insurance Guaranty Corporation which would guarantee that people get paid should the insuror go down. It is a modest proposal, but industry officials and leaders of the National Association of Insurance Commissioners are against it. They dread federal intervention. About two-thirds of the auto insurance is issued by stock companies, that is, firms that sell shares. Mutual companies account for the other third.

Half the insurance is written by stock and mutual companies which belong to rating bureaus. These bureaus, in effect, set the rates for members. They lead the way in proceedings before the state insurance commissioners, whom they badger for rate hikes. Behind the bureaus come the independent companies, which generally ask for less of an increase. (The independents often can afford to do this because they don't have an elaborate agent network to support.)

As justification for rate increases, insurance companies will cite inflation, the growing number of lousy drivers cracking up cars, and high jury verdicts awarded accident victims brought about by clever plaintiff lawyers. All of this is bolstered by a mass of actuarial data, which neither the commissioners nor anyone else attending the proceeding fully understand. Indeed, the state commissioners don't have the staffs to determine whether the companies are telling the truth, and many have never defined laws which say vaguely that rates must be "adequate" or "not excessive."

In 1964 the American Trial Lawyers Association, which represents 20,000 claimants' lawyers, feared insurance company publicity had finally got to the juries, and they were, in fact, returning reduced verdicts in accident cases. Joseph Kelner, then vice president of ATLA, sent around kits of publicity material to key association lawyers in each state. The kits told how to fight back. Studies showed, for example, that only 10 percent of the claims ever result in suit; only a tiny portion of this total are tried, and insurance companies win half the cases tried. Kelner also sent articles prepared especially for ATLA that demonstrated that auto insurance companies were not losing money as they claimed, but because of odd bookkeeping devices actually were hiding substantial earnings. In Richmond, Virginia, George E. Allen Jr., an ATLA attorney, who with his father and brothers runs a vast, semiautomated personal injury law firm, was sent one of Kelner's kits, which he examined with interest. Allen was concerned about lower jury awards, and he also thought the industry was pulling a fast one with the continual rate hikes. He joined with three

Norfolk ATLA lawyers who also were worried about rising rates. One of them was Henry Howell Jr., a state senator, who had been trying to get Virginia to set up a consumer bureau. He wanted an independent staff to stand for the general public before the state regulatory agencies. Howell thought insurance ought to be regulated like a monopolistic public utility. This is wild stuff for Virginia and Howell's bill got nowhere in the legislature. In 1965, the auto insurance companies asked for yet another rate increase. Allen, Howell, Stanley Sachs and H. Lee Kanter decided they would oppose the insurance companies in proceedings before the State Corporation Commission, the regulatory agency. This would combat the bad publicity the lawyers were getting as well as show what public defenders could accomplish. The lawyers raised $1,000 and in the spring of 1965 hired T. Grayson Maddrea, a Richmond accountant, to analyze the industry's books.

•

Maddrea began by assuming nobody could understand the actuarial statistics produced by the companies. He concentrated on unraveling the industry's finances, which he discovered were peculiarly handled.

Auto insurance companies, he demonstrated, use sleight-of-hand in accounting procedures which make the business seem as if it is in the red, when actually it is turning a profit. This trick is accomplished by mixing the accrual method of accounting (in stating income) with the cash method (in listing expenses). A hypothetical example may help to show how the dodge is worked. Say you take out auto insurance December 1, 1966, and on that day write a check for $120 to cover the premium. The company works by the calendar year and closes its books December 31. Since only one month is left in the year, the company shows only one-twelfth of the premium, or in this case, $10 as income. This is the accrual method, with the rest of the income spread out over the coming year. In the expense column, however, the cash method is applied: The company lists total agent's commission, production expenses, taxes, office expenses and profit. This totals about 35 percent of the premium and in the example comes to $42. Thus, while the company actually took in $120 on this premium in 1966, the books show a loss of $32. As long as the companies increase premium income each year, which they do, they will appear to be losing money.

Premiums, of course, are collected in advance and earmarked for a fund called the unearned premium reserve. Money in this fund, which last year for all companies totaled $3.7 billion, is counted in making rates. On the other hand, the company charges all losses as expenses when first reported, even though settlement of the loss claim may take years. This, as Maddrea suggests, results in a rather conservative picture of the business.

The unearned premium reserve is a windfall for the company in more

231

ways than one. Because of a rule drawn up in behalf of the industry by the National Association of Insurance Commissioners—the association that is supposed to be regulating the companies—no money in this enormous reserve is subject to federal income tax. The government adopted the NAIC rule. In most other kinds of corporations such funds would be taxed as income. This arrangement looks like a bigger steal than the oil depletion allowance. In fact, many insurance companies pay small federal taxes or none at all.

The auto insurance companies profit in another way: the money in their unearned premium reserve is invested and produces a return of four to five percent.

The company also sets aside funds in a loss reserve to cover claims. (The loss reserve often is half the size of the unearned premium reserve.) The loss reserve is invested for a return of four or five percent. The loss reserve is really a kind of trust fund, where money for an accident victim is held over the three to five years until the claim is settled.

None of the investment income from either of these huge reserves is counted as profit by the company when it asks for higher rates.

Maddrea figured out what the insurance companies actually made in Virginia by applying a cash accounting method for 1965. All companies showed a net profit before taxes of $11.3 million, or 9 percent profit. The supposed profit in that state is 5 percent.

Maddrea's approach has been used before by security analysts who want to convince investors that auto insurance stock is not the bum deal it seems.

As the Virginia proceedings wore on, Maddrea's reputation traveled through an underground of ATLA lawyers who were preparing cases in other states. He next appeared in Maryland as an expert witness for George Shadoan, a trial attorney who had intervened against a rate increase in behalf of Rockville, a town in the Washington suburbs. Shadoan ran Maddrea through his paces, and then cut to pieces the industry witnesses whom he caught misquoting court decisions. The state insurance commissioner, Francis B. Burch, turned down the appeal for rate increases. Adopting much of Maddrea's approach, he ruled the companies must change their accounting methods and include investment income from unearned premium reserves in calculating rates. The industry appealed to the courts, which upheld Burch. Maddrea has also appeared as an expert witness for ATLA lawyers fighting rate increases in Maine, West Virginia, and Indiana.

In Virginia, to get some independent advice on how rates should be determined, the State Corporation Commission spent $30,000 and hired Woodward & Fondiller, a New York firm specializing in actuarial consulting. Woodward & Fondiller came in with a lengthy report urging the state to abandon any attempt at regulation, and instead allow the companies to succeed or fail according to the principles of free enterprise. Under cross-examination, Senator Howell drew from the company representative that while preparing the report for Virginia, Woodward & Fondiller was also in the employ of Continental Casualty, one of the insurance companies seeking a rate increase in the same proceedings.

•

As the four Virginia lawyers drove ahead with their cases Joseph Kelner, who in 1965 became president of ATLA, apparently lost his enthusiasm for the reform he had helped begin. Nobody really knows what happened to Kelner, but he began calling up lawyers involved in the rate cases. Kelner says he only wanted information, but some took what he said as instructions to "call off the dogs," as one of them put it. Kelner says he never tried to change anybody's mind, but sources within ATLA suggest he felt the lawyers had gone too far and was anxious to arrange a "truce" with the industry. In this endeavor, according to one story, he got in touch with James Donovan, counsel for the National Bureau of Casualty Underwriters, the rating bureau that represents many of the stock companies. The idea was to somehow get the industry to stop insinuating that spiraling rates were due to high jury verdicts. For its part, ATLA would lay off its attacks on rates. At the time, ATLA was involved in a number of other political battles, and Kelner may well have thought the insurance fight was too much to handle. Kelner insists he didn't try to influence anybody. Donovan says there is nothing to the truce story. However, Donovan said he talked with Kelner and other lawyers in an effort to avoid having the "image of the bar" damaged because of these cases. It probably seems ungentlemanly for a few rambunctious ATLA members to be locked in a knockdown dragout with insurance lawyers belonging to the American Bar Association.

While Kelner's calls were credited with slowing some of the cases, he only made the Virginia lawyers mad and more determined than ever.

But a state-by-state change in rates will take ages. The real possibility for reform lies in ATLA's taking up the case of restructuring insurance rates, much as it did in supporting automobile safety laws, and going before Congress where at long last there is some interest in the auto insurance mess. This is not likely to happen. Instead Congress will probably work on the Dodd insolvency bill, a measure practical politicians see as the only possible thing to squeak past the industry's defenses.

But auto insurance needs a far more basic reform than the Dodd bill offers. The interests of this industry too often work against those of the general public. Through the Insurance Institute of Highway Safety, for example, the auto insurance companies supported the President's Committee on Traffic Safety, a Detroit front that determinedly opposed a federal role in traffic safety, and refused to accept the idea that vehicle design was a factor in accidents. They even opposed construction of a federal traffic safety research center because, the insurance companies claimed, it

233

was the beginning of a government monopoly in research. From their accident reports, the insurance firms might well have told us a good deal about why accidents happen and what can be done to reduce them. But they haven't.

Instead of the inane competition for preferred risks, insurance firms could be using their immense political leverage to argue for safer cars, better roads and uniform national licensing provisions for everyone who drives, all of which would lower underwriting costs. They ought to be arguing for less driving in metropolitan areas. They should stop basing rates on age, race and geographical area, and instead write insurance uniformly on the basis of experience, and in the case of youngsters on their training. As Maddrea makes clear, rates could very probably be lowered by insisting that the companies give a more realistic account of their business. And the companies should probably be balancing preferred risks with bad risks in writing single reasonable rates for drivers throughout the country. The business needs a thorough reform and stiff federal regulation.

More on Auto Insurance

by JAMES RIDGEWAY

The states have granted automobile insurance companies one price hike after another over the past five years, so that they might continue to insure the general public. But the companies are locked in a deadly competition for the relatively small number of preferred risk drivers—perhaps 30 million of the nation's 100 million drivers—and they are canceling or refusing to renew policies for growing numbers who are not in the preferred risk category and are viewed as "suspect." These are the people who are forced to buy insurance from the fly-by-night, high-risk operators who hang about the fringes of the insurance markets.

To get an idea of how difficult it is for people to buy insurance, here are a few cases that have come to members of Congress:

In December 1966 Nationwide Mutual Insurance Co. canceled the insurance of a South Carolina man. Asked why, the company said, "Investigation reveals that your automobile coverage was terminated due to circumstances surrounding a parking ticket which your wife received recently." The woman had protested the ticket to the police, because, she said, the meter was broken. Nonetheless she paid the fine. (In this case, the best guess is that by protesting the ticket, she gave the company an opportunity to define her as an unsuitable customer.)

State Farm Mutual Automobile Insurance Co. dropped an Alexandria, Virginia, resident because of "loss history." The man was involved in one accident during the fall of 1965; the other driver was charged by the police and his insurance company had reimbursed State Farm for repairs. In addition, there had been one $6 charge against the policy for towing the car out of deep snow and two charges totaling $4 for mechanics. This man was 43, had been driving since 1938 and had never had a moving charge brought against him. Unable to see why he should be canceled, he protested to the Virginia regulatory agency, which got in touch with State Farm. State Farm then reversed itself and said it would renew the policy if the owner would drop the road-service provision. Apparently the $10 in towing and mechanics' charges constituted a "loss history" which was too much for State Farm.

"Have you ever had to turn down a request from a friend, a customer or business associate?" begins a letter to a New Jersey man from Sentry Insurance, of Syracuse, New York. "If so you know it's not an easy thing to do. Unfortunately, we too occasionally are faced with this problem—telling a policyholder that we cannot continue his insurance protection." The letter went on to announce cancellation of the man's auto insurance policy because it no longer met Sentry's "underwriting requirements." When pressed for details, Sentry replied:

> All insurance companies are permitted to set certain standards of underwriting and apply these standards to the policies that they accept or renew. It is not our intention to appear arbitrary, but under certain circumstances, misunderstandings occurred where our specific reasons for retirement have been given, resulting in embarrassment to either the insured or the companies or both. For this reason we prefer to follow the general practice of insurance companies and ask that we be excused from giving the reason for cancellation.

This didn't mean anything to the New Jersey man and he further pressed the company for an explanation. This time he got a tart reply: "I am sorry that my first letter did not satisfy you. I hope I can do better this time, but unfortunately I must reiterate my comment in my previous letter concerning the confidential nature of our file." The letter went on to say there was a record of losses in 1963 and in 1965 (about $150 for repairs to the car) and a speeding violation.

"There are other factors that enter into underwriting decisions which must number in the hundreds," the Sentry letter said.

> It would be impossible for me to list them all here but I am sure that you can think of a few yourself. For instance, how a car is used, where it is used, who uses the car, the age of the drivers, and many others would enter into an underwriting decision. Not all of the underwriting factors apply in any one case but when our underwriting information reveals that a particular policy does not meet with our present requirements we have no choice but to not renew the policy.

Servicemen and young veterans have a difficult time getting insurance. A veteran wrote the Michigan Insurance Commissioner:

> I have just come home with an honorable discharge after serving four years in the Navy. I have had a driver's license since I was 16 years old. I had insurance on my car when I left for the service. A few days ago I bought a new car and immediately applied for insurance. However AAA Insurance Co., Detroit, and Michigan Mutual Auto Insurance Co. of Traverse City have refused me insurance because they class me as a bad risk. I have taken driver's training and have never had an accident.

"I'm 46 years of age and have worked at the same plant for better than 19 years," wrote a West Virginia car owner.

> I received my driver's license two years ago and bought a car. Nationwide carried me for six months and then sent me a cancellation notice, no explanation at all. When I couldn't find out why they canceled me I secured insurance with Insurance Co. of North America. In the meantime, I bought a new '66 Dodge through a local bank. To make a long story short I've received a notice of cancellation from this company. I've never been in a wreck, never been arrested, and I do not have one point against my license. No teen-ager drives this car. I just don't understand why they can do this.

Charles W. Gambrell, South Carolina's insurance commissioner, says that rate increases in his state have not resulted in wider markets, but instead have made the cancellation problem worse. In South Carolina, insurance companies are required to disclose the "guides" agents follow in writing policies. Gambrell said 83 percent of the companies doing 65 percent of the business in the state refuse to write new business with over-age drivers, that is, drivers between 62 and 70. Sixteen percent of the companies won't do business with divorced people. The theory is that a divorced person, especially a woman, is emotionally unstable and likely to run around a good deal, thereby increasing the chances of an accident. If a divorcee did get into an accident and it wasn't her fault, no jury would believe her. So it's better not to insure divorcees at all.

Gambrell said guides for different companies doing business in the state list the following categories of poor risks, or as the trade calls them, "suspect": garbage collectors, amusement park workers, bartenders and tavern owners, bowling alley or dance hall attendants, pawn shop proprietors, watchmen, farm laborers, professional athletes, entertainers and people who live at the YMCA. Gambrell said these guides probably apply

237

throughout much of the country and are in many instances simply veiled discrimination against Negroes.

•

In April 1966 Orman Vertrees, a reporter for the *Seattle Post-Intelligencer*, got hold of an agent guide, then in its fifteenth printing. It warned agents away from selling auto insurance to people in the "lower laboring classes," including those who worked for aircraft companies and as longshoremen. The guide told agents one could determine a good customer by looking at the children's haircuts. If the man is called "Shorty" or "Scotty," he might not be conservative enough to get auto insurance. If his wife works in a "reject qualification," for example, as a waitress, that lessens chances of getting insurance. Since then, a committee of the Washington state legislature has urged that insurance companies be made to state grounds for cancellations before issuing the policy, and then state the reasons when cancellation is made.

Narrowing the market for auto insurance can have a startling effect. The National Bureau of Casualty Underwriters, the rating bureau that represents the big stock insurance companies, asked for a rate increase in Kentucky. At the rate hearings called by Commissioner S. Roy Woodall, Jr., testimony showed that of 1,150,000 private passenger cars registered in the state, 35 percent are uninsured. In arguing for higher rates, the National Bureau said its member companies couldn't afford to do business at current levels. The cost of claims was rising so fast, the bureau argued, that member companies were forced to reduce risks by canceling policies, some of them held by people who under more ordinary circumstances would be considered good customers.

Both the state insurance department and the Louisville Auto Club, however, claimed business was not so bad as the National Bureau made it out to be, and that insurance companies were making 7.6 percent profit, instead of the usual 5 percent. (It is interesting to note that net income before tax for all stock property and casualty companies in the US rose to an estimated $1.03 billion for 1966, up from $561 million in 1965.)

As the auto insurance market got tighter in Kentucky, state officials reported finding "blackout" maps in the offices of some companies. These maps show marked areas of Louisville, mostly poor sections, where insurance is not to be sold. Moreover, state officials claim there is an effective blackout for all kinds of casualty insurance in the depressed Appalachian region.

Probably the simplest way to stop the capricious cancellation policies of the insurance industry would be for Congress to insist that cancellations be based on sizable loss experience alone. This might be accomplished by amending Senator Thomas Dodd's bill setting up a Motor Vehicle Insurance

Guaranty Corp., which aims to protect insured motorists against their insurance company's becoming insolvent.

During its investigation into auto insurance practices, Senator Magnuson's Commerce Committee might well look into some other ideas for making auto insurance more equitable and less expensive. Professors Robert E. Keeton and Jeffrey O'Connell have worked out a basic protection scheme, which would have insurance handled rather like Blue Cross payments, regardless of who is at fault. This would do away with much of the lengthy legal work, speed up payment and reduce costs by 15 to 25 percent, mainly by getting the lawyers out of the picture.

Because of the strong lobby of insurance agents, it is impossible to buy group automobile insurance in the country. Group insurance has helped to reduce the cost of life and accident and health insurance. Here savings would be made by doing away with the agent network. The agent often gets 20 percent of the premium as commission. In a group of 1,000 people paying premiums of $150,000, agents would stand to make $30,000 in commission. On the group basis, however, one agent might make about 2.5 percent (the rate paid a life insurance agent for a group policy). Thus, commissions would be reduced from $30,000 to $2,500. In addition, the group would get lower rates if its members weren't involved in accidents, which would work as an incentive to safer driving.

Neither of these proposals, however, deals specifically with the main issue of a narrowing insurance market, a problem which is not likely to be solved without federal regulation of the market.

239

Taken for a Ride

by GILBERT B. FRIEDMAN

A well-dressed man in his forties came into my law office very distressed. About a month before, he had been in an auto accident in which the other driver was injured. He had given the other driver his license number and the name of his insurance company. He told me:

> I thought everything would be taken care of. I bought my insurance from the dealer that sold me my car, and he told me I was fully covered. But after the accident my insurance company sent me a letter saying my insurance covered only damage to my own car. Then I got a letter from the state telling me to post a $1,300 bond or lose my license. I can't come up with $1,300."

"How was the insurance you bought sold to you?" I asked. He explained:

> After we negotiated the price and down payment, etc., and the salesman was writing up the papers, he asked if I had a broker to get insurance. He said, "You know that we can't let you drive the car out unless you have insurance." I said that I had no special broker or insurance company. The salesman said, "We can handle the insurance for you, and add the charge right into the contract." That sounded pretty good since I didn't have too much cash after making the big payment on the car. The salesman then wrote in the insurance on the policy, and added the cost, $250, to the total charge. It just made my payment slightly larger.

I asked my client why he felt that he was fully covered. "My God," he said, "for $250 even in San Francisco that should fully insure anyone for most everything."

Logical but untrue. The insurance he bought was a two-year, $100 deductible collision and comprehensive policy covering only damage to the insured car. It does not cover liability for injury or damage caused by the insured to others. Thus my client's problem. Without liability insurance, he failed to meet his state's financial responsibility law.

All of the 47 states without compulsory insurance have such a law. It requires a person in an accident to demonstrate that he is "financially responsible" by either having liability insurance or posting a bond. If he can do neither, his driver's license is suspended. The amount of the bond is determined after estimation of injury and damage to the other party, and can run as high as $25,000.

The question of who caused the accident is relevant in only six states. Colorado's Supreme Court declared its state's law was unconstitutional as a denial of due process, because it failed to provide a person a hearing to demonstrate he wasn't at fault before his license was suspended. In April 1968, a California trial judge came to the same conclusion. But in 34 states, even if my client had been stopped at an intersection and a drunk had run into him, he would have lost his license if he couldn't come up with the money. Once suspended, he might have to wait one to three years before recovering his license. Twenty states require that he obtain liability insurance before having his license reinstated.

My client could not raise the $1,300 and, therefore, had his license suspended. Later I asked numerous other practicing attorneys if they had run into this situation. Their answer invariably was, "It happens all the time."

How does this sort of thing happen? Most cars are bought on credit. The purchaser pays a portion of it, and the remainder is through a loan from some financial institution. Loans on cars are a huge business. In one month, November 1966, the Federal Reserve Board reported that $2.46 billion in new auto loans were written.

Now it is reasonable that when a bank or other financial institution gives a loan on a car, it wants to protect its security. For in a transaction such as this, the financial institution is the legal owner, while the purchaser is only the registered owner until the loan on the car is paid in full. Naturally the financial institutions want to make sure that if anything happens to the car, their interest in it will be protected. The loaning institution accomplishes this through insurance. If the car has collision insurance, then, if the car is in an accident, the bank knows that the car will be repaired to its original condition, over and above the deductible portion. If the car is covered by comprehensive insurance, then the financial institution knows it will be repaid by an insurance company if the car is stolen, and that the car will be repaired if vandals damage it.

The general rule, therefore, is that a car dealer won't allow a car bought on credit to be driven from the showroom unless the required insurance is purchased first. Where the buyer does get the car before the required insurance is purchased, the bank will in some cases buy the collision and comprehensive insurance policy, send the bill to the buyer and have his monthly payments adjusted for the cost of the policy and interest on that cost. The sales contract for the car allows the financial institution to do this. However, in most cases, the arrangements for insurance are made right at the showroom.

The dealer that sells the car isn't an insurance agent, of course, nor is the institution that finances the car. They are in the business of selling cars on credit, and the only reason they involve themselves in insurance is to protect the financier's interest in the yet unpaid-for car. They may know that the collision and comprehensive insurance is completely inadequate to cover the buyer of the car, and that the buyer should also purchase liability insurance. But that is not their affair; besides they don't want to bother with liability insurance because of the possible difficulty in placing the insured because of his driving record, or because of the arbitrary underwriting policies of many companies. Furthermore, the extra charge might scare the buyer away! So they don't mention liability insurance, and in many cases try to make it appear as if the insurance they have sold the buyer with the car fully covers him.

In many states, if a dealer sells only collision and comprehensive auto insurance, that must be spelled out in the conditional sales agreement. But how many buyers read their conditional sales contract with all its fine print? Even if they do, they don't know what the different types of auto insurance are. If someone did read the conditional sales contract, and it clearly said that he was being covered only by collision and comprehensive insurance, it is not unusual for him to conclude that he has what he needs, "comprehensive" insurance. Can you think of a more misleading word in the entire English language than "comprehensive," used to cover insurance for only fire, theft, vandalism, and loss of $100 worth of personal property from your car if by fire and lightning?

Suppose a buyer had been led to believe he had complete coverage, when, in fact he had been sold only comprehensive and collision. What could he do after an accident? Sue the dealer? He could try. The insured received a copy of the insurance policy. Why didn't he read it? The policies all say on their covers, "Please read carefully." This is no easy case to win. Probably very few attorneys would take this type of case on a contingency fee contract, though they do sometimes. In a 1964 Minnesota case, *Hochemyer v. Motor Insurance Corporation*, the buyer of an automobile on a conditional sales contract sued the insurance company for negligent failure of the seller to provide liability insurance. The seller of the car was also the agent of the insurance company. The insurance company was not authorized by the state of Minnesota to sell liability insurance, just collision insurance. The Supreme Court of Minnesota decided the case in favor of the insurance company, on the grounds that since it could not sell anything but collision insurance, its agent, the car dealer, could not have any greater authority, either express, implied, or apparent than the principal itself had.

Obviously, Motor Insurance Corporation in Minnesota is one of the insurance companies that sell collision insurance so as to protect the lending institution's loan. These companies exist in every state. Most large banks have their own insurance company to write the collision insurance when they make a loan on a car and the other party has no insurance, and if they don't actually own a company, they have one to feed it their business.

For example, the Premier Insurance Company of San Francisco, which writes insurance for people financing purchases through the Bank of America, sold $9.8 million net worth of collision and comprehensive in the year 1966. But Premier carries no liability policies at all. A January 1967 study entitled "Report to the [California] Legislature" told of an informal survey taken of drivers who had their licenses suspended for failure to comply with the financial responsibility law. Over 15 percent said that they "thought" they had liability coverage meeting California requirements.

But there is another unsavory feature about this selling of insurance to car buyers. In many cases where insurance is bought through car dealers, even the collision and comprehensive insurance does little to protect the buyer.

All the unsuspecting car buyer has usually been sold is a vendor single interest policy. Besides being extremely expensive, this policy protects only the financial institution which financed the car. If the car is in an accident and there is $300 worth of damage, the insured will have to pay everything; unless, of course, he can sue the other driver. The only time the insurance company pays is if the car is stolen or totally wrecked. Then the insurance company will pay the bank for its loss. But since it is a "deductible" policy, the insurance company will pay the bank for the loss of the car minus the deductible portion, usually $100, and that must be paid by the insured. In short, the insured pays the premium and the bank collects the money. According to Premier's president, 17.7 percent of the policies sold by Premier in 1968 were vendor single interest.

•

The only other insurance that even compares with the "Vendor Single Insurance" is the credit life and disability insurance that is also sold along with car purchases. Under these policies, which are included as part of the sales contract, any remaining payments on the car are paid by the insurance company in the event of the death of the buyer, and payments

243

missed by the buyer due to illness are also paid. Many people who buy cars from a dealer are sold this insurance, although it is one of the worst buys available. Premiums are fantastically high and any regular insurance agent can sell you a much better policy for half the price. A credit life insurance policy costs $34 over three years to protect a $3,000 debt. It should cost about one-third of this.

In the first place, each month as you make a payment the risk to the insurance company decreases, since the amount they might have to pay is decreased by the amount of the payment you have made. Therefore, if your payments are $100 a month for 30 months on a $3,000 loan, before the first payment the insurance you are buying is for $3,000, but after the first payment it drops to $2,900, the new balance on the loan, and so on until before the last payments you have insurance for only $100, the balance on the loan. You are thus not really paying $34 for $3,000 worth of insurance but for a much smaller amount over the three year period. Congressional committees have held hearings on the abuses in this field of credit insurance. Some companies paid only 15 cents out in benefits for every 75 cents they took in as premiums.

The very nature of these companies deserves mention. Many operate out of states where insurance regulation is very weak, for example, Texas and Pennsylvania. If there is a claim to be made, where do you go? The car dealer who sold you the policy says he has nothing to do with claims; he was just the agent for the company. The company has no local offices or even offices in your state. You must write their home office in Texas. They fail to answer your letter, or they quote some provision of the policy in small print which excludes you. What can you do? You can sue in your own state, but the whole burden is on you.

Besides this, the loopholes in these policies are notorious. By far the most prevalent one is that if the condition which causes you not to be able to make your payments were a *preexistent* condition, then the company need not pay. This is rarely made clear to the buyer. Millions of persons suffering from a wide variety of illnesses from heart trouble to multiple sclerosis are sold these health and accident policies. Subsequently, when they have an attack or these diseases stop them from making a payment, the company says they're not covered; they had this disease previously. And that's not all. A woman client of mine just purchased a car on time. She was sold a health and accident and a life insurance policy. Three weeks after she bought the car she discovered she had tuberculosis. Her case was serious and she would have to go immediately to a sanitarium for at least several months. When she first applied to the insurance company, she was told she was not covered because she had the condition prior to her buying the policy: tuberculosis takes years to develop. The fact that she was unaware of the condition did not change the insurance company's position. After I got into the case and threatened suit, the insurance company started to make payments—but only out of the generosity of their hearts—still denying that they were in any way liable. After they stopped, I again threatened suit. Rather than pay the legal expenses to fight this case or perhaps even more to keep this specific issue from being litigated, they again renewed payments. Unless you have an attorney who threatens suit, these companies just don't pay. If the illness prevented your making a few payments, the suit would not be worth enough money for a private attorney to take it. No one denies the right of a bank to protect its security in the car, but how long must millions of Americans drive around with nothing but collision and comprehensive insurance, thinking they are fully covered?

Present state laws, which require the conditional sales contract to state in large print that the insurance sold contains only collision or comprehensive or that it doesn't include liability, are meaningless. Meaningful legislation would require that a dealer be prohibited from selling any auto insurance without simultaneously selling liability insurance. This would prevent millions of Americans who do want insurance from being misled. The bank would still have its interest protected, but not at the expense of the public or purchaser. Despite the protestations of the car dealers and banks, there is no evidence that the sale of cars in New York, Massachusetts, or North Carolina where liability insurance is compulsory has slowed down.

No Risks Preferred

by JAMES RIDGEWAY

Efforts to reform automobile insurance are dragging along. The Senate antitrust subcommittee, led by Philip Hart of Michigan, held one set of hearings in the summer of 1968 and another is planned for the spring of 1969. The Transportation Department is in the midst of a two-year study of the insurance system.

The insurance companies are plunged into internal warfare over what to do about the government. Companies in the American Insurance Association, which writes 35 percent of the business, aren't opposed to federal regulation in principle, and they are for changing around the business to make it more efficient and fairer. But the mutuals and big independent firms, State Farm and Allstate, so far are against government interference. The lawyers are banked solid against any change whatever: they stand to lose money. The agents, represented in Washington by President Nixon's former law firm, are fearful they will be sacrificed in a reform. In fact, there isn't much prospect of any change soon. The Secretary of Transportation, Mr. Volpe, opposed reform of auto insurance while he was governor of Massachusetts, and the possibility of an anti-industry study emerging from the department is dubious. President Nixon himself has maintained close ties with the insurance people, most recently as a director of Mutual of New York and over the years through a friendship with the Kemper family, which runs Lumberman's Mutual, a prominent auto insurer.

Yet the reasons for a change in this industry are pretty compelling. The companies, which do about $10 billion in business a year, are charging higher and higher rates, while at the same time refusing to insure a growing number of people they deem to be poor risks. The insurance companies maintain their only consideration in issuing policies is whether a person has a bad driving record. They deny accusations of discrimination by color and class.

•

At an inquiry into the industry's practices, Senator Hart tried to find out how the companies determine who is eligible to buy insurance.

Jasper Reports, Inc., of Chicago, makes a business of providing insurance companies with reports on prospective policy holders. The Hart committee asked Fred Jasper, president of the company, to tell the committee about his work.

Hart asked Jasper:

> ... One of the reports contains information to the effect that the inside housekeeping of the person who is being investigated was satisfactory. Now what has that to do with driving ability?"
>
> Jasper: Oh, I do not think it has anything to do with driving, but I think it perhaps to some degree portrays the general overall reputation and I think perhaps a case might be made for the fact that an individual who lives in what you might classify as a pigpen might conceivably take the same care of their automobile from a mechanical standpoint. It is conjecture very obviously, but I think this would be a consideration and I think this is what underwriters were looking at if they found that people were living in a pigpen, a little concerned that they were careless in the care of their automobile.
>
> Hart: Well, how about the report that shows that the person was married and divorced before she was 20 and her family was very "standoffish." Now, what relevance is that to the driving ability of the lady?
>
> Jasper: Let us take the first part where you said she was married and divorced before she was 20. Nothing other than perhaps to portray instability.
>
> Hart: Or bad judgment with respect to mates but not necessarily to traffic?
>
> Jasper: A degree of irresponsibility ... but we are always weighing these things. We are reporting them as we find them and an underwriter uses this along with many other things.
>
> Hart: And the fact that her family was standoffish?
>
> Jasper: Well, that—no. I think perhaps the inspector may have been using that in defense of being unable to develop as much personal information as he might have been unable to otherwise. That is a defensive explanation.
>
> Hart: ... You have got a report in here that indicates the sub-

ject was living with a woman suspected not to be his wife. Now, how does this bear on his driving ability?

Jasper: I do not know that it would affect the driving but it might portray a situation where they were completely disdainful of the accepted mores, the accepted patterns of behavior, a little disregard for anybody else.

Hart: Well, with respect to these three categories—slovenly housekeeping, early marriage, and divorce, and living with somebody not your wife—what, if any, statistical data exists to show that these individuals are bad driving risks?

Jasper: Well, we do not compile any statistics at all. We are only in the reporting business and we are reporting information to the companies which down through the years they have requested be included in the reports. Now this is a constantly changing thing. Things that were important five years ago are no longer regarded as being important by many companies.

Jasper is the author of "A Confidential Report on Environmental Conditions in the Metropolitan Chicago Area." The book is provided to the industry as a guide to underwriting auto insurance. In the Confidential Report, Jasper breaks down metropolitan Chicago into ethnic areas: Polish, Jew, hillbilly, black. Of the Mexicans, he has this to say: "These Mexicans are for the most part well behaved, but a few do drink to excess and many of them are illiterate and many cannot speak English. These Mexicans should be inspected carefully for auto insurance."

Jasper Reports is not a little company. Customers for its ethnic guide include more than 50 of the largest insurance companies in the nation, including Allstate and State Farm, the two giants.

Insurance people deny they discriminate against blacks. Jasper said that only one-third of his customers worried about race, and he decided to drop the category lest he get caught at some later date. Joe T. Kelly, president of the Georgia Association of Independent Insurance Agents, put it this way:

No company represented in our office, and no other company that I am familiar with employs a blanket prohibition on either race, color or creed. Although it is true today, up until about 12 or 15 years ago the opposite, on a very limited basis was true. Admittedly, Negroes—who comprise, I suppose, about 25 percent or 30 percent of the population in my areas—have more difficulty buying automobile insurance at the more attractive level than is true of white people. However, race is not the reason for this: the reason is the higher incidence of undesirable risk history.

248

J. Victor Herd, chairman, Continental Insurance Companies of New York, gave the subcommittee a copy of his firm's underwriting manual. It warns the underwriter to watch out for bad risks, including merchant seamen, oil field employees, farm workers, waiters, janitors, painters, bellhops, unemployed persons and taxicab drivers. The manual goes on to tell the agents to be on the lookout for different sorts of bad risks:

> The divorced or separated male is, in our opinion, more undesirable than the man who has never married. The same is true in comparing the divorcee and the unmarried female. Some divorced persons are the innocent victims of circumstances. Others . . . because they are emotionally unstable. That is almost sure to be the situation with the person who has been divorced twice. We should leave them alone.

The manual says, "Also stay away from the exhibitionist who overdecorates his car with fox tails, fender fins, mud flaps, boxing gloves, baby shoes, spot lights and other ornaments. He is not likely to be a very conservative or considerate driver."

The insurance companies make this sort of arbitrary judgment about whom they sell to in order to narrow the market to those "preferred risks" who have not had an accident and aren't likely to have one. So while the population generally increases and the need for insurance mounts, the industry works to narrow its market. While the companies skim the preferred risks, they are forever asking the state insurance companies for higher rates. They claim drivers are getting worse all the time and inflation is running costs up with the result that they are losing money and in some cases are on the verge of going out of business.

•

The companies are able to make these claims for several reasons. For one, the insurance commissions have been allowing them to mix methods of accounting, shifting off in midstream from accrual to cash—which gives the impression of a loss when in fact there is a profit. Moreover, the companies have not taken into account investment income in setting rates. In addition, they play a political charade with the commissions. Inefficient companies make a plea for higher rates through a rating bureau. The big companies support the request. Once it is granted, the big companies undercut the ceiling, creating the impression of a bargain.

Senator Hart introduced figures at the hearings which showed that in 1967 the 10 largest stock property and casualty companies reported an underwriting loss of $273 million. But when the accounting method was changed to the type generally accepted by corporations, the loss turned into a profit of $55 million. Neither of these figures included net income from investment of the same 10 companies. That came to $1.7 billion.

Richard Norgaard of the University of Southern California testified before the subcommittee that casualty insurance companies are earning greater rates of profits than 90 percent of some 640 leading American corporations. For instance, his study showed that Allstate, an industry leader, had a 24.6 percent profit. (However, a study by Arthur D. Little Co., commissioned by the industry, claimed that over a 10-year period the return was only 4.4 percent.)

The arguments over whether the auto insurance companies are making or losing money are muddy. But it's possible to get a clue to the business by looking at the way the companies themselves discuss income to their stockholders. Continental, for instance, reported to stockholders in 1966 and 1967 that it lost 28 cents a share, based on statutory accounting; but once the income was adjusted, it showed an underwriting profit of $1.61 per share. (This did not include investment income.)

These figures don't convince the state insurance commissioners, who long have been pawns of the industry. In 1965, there were rate increases in 40 states; the next year rates went up in 23; in 1967, they were allowed to increase in 25.

A few commissioners and small groups of lawyers have opposed the industry's demand for higher rates in Virginia, Maryland, Kentucky, New Jersey and a handful of other states. But it's a losing battle. When Charles Howell, the New Jersey commissioner, disapproved a proposed 20.6 percent rate increase in 1968, the industry retaliated. William T. Cahill, a New Jersey congressman who wants to reform the industry, says 50,000 cancellation notices were sent motorists, business people and homeowners in the first few months after the decision. Agents' commissions throughout the state were slashed, and the agents were denied binding authority to write insurance. Cahill quotes a letter from a major insurance company to an agent that says:

> It is required that you not bind us on any new private passenger-automobile risks . . . after receipt of this letter . . . you may submit applications without binders for new family automobile policies when we are, in your judgment, the logical carrier because of other lines that we now have for the applicant.

In other words, the only way to get auto insurance was to take out home, fire and life insurance along with it. Or it was possible to get insurance by signing a "consent to rate" provision in the New Jersey law, a clause which in effect waives the individual's rights to legal rates and allows the company to charge him higher prices at its discretion.

The object of perfecting techniques to exploit the "preferred risk" market is to assure the insurance companies a steady flow of cash that can be plowed into investments. Insurance companies are really disguised investment trusts. The investment side of the business is the most interesting and profitable line of work, and in recognition of the possibilities the entire industry has been on the move to reorganize itself so as to take better advantage of the insurance company as investment bank. In some cases this has meant merging with an industrial conglomerate; in others shifting the stock of the insurance company to a holding company, which then buys other types of businesses, and in effect, turns the business into a conglomerate. Here are examples of this trend: Teledyne, an electronics-based conglomerate, has bought six insurance companies and is bidding on a seventh. ITT, which already owns one insurance company, is bidding on a second. Lykes Co., the shipbuilders, and Walter Kidde & Co., well known for its fire extinguishers, both have purchased insurance companies. Leasco, a data processing firm, picked up Reliance Insurance. Gulf & Western bought Providence Washington Insurance; American Express purchased Fireman's Fund.

At the same time, insurance companies have transformed themselves into "hybrid conglomerates," as they are sometimes called—hybrid because they specialize in financial services related to insurance such as mutual funds, small loans, variable annuities, etc. For example, the Continental National American Insurance group (CNA) formed the CNA Financial Corp., a holding company, which controls the insurance company stock. CNA Financial then bought out Tsai Mutual Fund and General Finance Corp., thereby entering the fields of both mutual funds and small loans as well as insurance.

A conglomerate offers the possibility of tie-in markets (selling insurance to your own employees), as well as the steady cash flow that permits further acquisitions. Or the insurance company's bank can be put to such use as in the following case: In 1968 National General Corp., a Los Angeles-based company that distributes movies and develops real estate, bought 75 percent of the stock of the Great American Holding Corp., which owns Great American Insurance Co. National General put 14 men on the insurance company's 17 member board of directors. In the same year, Great American paid a dividend of $2.80 per share. In January 1969, however, the new board of directors voted a stock dividend worth $55 a share.

Banks and insurance companies are moving from opposite directions toward the re-creation of the old-fashioned investment trust. As Congressman Wright Patman's (D, Tex.) long study of banks indicates, insurance companies already own a considerable amount of bank stock, and the two businesses are intimately connected through a series of interlocking directorates. Patman's study shows 81 people holding interlocking positions among six New York commercial banks and various insurance companies. First National City Bank has bought Chubb & Son, a management company that owns insurance companies. The acquisition puts this huge bank directly into the insurance business. CNA Financial, the insurance holding company, controls a bank in Chicago. Thus, through the holding company device a large insurance company goes directly into banking. Banks and insurance companies aren't the only kinds of companies that are moving to form investment trusts. This is a general business trend. Model conglomerates are organized around a bank of some sort and a management core. The management acts as a brokerage, dipping into the bank to buy subsidiaries. When they don't produce, they are sold off.

•

The point is that while the Transportation Department works on studies of insurance systems, the entire industry is changing. In all likelihood any study of the insurance business will turn out to be irrelevant, unless it is accompanied by some effort to come to grips with the new investment conglomerates.

A moderate reform of automobile insurance probably would require devising a more "efficient" system—removal of lawyers who argue the cases and run the prices up, or getting rid of agents whose commissions jack up the price. The government might also assume general supervisory powers over insurance, and through a corporation modeled on the Federal Deposit Insurance Corp., check books, make sure the companies stay solvent, that they don't discriminate against blacks or Mexicans and that there is competition in the industry, which, in turn, will bring about reduced rates. Proposals along these lines are coming from within Congress as well as from the more progressive sector of the industry.

But such reforms won't change the insurance industry's ability to fix rates. The object of the game will stay the same: milk the driver to feed the investment trust.

Congressman William T. Cahill (R, N.J.) suggests removing small auto insurance claims, which constitute the bulk of the business, to a federal agency that would compensate victims of accidents regardless of fault for out-of-pocket expenses to a maximum of $2,500. The simplest and most expeditious way to provide automobile insurance is for the government to run the business, perhaps through the social security system. Everyone in the nation should be covered by automobile, life and accident and health insurance. Medicare is a feeble beginning in this general direction. Perhaps Senator Hart can be persuaded to broaden his antitrust inquiry into the insurance business and compare the US system with insurance programs in places like New Zealand and some of the Canadian provinces.

252

Dirty Deal in Small Loans

by JAMES RIDGEWAY

Finance companies are making a killing on insurance. Tacked on to their high interest rates is an exorbitant charge for insurance, used to repay the loan in case the borrower dies. It takes the risk out of lending.

But what the customers probably don't know is that relatively few borrowers die before loans are repaid. Much of the premiums are pure profit, and a good bit of it is funneled back to the finance company either in the form of commission or because the loan company owns the insurance company.

In a speech in Chicago in October 1966, Dean Sharp, an assistant counsel of the Senate antitrust and monopoly subcommittee, said an unpublished committee report on credit life insurance indicates that borrowers have been overcharged $700 million since 1959.

About 80 percent of the $72 billion in outstanding consumer debt is covered by credit life insurance. This is financing for automobile and household appliances as well as personal loans.

Premiums for credit life vary around the country, and run from a low of 37.5 cents per $100 borrowed per year charged by General Motors Acceptance Corp., the biggest finance company, to $2 per $100 asked by the small loan companies located near military bases. A usual premium is $1 per $100. The insurance usually is calculated on the whole loan and must be paid at the outset. This can add up: A Washington finance company recently quoted a price of $30 for insurance on a three-year, $3,000 loan.

Credit life is a relatively small part of the insurance industry, but it is the fastest growing. The business is lucrative because costs are low, and

Reprinted by permission of the New Republic, © *1966, Harrison-Blaine of New Jersey, Inc.*

borrowers seldom howl. Once in the hands of a finance company they are too beaten down to figure out the different charges which frequently are hidden. Last year 63 million borrowers paid insurance companies $590 million in premiums for credit life. The major costs to the insurer are death payments, but they only came to $280 million. James H. Hunt, Vermont's insurance commissioner, and one of the people concerned about the high cost of this insurance, said that actuarial studies showed the cost of a claim to be only 30 cents per $100 borrowed. The insurance companies themselves have said that administrative expenses run a bit under 5 cents per $100. This brings total cost to 35 cents. So, if a company charges the usual $1 per $100 rate, it comes out with a profit of 65 cents.

This system can result in rosy profits. For example, Old Republic Life Insurance Co. of Chicago is one of the biggest firms specializing in credit life and writes little else. In 1965 Old Republic reported premiums of $62.6 million and paid out death benefits of $23.3 million. This suggests a gross profit of 63 percent.

The interests of the finance and insurance companies frequently coincide. The insurance company pays the finance firm a commission on the credit life sold and, of course, the more made in premiums, the higher the commission. At the end of a good year, it is common practice for the insurance company to kick back profits to the finance company. This is known in the trade as the retrospective rate credit. Thus, competition works in reverse. Instead of looking around for the cheapest insurance for its borrowers, it is very much in the interest of the finance company to work the rates as high as possible.

Moreover, some of the biggest finance companies own the insurance companies that write policies on their loans. Under this double-headed arrangement, the parent finance company makes money on interest as well as from premiums, and it can charge the insurance subsidiary management fees for handling the records.

There are even more subtle renderings. Commissioner Hunt has said,

> In examining the statement of a very large and well-regarded stock insurance company, I noticed that most of their credit life business was being reinsured. There was no actuarial reason for this, so I made some inquiries. It turned out that this company wrote credit insurance for a large finance company. The deal was that the insurance company reinsured over 95 percent of the incoming credit business with an insurance company controlled by the finance company. About 45 percent of the premium was profit, and, of course, all but a prenegotiated part of this went to the wholly-owned subsidiary of the finance company. For a price, then, the finance company bought the good name of the insurance company and,

to boot, avoided the appearance of controlling the business, whereas, in fact, they did.

Mr. Hunt makes this seem all rather conspiratorial. But there are no laws prohibiting finance companies from owning insurance companies; nor in most places are there any restrictions on their dealings with insurance companies. These transactions are in the open and apparently regarded as a common business practice, as the following examples suggest:

CIT Financial Corp., second biggest finance company in the country, buys credit life from Connecticut General, which then reinsures these policies with a wholly-owned subsidiary of CIT called North American Co. (Figures for North American were not readily available. But Connecticut General says that it took in $13.5 million in credit life premiums in 1965 and paid out $6.7 million in death benefits for a gross profit of 50 percent. As a reinsurer North American shared in the risks and the profits.)

Associates Investment Co., another of the largest finance companies, also owns an insurance subsidiary which writes some of the credit life on its loans. The way it got into the business is interesting. In 1953, Associates wanted to move into the insurance field. At the time, Old Republic was issuing credit life policies for the finance company. Associates then set up an insurance subsidiary called Alinco. Old Republic reinsured Associates' business with Alinco and handled the administrative details. Alinco had no office or any salaried employees. An accountant employed by another of Associates' subsidiaries spent one day a month taking care of the books. Despite the simplicity of its operation between 1953 and 1959, Alinco's financial success was striking. Its net gain from operations during that period, before federal income taxes but after paying its expenses and share of death benefits, was in excess of $28.5 million. In 1957 Associates acquired Capitol Life Insurance Co. of Denver, an old line insurance company, and subsequently shut down Alinco.

An Associates' official said insurance rates range from 50 to 75 cents per $100 borrowed. In 1965 Capitol Life, which writes half of Associates' policies, reported premiums of $4.3 million and death payments of $1.6 million (gross gain of 63 percent).

Other companies have insurance subsidiaries. Commercial Credit Co. owns American Health & Life Insurance Co. which writes policies on the parent's loans. An American official said an insurance rate is $1 per $100. American showed premiums of $10.6 million in 1965 against death payments of $5.8 million for a gross gain of 45 percent.

Financial General controls Bankers Security Life Insurance Society. The Transamerica Corp. owns Pacific Finance Corp. which, in turn, controls Pacific Fidelity Life Insurance Co.

In general, the profits for insurance companies in this business range

255

from about 36 percent to 60 percent. Commenting on this situation, Commissioner Hunt said, "If normal competition, rather than reverse competition, could exist there would be a tremendous reduction in costs of credit insurance passed on to borrowers. I would estimate that, based on current premium income, the savings would exceed $100 million nationwide annually."

Payment of death benefits probably has risen during the past year because of the war. Many finance companies thrive on army camps. One congressional investigator reports helicopter pilots at Fort Rucker, Ala., about to leave for Vietnam, are buying automobiles and household appliances. They borrow the money and it is insured against their death at rates up to $2 per $100. The Defense Department has approved 93 life insurance companies to solicit business on military posts. One-third of these write credit life, and include companies charging high rates.

As in the case of all insurance, regulation of credit life is left in the hands of the states. Thirty-one states have no effective regulation over rates charged. Massachusetts recently sought to bring down rates by limiting the premium to 50 cents per $100 per year. Both Vermont and Connecticut have passed laws prohibiting lenders from making a profit on credit insurance in the small loan field.

In his Chicago speech, Dean Sharp called for federal regulation. Credit life insurance on any loans under $1,000 should be banned outright. The risks to the finance companies are too slight to bother with. And the Congress should make it illegal for a finance company to profit on insurance.

The Repossessed

by GILBERT B. FRIEDMAN

Mr. Jones sits nervously in his chair talking across the desk to his attorney. "If they attach my wages," he says, "I'll be fired from my job. I had a buddy at work who was fired just last week on his first attachment."

"What is the basis of the claim the collection agency is suing you for?" his attorney asks.

"I don't really understand," says Mr. Jones.

> A few months ago I bought a new used car and I got behind in the payments. Ninety-eight dollars a month was just too much. So they came and took the car. Then I received a notice that they were going to sell the car unless I paid the full balance of $1,300. Fat chance! If I can't pay $98 a month, how am I going to pay $1,300 all at once? So they sold it, but now they want $500 more from me. How can they do that after they sold the car, anyway? I have no way of getting that kind of money, and if they attach my wages, I'll be fired for sure. What can I do?

This sort of conversation takes place in attorneys' offices throughout the country. The $500 for which this man is being sued is the amount named in a legal action known as the "deficiency" judgment, and it is a last step in a common and rather unsavory chain of events.

The story goes something like this: Mr. and Mrs. Jones see an ad that says, "Come on in to Uncle Steve's Friendly Used Car Lot and pick out the new used car of your choice. No money down, low monthly payments, and 36 months to pay." So they go on in and pick out a shiny late-model sedan with a placard in the windshield saying "Only $50 a month!" They talk to Uncle Steve, their friendly used car dealer, and things get a bit more complicated. First there is a $500 loan from Sharkskin Finance Company for the first month's payment. Sharkskin will have the Jones' household furniture as security and Uncle Steve gets a kickback from Sharkskin for steering in the Joneses. Then there are the finance charges, the credit life, health and accident insurance, and a few other charges. By the time Mr. Jones has signed all the papers he's agreed to pay $98 a month. The funny thing is that as he drives the shiny new car out of the lot, Mr. Jones doesn't know that he's paying more than $2,000 for the car.

For several months the Joneses get those payments in promptly. But pretty soon they're feeling pinched; they can't afford the car, and besides it isn't running all that well. So they stop making payments; Uncle Steve sends them a couple of letters; then one day Mr. Jones comes out to get into his car, and it isn't there. It has been repossessed.

When a car is "repossessed," it is usually taken back legally. There are firms whose specialty is "stealing" back cars of buyers who fail to keep up on their payments. They spot the car from its license plate and description; hot-wire it, if necessary; and simply drive it off. These firms are acting entirely within the law; since Mr. Jones didn't pay for the car in full, he is merely the registered owner. The legal owner is Uncle Steve or the financer that made the principal loan.

When Uncle Steve gets the car back, he sells it to a wholesaler—not for the $2,000 plus, but for $900. And this is where the deficiency judgment comes in.

When the car is repossessed, Mr. Jones still owes $1,300. Uncle Steve has sold it for only $900. So he sends Mr. Jones a bill for the difference plus repossession charges and "reasonable" attorney fees, $500 total. Since Mr. Jones can't come up with the money, Uncle Steve goes to court and gets the deficiency judgment. Nor is that all. Mr. Jones still owes Sharkskin Finance Company that $500 he used to make the first payment, and if he stops making monthly installments on that, they'll come and get his furniture. Quite likely there will be another deficiency judgment.

Every state allows deficiency judgments. It's big business. Merchandise is sold at ridiculously high prices with little or no down payment required. What is stressed is the monthly or weekly payment, never the total cost. It used to be that merchants gave credit to make a profit on the product they were selling; today many merchants sell merchandise to make their main profit on the finance charges.

When a person is served with a summons and complaint notifying him that he is being sued for a deficiency judgment, he is also usually served a paper informing him that his wages are to be garnisheed, a modern parallel to debtor's prison. Garnishment means that the court orders the employer to withhold a certain amount of an employee's earnings, as much as one-half depending on the state, to satisfy the judgment. The employer must withhold this amount of the employee's wages and turn it over to the sheriff. If the employer doesn't do this, he can get himself into legal difficulty for failure to obey a court order. The garnishment can be made even before Mr. Jones has a chance to argue the case in court. The bank or finance company needs merely file suit. The wages are then attached and the sheriff holds the money until the outcome of the suit is decided.

In most states, Mr. Jones can file a "claim of exemption," contesting this garnishment, but this is seldom done. The claim of exemption is technical and rarely done without the aid of an attorney, and, even then, it often proves useless since the attorney for the other side can demand a court hearing. If the original item purchased was a necessity, usually no claim of exemption is allowed.

Most employers find the whole procedure of having their employees' wages garnisheed a bother to their office payroll staff. It has been estimated that it costs some large employers as much as $60,000 a year just to process these garnishments. In addition, many employers take garnishments as a sign of their employees' unreliability. So many employers, large and small, fire the employee. Thousands of employees each year are discharged from employment for this reason: their wages were garnisheed once too often.

What can an attorney do for a person thus threatened? He can look to see if there has been any violation of any of the technical laws surrounding the sale of the car. If so he can write the dealer that his client wants to rescind the contract, and he states that if they sue, he, the lawyer, will defend all actions. Sometimes that ends it. Sometimes, even if everything is proper and only a fairly modest judgment has been brought against the person, some type of pay plan can be worked out after compromising the claim anywhere from one-third to one-half. But if there is no hope for a settlement, the only thing the attorney can do is advise his client to go through bankruptcy proceedings, wiping out this along with all his other debts.

Unfortunately filing bankruptcy is sometimes not the end. If the finance company cannot get the debtor to reaffirm the debt in writing after he files bankruptcy—and the finance companies have a whole chapter in their manual on the various techniques to do this—then they try another device. The rule is that if a creditor can prove that the debtor obtained the credit (loan on a car) through fraud, then this debt is *not* discharged.

On an application for credit or a loan, there is always a space on the form where the customer is supposed to list all of his debts and financial obligations. But on most forms of this kind, the space allowed is about three lines, hardly room for the majority of customers who buy heavily on credit. In addition, the man helping the customer will often gloss over this portion of the form, allowing the customer to believe that this portion is not of great importance. Nevertheless, the customer, on the bottom of the form signs a statement which certifies the completeness and truth of all replies. After bankruptcy is filed, the finance company can claim that there is a discrepancy between the amount of money the debtor listed in the three lines provided and the total debts listed in the bankruptcy action. If they had known his true situation, they say, they would never have made the loan. In short, the debtor through fraud and deceit has tricked the poor finance company. Although few of these suits are successful, they continue to keep a cloud over the debtor's head and can be used to force some kind of settlement of the claim.

Bankruptcy takes paperwork and time, and if, upon hearing that the debtor intends to file bankruptcy, the finance company, nevertheless, goes through with the wage attachment, the debtor may find himself a *jobless* bankrupt. The most frequent victims of this system are people with low incomes, often in minority groups, for whom the easy credit policies so widely promoted and advertised seem an ideal way to get ahead. (The President's Commission on Civil Disorders found that deceptive sales and credit practices are among the 12 bitterest grievances in American ghettos.)

•

One way to break the system would be the elimination of deficiency judgments and garnishment of wages. In 1961 California passed a law outlawing deficiency judgments. Unfortunately, it left one exception: automobiles, which account for 42 percent of all credit sales. A law prohibiting deficiency judgments would make auto dealers check a prospective purchaser's credit more carefully, or at least not let the purchaser become committed to payments he obviously can't keep up, in view of his income. And if the dealer did sell the car and payments weren't made, the dealer would have to choose *between* the car and the payments. *Today, he can get both.*

The case for the elimination of wage garnishments is even stronger. Three states, Florida, Texas and Pennsylvania, have laws prohibiting attachment of wages. Comparable legislation in the rest of the states or by the Congress would provide a new kind of security to millions of Americans who live in dread of being fired. They would know that their job was safe from creditors and that the money needed to feed their families would be there. The welfare rolls would be reduced by the number of families forced into unemployment because their bosses wanted to eliminate unnecessary wage expense.

There are two arguments made by the commercial world against this change in the law. One is that credit will not be given as easily, and the poor man will suffer most because he is least able to pay cash. Even if you accept this premise, the fact, as given by the Associated Credit Bureau, is that there is just as much credit given in states where garnishment of wages is not allowed as there is in states where it is. This is measured by the ratio of installment credit to retail sales, and it is approximately $1 installment credit for every $4 retail sales in all states regardless of what their garnishment law is.

The second argument is that the percentage of recovery on accounts assigned to collection agencies tends to be lower in states where wage garnishment cannot be freely gotten. This argument does not hold up either. In New York where the creditor can garnishee only 10 percent of a man's wages, or New Jersey or Nebraska where he is limited to 20 percent, there is a higher percentage of recovery of debts than in California where the creditor can get 50 percent of a man's wages.

There is a direct relationship between the ease of garnishment and the rate of bankruptcy filing. The easier it is to garnishee a worker's wages in a state, the higher the number of bankruptcies filed. And once a straight bankruptcy is filed, most creditors don't get a cent. The number of bankruptcies that are filed is increasing by a rapid rate, and 90 percent of them are not businesses but individual working people.

Two versions of a Truth-in-Lending Law, making creditors spell out the yearly rate of interest, have passed the Senate and House. The House version has a more significant and less publicized provision on garnishment. Spurred on by Representative Leonor Sullivan (D, Mo.), the House version outlaws the garnishment of wages on the first $30, permitting garnishment of only 10 percent of wages for a family over $30. If this provision isn't killed in Senate-House conference, we shall have taken a long step forward.

Big Brother Keeps Tabs on Insurance Buyers

by STANFORD N. SESSER

In 1967 Retail Credit Co. supplied 35 million reports on people to 40,000 customers. From its 1,800 offices across North America it took in $135 million in revenues. Yet it has retained almost complete anonymity. Operating in a shroud of secrecy and beyond the scrutiny of any federal or state regulation, this Atlanta-based firm has built up files on 45 million Americans; and not just statistics on names, addresses and family. Retail Credit inspectors scrutinize the drinking habits of everyone they investigate. A given file might touch on any number of allegations, including rumors of extramarital affairs and homosexuality. The individual concerned has no idea the investigation is taking place and never has the opportunity to answer any of the charges.

The name Retail Credit is misleading. Except for a subsidiary operation, it does no credit checking. The vast bulk of its business comes from investigations of people who apply for insurance; Retail Credit brags it works for every major insurance company in North America. The second largest source of the company's revenue stems from investigating job applicants.

Here's how it works: Mr. X applies for, say, life insurance; the insurance agent tells him the company will let him know if he can get a policy; the company contacts Retail Credit, which assigns an inspector to do a report on X; the inspector visits X's neighbors and business associates, writes up a report and sends it to the insurer, who decides on the basis of the report whether coverage should be granted.

Reprinted by permission of the New Republic, © *1968, Harrison-Blaine of New Jersey, Inc.*

Thus the prejudices of insurance companies must of necessity be the prejudices of Retail Credit. If they don't want to insure homosexuals, Retail Credit must find out if the applicants *are* homosexuals. If they decide not to write policies for Negroes, Retail Credit must pay attention to the applicant's race.

Retail Credit's *Inspector's Handy Guide*, copyrighted in 1962, revised in 1965, and dropped only in the fall of 1967 after excerpts from it appeared in *The Wall Street Journal*, lists the points that should be covered in the inspection report. Under a section headed "West Indian Island Races" (including Puerto Ricans) it asks: "Is the applicant pure Caucasian or a mixture? Describe the individual if a mixture of races to show whether predominantly Caucasian or Negro. It is not practicable to attempt to estimate percentages."

The guide has the following questions about applicants for insurance who are Mexican-Americans: "Is he a permanent resident or the floater type?" "Does he occupy a hovel type of residence or a good substantial home?" "Does applicant associate with Mexicans or with Anglo-Saxons?"

When a church applied for fire insurance, the inspector was required to note "whether Baptist, Episcopalian, Methodist, etc., and whether the congregation is composed of Negro or white people, or general racial makeup of congregation." Information about apartment houses included "racial descent" of tenants, and a report on workmen's compensation would state "predominant races" in the neighborhood.

Retail Credit claims it cut out such reporting practices last year, and that it will no longer supply racial information unless insurance companies specifically request it. According to Charles M. Watt, Retail Credit vice president and secretary, 100 auto insurance companies and 16 life insurance companies have already made such requests. Mr. Watt won't name the companies or give their size.

Retail Credit officials are hesitant to discuss in detail their investigative techniques. But no such reluctance exists on the part of their main competitor, Hooper-Holmes Bureau Inc., which has files on nine million people. Hooper-Holmes and Retail Credit both say their operations are identical.

In his headquarters in Morristown, N. J., Frederick E. King, president of Hooper-Holmes, describes the procedure of an inspector suspicious of an extramarital affair: "You go to a neighbor and establish rapport," he says. "Then you ask, 'What's your opinion of X's home life; how do you think of him as a family man?' This will usually elicit some hint—through the expression on their faces or the way they answer. Then you start digging. You press them as far as they go, and if they become recalcitrant, you go somewhere else. If you go to enough people, you get it." Homosexuality, Mr. King asserts, "is one of the most difficult things to determine." But, he points out, "If you have that sixth sense that something is wrong, you dig. The tip-off is their mode of living, their circle of friends and the organizations they belong to." In defense of this line of inquiry, Mr. King says that insurance companies are interested only in the odds, not the morals, and that "a life insurance applicant who is a homosexual is a greater risk."

When this information goes into a file, it is available to almost all comers. The State Department, FBI and other federal agencies as a standard practice use Retail Credit's and Hooper-Holmes' data. "The FBI is constantly in our files," Mr. King states. For a price, anyone can buy the material. You simply have your company make an inquiry under the guise of an employment check, and the report gets mailed out.

There is one exception to easy access—the person who wants to see his own record. Suppose an insurance company turns you down because a neighbor characterized you to Retail Credit as a homosexual. Under the contract with Retail Credit, your insurance agent can tell you only that you were considered a bad risk. He can't repeat the charge, tell you an inspection report had been done, or even mention Retail Credit's name. If you should get wind of what happened and go to Retail Credit, it won't do you any good—the company will refuse to confirm or deny it did a report on you. According to Mr. Watt, Retail Credit will merely invite a person to write a statement about whatever might be bothering him, and "we tell him if we did a report, we'll send the statement to anyone who asked about him."

No one at Retail Credit claims the information on all of the 45 million records is correct. A Pennsylvania man tells what happened when his wife was turned down for major medical coverage by an insurance company:

> I refused to accept this decision and carried my complaint in a direct visit with the New York office of the insurance company involved without satisfaction. I further carried my complaint to the insurance commissioner of Pennsylvania and he was unable to learn the specific reason for this rejection. Retail Credit refused to grant me an interview and thus my only recourse was through the courts. But the best attorneys advised me that it was virtually impossible to inspect their confidential files.
>
> Through considerable expense and through a means that I do not have liberty to state, I was able to learn that my wife was charged with being an alcoholic. Yet my wife has never consumed more than a dozen drinks in the 20 years of our marriage. To this day no major insurance company will cover her, yet I have never been given the opportunity to correct this horrible fallacy.

Retail Credit also owns, through a subsidiary, 62 local credit bureaus from Atlanta to Montreal that contain files on millions of additional people. But unlike the insurance inspections, the credit files concentrate on financial rather than moral hazards, covering income, nonpayment of bills, lawsuits.

Retail Credit credit bureaus are all affiliated with the Associated Credit Bureaus of America Inc., an organization of 2,200 local bureaus that allows each one access to the combined total of 110 million files. All of which raises an intriguing possibility: If Retail Credit and the ACB of A ever decided to combine credit files with insurance inspection reports, the network would encompass virtually the entire life history of every adult American.

The Unbondables

by GILBERT B. FRIEDMAN

In 1966, the University of Southern California proposed building a multi-purpose health center in Watts. A group of Negro civic leaders and businessmen had the vision of using local Negro labor for the construction work, and with this in mind the BBWC Construction Company was born. This company was accepted as the lowest bidder. The lowest subcontractor to BBWC for the plumbing work was Cecil Hamilton, a Negro plumber with 20 years' experience. The lowest bid on the electrical work was submitted by Cliff Allen, who had an integrated electrical contracting firm. The first firm accepted to work on the job was Bailey's Construction Company. Lloyd Bailey, who heads this firm, was born in Watts and has lived there 50 years. He employs local men, as does every other subcontractor working on his team. Fifty Watts men were hired by agreement with the local union.

The university's contract with BBWC was negotiated, however, on the understanding that the company would be able to secure the necessary surety bonds. It wasn't. And it did not merely try one or two companies; it tried a dozen. No insurance company would furnish them with the necessary bonds for this $500,000 job.

Every time government money is used, as it would be in this instance, contractors must submit surety bonds guaranteeing reimbursement in case the contractor does not perform as required. This rule applies in various guises whether the financing is local, state or federal. For example, the Miller Act requires surety bonds in the construction of all federal buildings. Under other departments, such as the Department of Housing and Urban

Development (HUD), surety bonds are required under a policy decision. Many private developers also require surety bonds of contractors and subcontractors. The practical effect is that small minority contractors are denied work.

This system of surety bonds even controls who can bid on a government-financed job. In order to submit a bid, the contractor must also submit a "bid bond." This bond insures the developer that the lowest bidder will be able to get the *other* bonds for the job. If he does not get these bonds, then the bid bond, usually 10 percent of the bid, is forfeited. Assuming the contractor does get the job, he must then post two bonds. One is a performance bond as security for the faithful performance of his contract. The other is a labor and material bond of not less than 50 percent of his contract price as security for the payment of all persons performing labor and furnishing materials. The total coverage of both bonds equals 100 percent of the cost of the project. It is next to impossible for a small contractor to "lick the system." Even if he could raise the required 10 percent of the contract price, he could hardly be expected to raise 100 percent "cash on the line" of the total contract price in place of the unobtainable bonds.

It would be nice to report that in the case of BBWC the various community groups sat around conference tables with the insurance companies, "reasoned together," and got around the obstacle of surety bonds. But it didn't happen that way. Instead, the "Tony Jacquett Compliance Plan" went into effect. Tony Jacquett was a young black man in Watts who told the various authorities that unless black men were allowed to build this health center in Watts, he was going to burn it down after the white men built it. This was how the BBWC Construction Company overcame the seemingly insurmountable obstacle of the surety bond. Not very businesslike, but effective.

Other small contractors have not been so fortunate as BBWC. Alladin Electric Inc., for example, is an electrical contractor in Berkeley, California. Ray Dones, its founder, has been in business since 1953. Alladin employed six full-time electricians, all of them Negroes, and an Oriental office manager. Alladin used to do most of its work on single-family, small duplex buildings. But with the recent slump in construction, this kind of job has come to a near standstill. There is, however, a great deal of building going on, most of it government-financed. But Alladin can't get the surety bonds. As a result, Alladin Electric has had to lay off two of its six electricians.

In 1967, the Oakland Council of Churches sponsored the construction of a housing development for the elderly, called Satellite Homes. The project was 100 percent federally financed. Officials of the council called Mr. Dones and others from the community and specifically asked how they could make sure that there would be adequate minority representation in the work force. Mr. Dones suggested that the four separate apartment houses to be built be let out as four separate jobs. Six minority contractors

267

of the San Francisco Bay area had pooled their resources and formed the Trans-Bay Construction Company so they could bid as general contractors on one job as joint venturers. They suggested four separate bids, because they knew that they would never be able to get a bid bond for the total project—$2.3 million. The council architect and others refused to accept this or any of the other suggestions of the minority contractors. The Trans-Bay Construction Company was unable to obtain the bid bond. Satellite Homes today is being built with only a token force of blacks on the job and no black contractors. As of July 1968 there is not one black contractor in the San Francisco Bay area on any sizable federally financed construction, although there are about 125 black contractors and subcontractors in the area.

In April 1967, Alladin Electric submitted a low bid for $130,000 electrical subcontract to the general contractor on a Navy job at Hunters Point in one of San Francisco's ghetto districts. Alladin was required by the general contractor to get a surety bond. Mr. Dones knew that he could not get one for the whole job, so he subcontracted $50,000 worth of the contract. Continental Insurance Company then stated they might issue the surety bonds if Alladin got $10,000 more in cash in its business. Alladin did. Next Continental Insurance Company suggested that if Alladin got a $25,000 bank letter of credit, a loan the bank agrees to give you if you need it in the future, they might issue it. Alladin got that. Continental continued to delay. They never said no; they just wouldn't say yes. Finally the general contractor gave the job to the next lowest bidder because Alladin could not get the surety bonds. This is what minority contractors face.

•

Some contend that the main reason black contractors have not been able to get surety bonds is that they do not furnish the necessary information to the insurance company in sufficient time before the deadline for the company to do the necessary underwriting investigation. This is partially true. But the reason is that most general contractors who get the job do not usually require their subcontractors to furnish surety bonds. When, however, a general contractor wants to throw a stumbling block in the path of the lowest subcontractor, one thing he can do is require him to get a surety bond. The subcontractor is left with only a limited time in which to apply for the bond. (This argument does not apply when the black contractor is bidding as a *general* contractor and cannot get the surety bond, as in the Watts Health Center or the Satellite Homes project.)

On June 9, 1968, the Ford Foundation announced a $300,000 grant to the General and Specialty Contractors Association of Oakland for a model community action program aimed at providing a system through which target area contractors and subcontractors can become employers of the disadvantaged construction worker. One of the chief aims of the program is to increase the bonding capacity of the small general and subcontractors.

With the Ford grant, a Credit Bank will be created which will provide a portion of the training costs for the upgrading of minority construction contractors and, simultaneously, assist the small contractors willing to share in training workers. At present minority contractors' profit is too low to allow them to undertake a training program in any but the most limited scope. Under the Ford program, approximately 100 currently unemployed men will be trained and will have steady work over a three-year period.

The bonding companies require, among other things, that the contractor have an adequate amount of unencumbered working capital to ensure that he will be able to complete the job. As it is customary for the developer to hold back 10 percent of the contract price until the job has been completed, the bonding companies use this figure as the basis for their liquidity requirement. Therefore, in order for a contractor to obtain bonding for a $200,000 job, the contractor must have a minimum of $20,000 in cash which is not offset by a liability of any kind. Since even some big contractors cannot meet this stiff requirement, one contractor will often lend part of his bonding capacity to another for a percentage of the profits. But small contractors neither have nor can borrow any bonding capacity; their liquid cash position must be increased in order to make it possible, under the present system of bonding, to employ the men they want to train. The Ford grant will do this on the basis of a work plan submitted by the contractor in which he outlines the number of men that he would train. If a cooperating contractor submits a job he plans to bid on to the Credit Bank's board, and if the board decides the contractor's proposal is reasonable, they will advance him the necessary money, for example, $20,000 to meet the requirements of the insurance company. This advance is paid back by the contractor to the Credit Bank before his profit is taken out of the completed job. As this payment does not involve a financial obligation, either implicit or explicit, the funds could be used to meet the liquidity requirements, and thereby increase the bonding capacity by $200,000. However, if insurance companies continue to treat black contractors as they do today, this program will be merely a gesture. Relief on a nationwide scale is badly needed.

Ultimately, the question is whether surety bonds on government projects are necessary. Supposedly, they serve as assurance that the taxpayer's money made available will be adequately protected, will not be dissipated, and will be effectively used for the purposes intended. But this isn't at stake when there is a federally financed project. The government maintains very careful control. All buildings, public or private, are inspected during construction, but none so thoroughly as government buildings. At every step of the construction federal inspectors check to see that the work is properly completed. No one is paid until the work has met specifications.

Despite these precautions, surety bonds are always required. When one considers the fact that the government pays all the premiums for these bonds, the situation becomes absurd. The cost of the bonds is added into the price of the bid as a direct cost by the contractor, and the government ends up paying more. Would it not be more economical for the federal government to be a self-insurer, rather than indirectly pay the insurance companies huge sums in the form of premiums? Where there are federally controlled inspections and other safeguards, failures by contractors could be held to a minimum.

•

Even if surety bonds are essential, the present method of securing them is questionable. There are case decisions by both the federal and state courts which have held that similar delegations of authority to private organizations without standards or procedural safeguards were unconstitutional as violations of the aggrieved's rights to due process of law.

For example, a New York statute delegating to a private "Jockey Club" the power to license horse owners, trainers, and jockeys was challenged in the court by Mr. Jule Fink who had applied for a license to race his horses in New York state during 1949 and was turned down by the Jockey Club. The New York Supreme Court in upholding Mr. Fink's position said that the powers given to this private association were "such an abdication as to be patently an unconstitutional relinquishment of legislative powers." The case with the insurance company issuing surety bonds is a step further removed, because Congress has not delegated this function of who can qualify for surety bonds. The administrator has delegated it to the private party with no procedural safeguards against any arbitrariness, or unfairness on the part of the insurance companies. The insurance company is left to be the judge whether someone is "sound" enough to undertake a project. The federal government takes great pains and sets criteria for which insurance companies can sell surety bonds on federal building contracts. The limit of the amount they can sell is published in an annual list by the Treasury Department (Treasury Department Circular 570, 1967 Revision). An insurance company may request a hearing with the Treasury Department for a review of the decision. Yet once an insurance company falls within the criteria it is free in its own absolute discretion to say whether it will allow a contractor to place his bid. The contractor, however, has no right to request a hearing for review of the insurance company's decision.

New programs to create jobs for minority workers are needed, but it should be made clear that there are in America today skilled minority craftsmen in the construction industry, many of whom own their own business and employ minority persons, who have been frozen out by the present system of issuing surety bonds.

Perhaps the President, Congress, or the various government agencies

270

could set up standards. The Secretary of the Department of Housing and Urban Development, for example, might establish new regulations by which a contractor who is turned down by several insurance companies could apply to the Secretary for a waiver of the bond requirements. After an investigation by HUD, the bonds could be waived in certain situations and additional requirements set up in lieu of the bond if they were thought necessary to protect the government's interest. For example, smaller companies which do not have the large staff of business experts could be required to use companies such as Builders Control of Northern California, a company which oversees the financial aspects of construction work and makes inspections, etc. to see that the job is going properly and is often used in lieu of a surety bond on private jobs. The fee they charge is almost identical to that of the premium for a surety bond.

The National Advisory Commission on Civil Disorders' insurance report, entitled "Meeting the Insurance Crisis of Our Cities," touched on this problem. Its authors stated, ". . . Obtaining these necessary bonds is often difficult, if not impossible, for the small contractor who seeks to perform construction work in urban areas. This restricts the ability of these contractors to expand their business and reduces competition for construction work in the urban area." The commission proposed that a federal corporation reinsure these insurance companies that sell bid and performance bonds to small contractors in ghetto areas. This would mean the government's taking over all or some of the risk of the insurance companies. This suggestion becomes somewhat ludicrous, however, when one considers the fact that the federal government pays all the premiums to begin with, since the contractors just add the premiums into their bid. Under this approach all the insurance company would do is collect the premiums while the federal government would pay and then take the risk. It looks pretty— if you happen to be an insurance executive.

271

Cheap Life Insurance

by JAMES RIDGEWAY
and DAVID WIGGINS

A person can go mad trying to choose among the different companies selling life insurance. While the business is by nature complex, and made additionally so because of the agent's intricate sales pitch, you can begin to get a rough idea of how inexpensive insurance could be by looking at the State Life Fund, a bare-bones company operated by the Wisconsin Insurance Department. It was set up in 1911 following the big insurance scandals and amidst the Progressive fervor. In 1966 the Fund sold insurance at close to half the price of the commercial companies.

You can buy insurance from the Fund if you meet the physical requirements. You don't have to be a resident of Wisconsin, but just in the state long enough to complete the transaction. Because it neither advertises nor uses agents, the Fund doesn't do much business, accounting for less than one percent of all life insurance sold in the state.

Making true cost comparisons between life insurance companies is taxing to the mind, and even the experts disagree on the right way to do it; but you can appreciate the advantages of buying from the Fund by the following examples: A $10,000 whole life policy issued by the Fund to a 30-year-old man in good health would run $217.40, less a first-year dividend of $100.90 for a net cost of $116.50. Dividends get higher as time goes on. The same kind of policy issued by commercial companies would typically range from about $160 a year for a policy bought from a stock company (it doesn't pay dividends), to $180 for a dividend-paying mutual company. To pick one example, the Metropolitan Life Insurance Co. offers a whole life policy beginning at age 30 for an annual premium of $211.20. Dividends begin in the second year at $17.

Reprinted by permission of the New Republic, © *1966, Harrison-Blaine of New Jersey, Inc.*

Term insurance, which generally has no cash value and can't be used as collateral against loans, is considerably cheaper than whole life. For $10,000 of term coverage beginning at age 30 and running to 65, the State Life Fund charges $161.50 a year, less a first-year dividend of $102.20, for a net of $59.30. A similar policy by a commercial company could run $120.

This is life insurance without frills, offering only a few standard types and with a limit per holder of $10,000. The Fund's office consists of some desks and filing cabinets in a corner of the Insurance Department in a state office building at Madison. The staff consists of three full-time workers. Factual information about the policies is reproduced cheaply and is available either at the receptionist's desk or by mail.

The Fund pays its own way, reimbursing state government for the floor space it occupies, for the time of the state employees utilized, and for the services of the state investment board which handles its investments. Critics sometimes argue the Life Fund is getting a free ride because it is so closely associated with the state government. But the state does not guarantee the Fund.

The Fund does not quite match the big private companies in investment earnings. Its success is the result of low operating costs, a negligible lapse rate and good mortality experience. In recent years the Fund's expenses amounted to only 3.9 percent of premiums written. By contrast Metropolitan Life Insurance Co. had expenses amounting to 16.5 percent of premiums. The Fund's lapse rate was less than 1 percent; rates of 5 percent and higher are common in the industry.

It saves money by not hiring agents, who substantially increase insurance costs. An agent usually gets 50 or 55 percent of the first-year premium. He is likely to receive 5 percent of the premium payments for a period up to nine years. While the agents make themselves out to be professionals on whose judgment you should depend, in fact they are under relentless pressure from the company to sell; many of them work part-time and are poorly trained. It is not uncommon to run into agents who appear to know little more about insurance than the customer.

When the State Life Fund went into business, part of its purpose was to provide inexpensive protection to workingmen, farmers, and other low-income people. But the intended beneficiaries never took to the idea, and after the first six years of operation only 461 policies had been issued. Since then, the organization has been periodically attacked by the insurance agents as the sort of evil associated with the Industrial Workers of the World. Nevertheless, some of them know a good deal when they see it, and buy policies from the Fund. As late as 1959, the Fund sold only 89 policies in 12 months. In the early 1960's the insurance interests sponsored a bill to stamp out the Fund, and as a result of the oratory about "unfair competition," and "socialism," the word got out the state was selling insurance cheap. This unintentional publicity paid off: Fund policies in force doubled between 1959 and 1965 to 6,000 for a total of $30 million in insurance.

Another relatively inexpensive kind of life insurance is offered by mutual savings banks in Massachusetts, New York and Connecticut. It is sold over the counter in the banks and is generally limited to $10,000 coverage per person. Usually one must either live or work in the state to get it. Banks within a single state achieve economies by pooling various administrative functions. There are no agents. In New York the banks do some radio advertising and send out blurbs to their customers.

In New York, a 30-year-old man in good health would pay $167.10 a year for a $10,000 straight life policy. Dividends begin the first year at $13.50 and move higher. Like the Life Fund in Wisconsin, savings bank life insurance grew out of the scandals in the early part of the century. This kind of insurance was first made legal in Massachusetts, where Louis D. Brandeis led the campaign. He had hoped it would offer cheap insurance to people of little means. But the idea never has caught on. It wasn't until 1938 that Governor Lehman got through the New York legislature an act permitting savings bank life; Connecticut's law followed in 1940. The insurance industry opposes extension of savings banks into the insurance field and helped beat down a bill in New Jersey. As it stands, savings banks are so tightly regulated by law that there is little chance of their offering much serious competition to the insurance companies which, despite the feeble efforts of state commissioners, are to all intents and purposes not regulated and free to do as they please.

The Veterans Administration offers a final interesting example that suggests what might be done in offering inexpensive life insurance coverage. The VA handles a number of inexpensive policies for veterans of different wars, and while in some of them there is an element of government subsidy, in general they pay their own way. National Service Life Insurance, which applied to men in the Second World War, is the largest program. There were 4.8 million policies amounting to $32 billion of insurance outstanding at the end of 1965. In this program, a $10,000 policy for a 30-year-old man would run $184.70, less a dividend of $72, for a net cost of $112.70 a year. While the government pays the cost of administering this policy, the expense comes to a little less than $4 per policy annually.

INDEX

Abbott Laboratories, 70, 76, 79, 92, 93
Abraham & Straus, 129
Accame, Dr., 78
Adams, John G., 163
Additives, 48–52
Admirals of the Flagship Fleet, 168–170
Advertising, 12, 15–18, 22, 128–132; of cigarettes, 117, 121, 122–123; of drugs, 91–94; of mutual funds, 147
Advertising Age, 118
Advisory Committee on Obstetrics and Gynecology, 110
Agriculture, Dept. of, 4, 44, 88, 115
Air fares, 151–153, 154–159, 165–167
Air routes, 160–164
Alessandroni, Walter C., 143
Alinco, 255
Alladin Electric Inc., 267, 268
Allen, Cliff, 266
Allen, George E., 230, 231
Allen Products Co., 67
Alpo Dog Food, 67
Alsmeyer, R. H., 54, 55
Ambassadors Club, 168, 169
American Airlines, 151, 156, 160, 161, 162, 163, 170
American Cancer Society, 118, 123
American Express, 251
American Health & Life Insurance Co., 255
American Insurance Association, 246
American Journal of Clinical Nutrition, The, 71
American Journal of Obstetrics and Gynecology, 98, 100, 101
American Marketing Associates, Inc., 135
American Meat Institute, 45, 51
American Medical Association, 63
American Quinine, 90
American Review of Respiratory Disease, The, 195
American Trial Lawyers Association, 230
Aqua-Rama, 143
Archer, Victor E., 187
Armour Pharmaceutical Co., 92
Arthur D. Little, Inc., 10, 250
Aspinall, Rep. Wayne, 185
Aspirin, 81

Associated Credit Bureau, 260
Associated Credit Bureaus of America Inc., 265
Associates Investment Co., 255
Atlantic & Pacific Tea Company (A&P), 21
Atlas Credit Corp., 143
Atomic Energy Commission, 64–65, 184
Atromid, 5, 94
Aurichio, Rosemary, 169
Automobile Manufacturers Association, 139
Ayerst Laboratories, 94, 107
Ayres, Robert, 223

BBWC Construction Company, 266
Bac*Os, 54, 57
Bacon, 50, 64, 65, 68
Bailey, Lloyd, 266
Bailey's Construction Company, 266
Bankers Security Life Insurance Society, 255
Barash, Peter, 24, 25
Bartlett, Sen. E. L., 169, 197
Batten, William, 11, 12
Baver, Prof. Raymond, 10
Bayer aspirin, 81, 83
Beef stroganoff, 53–56
Berman, Harold, 202
Black Lung, 188–196
Blatz, Prof. Hanson, 199
Block Drug Company, 131
Bonding, 266–271
Bontrae, 57
Book Week, 203
Borden *vs* FTC, 14
Botulism, 38
Boycotts, 21–24
Boyer, Robert, 55
Brand names, 13, 81–85, 86–90
Brandeis, Louis D., 274
Brandow, Dr. G. E., 11
Braniff Airlines, 161
Bridenstine, Louis, 210
Bristol Laboratories, 93
British Medical Journal, 102, 110, 113
British Medical Research Council, 110
Bukarest, Bernard, 145

275

Burack, Dr. Richard, 89
Burch, Francis B., 232
Bureau of Commercial Fisheries, 37
Bureau of Labor Statistics, 21, 30–31
Burley and Dark Leaf Tobacco Export
  Association, 115
Busby, Horace, 163
Bush, Dr. Vannevar, 88
Business crime, 134–140
Business Week, 17
Buzzell, Robert D., 16

CIT Financial Corp., 255
CNA Financial Corp., 251
Cahill, William T., 250, 252
Califano, Joseph, 163
Callaghan, Richard L., 130
Calorie Control Council, The, 76
Camarata, Judge William J., 145
Capital International Airways, 165
Capitol Life Insurance Co., 255
Caplowitz, David, 31, 33
Carter, Cliff, 163
Casavan Carrara Marble Co., 125
Casavan Industries, Inc., 125
Casavina, Paul R., 125
Cerruti, Frank A., 125, 126
Chain Store Age, 23
Chase, Howard, 10
Chubb & Son, 251
Cigarette Advertising Code, 117, 120
Cigarettes, 115–126
Chamber of Commerce, 175
Children's Cancer Research Foundation,
  8
Citizens Committee for Metropolitan
  Affairs, 84
Civil Aeronautics Board, 150, 160–164,
  165, 168–170, 171–172
Clarkson, Dr. M. R., 42
Clayton Antitrust Act, 19
Clifford, Clark, 162
Clinton Prison, 71
Clipper Club, 169
Coal Mine Safety Act, 189
Coal pneumoconiosis, 181, 188–196
Codex Alimentarius Commission, 51
Coles, Robert, 188–196
Colonels Club, 169
Color Additives Amendment, 49
Columbia University, 124
Commercial Credit Co., 255
Committee on Medical Research of the
  Office of Scientific Research and De-
  velopment, 87–88
Commoner, Prof. Barry, 4
Communications Research Center, 60
Condon, Frederick Hughes, 202, 203,
  204, 209, 215
Confidential Report on Environmental
  Conditions in the Metropolitan Chicago
  Area, 248
Congressional Record, 46
Consolidated Coal Company, 189
Consolidated Credit Corp., 142, 143
Consumer Frauds Bureau, 34
Consumer Marketing Service, 51
Consumer Price Index, 15
Consumers Union, 5, 6, 37, 133
Continental Airlines, 161, 162, 163, 169
Continental Insurance Companies, 248,
  250, 268
Continental National American Insurance,
  252
Contraceptives, oral, 104–108, 109–114

Cook, C. W., 17
Corvit, 90
Cotton, Sen. Norris, 169
Coumarin, 50
Council on Foods and Nutrition (AMA),
  8
Covington and Burling, 5
Crescent Investment Co., 144
Cron, Theodore, 130
Crookee, John, 163, 165–166
Curtis, Sen. Carl, 201
Cutlor, Lloyd, 139
Cyclamates, 6–7, 49, 70–73, 74–77, 78–80

Dairy Industry Newsletter, 63
Dairy products, artificial, 58–63
Danner, Richard, 208, 209, 210, 212, 214
Davies, Aleo P., 45, 46
Davies, Rose-Hoyt, 90
Defense Supply Agency, 90
DeLaney Clause, 49
Denver, 21
Dershowitz, Prof. Alan, 139
Dexedrine, 89
Dichter, Dr. Ernest, 26
Digitalis, 90
Dodd, Sen. Thomas, 230, 233, 238
Dominick, Sen. Peter H., 169
Dones, Ray, 267
Donovan, James, 233
Dowling, Edward, 10–20
Drugs, 81–85, 86–114; contraceptive,
  104–114; quinine, 95–97; thalidomide,
  98–103
Dubos, Dr. Rene, 8
Dynapen, 93
Dwyer, John, 205

E. R. Squibb & Sons, 70, 83, 89, 94
Eastern Airlines, 150, 161, 163
Eisenhower, Dwight David, 160, 161
Electro-thermal industries, 126
Encyclopedia Brittanica, 135, 136
Engines, 223–225
Enovid, 107, 113
Epstein, Dr. S. S., 8
Equanil, 90
Erythrocin, 93
Estrogen therapy, 104–108
European coal and steel community, 182
Evans, Dr. Robley D., 185, 186
Evans, Rowland, 163

Family Circle, 114
Farm Journal, 61
Farmington, 188, 189
Federal Aviation Agency, 152
Federal Communications Commission,
  122
Federal Deposit Insurance Corp., 252
Federal Food, Drug & Cosmetic Act, 49,
  56, 66, 75
Federal Meat Inspection Act, 54
Federal Metal and Non-Metallic Mine
  Safety Act, 184
Federal Radiation Council, 185
Federal Trade Commission, 18, 21, 22,
  33, 118, 135
Feminine Forever, 104, 105, 107
Feosol, 90
Fiber-lum Corp., 142, 143
Field Enterprises, 135, 137
Filled Milk Act, 59, 61, 62
Filters (cigarette), 120–121, 124–126
Financial General, 255

Fink, Jule, 270
Finney, Thomas, Jr., 162, 164
Fireman's Fund, 251
First Mercantile of New Jersey, 144
First National City Bank, 251
Fish, 37–40
Flavor and Extract Manufacturers
  Association, 49
Fleming, Alexander, 87
Flying Tiger Airlines, 161
Foley, Rep. Thomas, 45
Food, 2–9; advertising of, 15–17; cost of,
  21–25; in Washington ghetto, 27–29,
  31; quality of, 12–14
Food Additive Amendment, 49
Food Additive Orders, 49
Food and Drug Administration, 4, 5, 8;
  and additives, 49; and cyclamates, 70;
  and fish, 38; and irradiation, 64–69;
  and Lasix, 130; and milk standards,
  63; and Weekly Recall Report, 6
Food lobby, 10
Food and Agriculture Organization of
  the United Nations, 51
Food Chemical News, 51
Food from Farmer to Consumer, 12, 19
Food Technology, 7
Fonda, Henry, 171
Ford, Henry, 55
Fountain, Rep. L. H., 103
Francechini, Ray, 56, 57
Freedom of Information Act, 133, 134
Freeman, Orville, 22
Friedman, Gilbert B., 154–159, 240–245,
  257–261, 266–271
Furness, Betty, 165

G. D. Searle & Co., 107, 108
Gambrell, Charles W., 237
Games (in supermarkets), 22
Gamma radiation, 50
Gardner, John, 116
Gardner, W. David, 70–73, 74–77
Garner, Douglas, 183
Garner, Eola, 183
Geigy Pharmaceuticals, 92, 94
Geller, Eric, 135–137
General Finance Corp., 251
General Mills, 54, 55, 57, 129
General Motors, 206–207, 208–210, 211–
  215
General Motors Acceptance Corp., 253
Genetics, 6, 7, 78–80
Get Smart, 118
Ghiani, Dr., 78
Gillen, Vincent, 203, 204, 205, 208, 209,
  210, 211–215
Gillilland, Whitney, 163
Glenn, John, 129
Goddard, James, 65–66, 67, 92, 93, 110,
  114
Goldberger, Herbert A., 170
Gordon, Jerome, 175–180
Grades (on food), 12–14
Graham, Malcolm D., 218, 219
Grange, George R., 51
Gray, Harold, 157
Great American Holding Corp., 251
Great American Insurance Co., 251
Greenbelt Consumer Services, 31
Greyhound Bus Company, 139
Griffin, Sen. Robert, 162, 163
Grocery Manufacturers of America, 10,
  11, 19
Grolier's, 135, 136

Grossman, Richard, 203
Grove, Dr. Arthur S., 78–80
Gulf & Western, 251
Guttmacher, Dr. Alan F., 113

Haagen-Smit, Prof. Arie, 223
Haddad, William, 31, 84
Haddon, Dr. William, 219
Ham, 65, 66, 68
Hamilton, Cecil, 266
Hand, Lloyd, 163
Handbook of Prescription Drugs, The,
  89
Hansen, Sen. Clifford, 134
Harper, Deputy Att. Gen. Douglas, 145
Hart, Sen. Philip, 11, 24, 26, 29, 39, 95,
  130, 246, 249
Harvard Business Review, 140
Hearing aids, 133–134
Hellman, Dr. Louis M., 110, 111
Hepatitis, 38
Herd, J. Victor, 248–249
Hertz, Dr. Roy, 113
Hochemyer v. Motor Insurance
  Corporation, 242–243
Hoechst Pharmaceuticals, 93, 130
Holifield, Rep. Chet, 185
Holland, Robert F., 59
Holton, Brenda, 52
Hooper-Holmes Bureau Inc., 263–264
Hormel, 5
Horn, Judge Herbert, 145
Housing and Urban Development, Dept.
  of, 267
Howell, Charles R., 144, 250
Howell, Henry, Jr., 231, 232
Hruska, Sen. Roman, 11, 12, 14
Huge, Harry, 188–196
Hughes, Gov. Richard, 144, 218
Hume, David L., 116
Hundley, Dr. James, 117
Hunt, James H., 254
Hygroton, 94

Icelandic Airlines, 155, 166
Indolon, 93
Industrial Valley National Bank, 143
Inspector's Handy Guide, 263
Institute of Experimental Pathology and
  Toxicology, 70
Insurance, 246–252; automobile, 229–
  233, 234–239; bonding, 266–271; and
  finance companies, 253–256;
  investigations for, 262–265; life, 272–
  275
Insurance Institute for Highway Safety,
  233
Interior, Dept. of, 37, 181, 184
International Air Transport Association,
  155, 166
International Council Club, 169
International Telephone and Telegraph,
  251
Investment Company Act, 149
Irradiation, 50, 64–68, 68–69, 197–200
Isotapes, Inc., 67

Jacobsen, Jake, 163
Jacquett, Tony, 267
Japan Airlines, 160, 161
Jarrell, Joseph G., 7
Jasper, Fred, 247–248
Jasper Reports, Inc., 247, 248
Jenkins, Walter, 163

Johnson, Lyndon Baines, 10, 160, 161, 162, 163
Johnson & Johnson, 87
Journal of the American Medical Association, 92, 114
Journal of the American Trial Lawyers Association, 202
Jungle, The, 41

Kadish, Prof. Sanford, 138
Kanter, H. Lee, 231
Kaye, Danny, 212
Keeton, Robert E., 239
Kefauver, Sen. Estes, 91
Kefauver-Harris Drug Amendment, 72, 75, 83, 91
Kelly, Joe T., 248
Kelner, Joseph, 220–222, 230, 233
Kelsey, Dr. Frances O., 98, 99
Kennedy, Sen. Edward, 150, 153
Kennedy, Sen. Robert, 201, 210, 213, 219
Kerner Report, 33
Kerr-McGee, 185, 186, 187
Kiehl, Elmer R., 11
Kimball, Dr. Richard A., 8
King, Frederick E., 263
King Coal, 196
Kirk, Grayson, 124, 125
Kirk, Kenneth, 39
Kleiner, Robert, 67
Kwitny, Jonathan, 141–145

Labor, Dept. of, 184
Ladies Home Journal, 114
Lakeside Pharmaceuticals, 94
Lambert, Thomas, Jr., 202
Larimore, Dr. Granville, 199–200
Lasix, 93, 130
Leaf Tobacco Exporters Association, 115
Leasco, 251
Lederberg, Dr. Joshua, 111
Legator, Dr. Marvin, 8
Lehman, Gov. Herbert H., 274
Leonard, Rooney E., 44
Ley, Dr. Herbert, 78, 93, 110
Lienhard, G. O., 87
Life, 131
Liljenquist, L. Blaine, 45
Lincocin, 93
Ling, James, 163
Loma Linda Foods, 53, 54, 61
Long, Sen. Edward, 207
Long, Sen. Russell, 84
Lung cancer (mining), 183–187
Lykes Co., 251

McAlpin, George W., 218–219
McCall's, 112
McCleery, Dr. Robert S., 93
McDonald, John, 23
McFarland, F. J., 49, 50
McNeil Laboratories, 87, 90
McPherson, Harry, 163
Maddrea, T. Grayson, 231–234
Magowan, Robert, 23
Magnuson, Sen. Warren, 11, 116, 123, 124, 135
Man from U.N.C.L.E., The, 118
Management Consultants, 205, 208
Manning, John, 133
Markham, Prof. Jesse W., 10
Marios, Hugh, 19
Martin-Marietta, 67
Masters, Dexter, 203
May, Rep. Catherine, 12
Mayfield, Dr. F. H., 221

Mead, Johnson Co., 94
Meat, 5; hamburger, 45–47; inspection of, 41–44
Meat Inspection Act, 41, 43
Medical Tribune, 93
Medical World, 86
Medical World News, 92, 93
Meeting the Insurance Crisis of Our Cities, 271
Menopause, 104–108
Meprobamate, 90
Merch, Sharp & Dohme, 84
Meselson, Dr. Matthew, 8
Meserue, William, 39
Metropolitan Life Insurance Co., 272, 273
Meyner, Robert B., 117, 118
Mike Douglas Show, 202, 203
Milk, 58
Milk Industry Foundation, 62, 63
Miller Act, 266
Miltown, 90
Minetti, G. Joseph, 152, 163, 170
Mining, 181, 188–196
Mintz, Morton, 91–94, 109–114
Modern Air Transport, 165
Mondale, Sen. Walter, 46
Monroney, Sen. Mike, 169
Monsanto Chemical Co., 10
Moore, Dr. George E., 120
Morgan, Dr. Karl, 198
Morse, Prof. Richard, 224, 225
Morse, Sen. Wayne, 84
Mortgage Finance Research, 142, 143
Mortgages, 141
Morton, Sen. Thruston, 11, 116
Motor Carrier Safety Act, 139
Motor Insurance Corporation, 242, 243
Mullen, Russell H., 218
Muller, Dr. Hermann J., 7
Murphy, Eileen, 208, 210, 212, 214
Murphy, Sen. George, 169
Murphy, Robert T., 152, 163, 170
Muskie, Sen. Edmund, 225
Mutual Funds, 146–150
Mutual Home Dealers, 144
Mysteclin-F, 94

NDGA, 50
Nader, Ralph, 48, 138–140; on food, 2–9, 37–47; on health, 175–180, 181–182, 197–200; on internal combustion engines, 223–225; and investigation by GM, 201–205, 206–207, 208–215
National Academy of Sciences, 4, 8, 51; and National Research Council, 74, 76, 78
National Advisory Commission on Civil Disorders, 271
National Aeronautics and Space Administration, 129, 130
National Association of Insurance Commissioners, 230, 232
National Association of Manufacturers, 175
National Association of State Departments of Agriculture, 45
National Bureau of Casualty Underwriters, 238
National Bureau of Standards, 133
National Canners Association, 51
National Crime Commission, 138
National Commission on Food Marketing, 10, 12, 15, 22, 29
National Dairy Council, 60
National General Corp., 251

National Highway Safety Bureau, 216, 219
National Institutes of Health, 44, 108
National Interagency Council on Smoking and Health, 118
National Service Life Insurance, 274
Nationwide Mutual Insurance Co., 235
Nelson, Sen. Gaylord, 84, 87, 206, 213
New Republic, 82, 209
New York Times, 14, 19, 92, 132, 212
Nickerson, John, 40
Nixon Pres. Richard M., 160, 161, 162, 246
Nixon, Mudge, Rose, Guthrie, Alexander and Mitchell, 164
Norgaard, Richard, 249
Norinyl-1, 94, 113
Norpramin, 94
Norguen, 94
Norse Chemical Co., 70
North American Co., 255
Northeast Airlines, 151, 153, 161
Novak, Robert, 163
Nulsen, Dr. Ray O., 98, 99–103

Oberdorfer, Don, 115
O'Connell, Jeffrey, 239
Odell, Arthur, 57
Office of Economic Opportunity, 31
Ohio Chemical and Surgical Co., 93
Old Republic Life Insurance Co., 254
Omega watches, 129, 132
100,000 Mile Club, 169
Oracon, 94
Ortho-Novum, 113
Ortho Pharmaceutical Corp., 87
Ottinger, Rep. Richard, 217
Overseas National Airlines, 165
Ovulen-21, 94
Oxford Consumer Discount Co., 144
Oxford Discount Co., 142, 143
Oxford Finance Co., 144

P. Lorillard, 117, 120
P. F. Colliers, 135, 136
Pacific Fidelity Life Insurance Co., 255
Pacific Finance Corp., 255
Pacific Southwest Airlines, 152
Palmer, R. G., 218
Pan American Airlines, 161, 164
Pantheon Books, 89
Parker, Andy, 23
Parker, Herbert M., 186
Parks, Robert L., 160, 161
Pastore, Sen. John O., 184, 185
Patlind, Inc., 144
Patman, Rep. Wright, 251
Paul J. Truran, Inc., 144
Penicillin, 87
Penicillin G, 83, 89
Pennex Products Co., 83, 89, 90
Pentids, 83, 89
Peripheral neuritis, 102
Peritrate SA, 93
Perth Amboy News Tribune, 144
Pesticides Chemical Amendment, 49
Peterson, Esther, 22, 23, 27, 30
Pfizer Co., 94
Pharmaceutical Manufacturers Association, 86, 87, 92
Physicians' Desk Reference, 81, 92
Pillsbury Co., 70
Pincus, Dr. Gregory, 113
Platt, Fletcher, 217
Pogge, Dr. Raymond, 99
Pollution, 6

Poor Pay More, The, 31, 33
Porter, Sylvia, 143
Posin, Daniel, Jr., 216–219
Post, Troy, 163
Power, Aloysius, 208, 210, 211, 213
Powers, Col. John "Shorty," 129
Poultry, 5
Poultry Products Inspection Act, 44
Premarin, 107
Premier Insurance Company, 243
Prescription Drug Industry Fact Book, 87
Presidents Club, 169
Price, Rep. Melvin, 185
Private clubs (airline), 168–170, 171–172
Private labels, 13
Procaine penicillin, 83
Proceedings of the Society for Experimental Biology and Medicine, The, 75
Proctor and Gamble, 61
Progressive Grocer, 23, 79
Provera, 107
Providence Washington Insurance, 251
Protein-bound-iodine, 71
Public Health Service, 39, 117, 122, 181, 186
Purcell, Rep. Graham, 11, 12, 45, 47
Purdue Airlines, 165
Py-co-pay toothbrushes, 129, 131

Quinine, 95–97

Ralston Purina, 55
Rankin, Commissioner W. B., 5, 38
Rasmussen, Dr. Donald, 195
Ratner, Dr. Herbert, 111
Reader's Digest, 87, 131
Reliance Insurance, 251
Renese, 94
Report of the National Commission on Community Health Services, 8
Repossession, 257–261
Resources for the Future, 223
Retail Credit Co., 262–265
Reuters, 110, 111
Ribicoff, Sen. Abraham, 201, 204, 206, 209, 211
Ridgeway, James, 26–32, 98–103, 150–153, 272–274; on auto insurance, 229–233, 234–239, 246–252; on Ralph Nader, 200–205, 208–210, 211–215; on small loans, 253–256
Ridolfi, Sido, 144
Riley, Royal, 216
Roche, James, 210, 211, 212, 213
Rock, Dr. John, 114
Rockefeller, Laurence, 162
Rockefeller, Nelson, 162, 164
Rogers, William P., 164
Rosenfeld, Mordecai, 146–150
Rosenthal, Rep. Benjamin, 24
Rubini, Dr. Milton, 77
Rusk, Dr. Howard, 91, 92, 93
Ruskin, Dr. Arthur, 112
Ryan, John C., 170

Sachs, Dr. Miriam, 179
Sachs, Stanley, 231
Sadow, Leonard B., 132
Sadusk, Dr. Joseph F., Jr., 113
Safety: highway, 216–219, 220–222; industrial, 175–180
Safeway stores, 21, 23, 31
Safrole, 49
Sales Management, 137

279

Sanford, David, 21–25, 48–67, 81–88, 128–132; on airlines, 160–164, 168–170; on Nader, 211–215
Saturn Airlines, 165
Sausage products, 5
Scalise, Larry, 215
Scheer, Julian, 131
Schroeder, Harry F., 24
Schrag, Philip G., 33–36
Schwartz, Hugh, 60
Science, 75
Seaborg, Glenn T., 66
Sears, Roebuck and Co., 21
Seattle, 135
Seattle Post-Intelligencer, 238
Secondary Mortgage Loan Act, 143
Securities and Exchange Commission, 147, 149
Security National Fund, Inc., 144
Senate Commerce Committee, 115
Senate Special Committee on Aging, 134
Serax, 93
Sesser, Stanford N., 262–265
Shadoan, George, 232
Sharp, Dean, 253, 256
Sheppard, Mrs. Annamay T., 145
Sherman Antitrust Act, 139
Sherwood, Frederick, 137
Sills, Arthur, 144
Sinclair, Upton, 41, 44, 196
Slater, Dr. Charles C., 10
Smith, C. R., 163
Smith, Henry Such, 216, 217, 218, 219
Smith, Kline and French, 89, 90
Smith, Neal, 41, 43
Snyder, W. S., 187
Sonosky, Jerome, 213, 214
Sorensen, Theodore, 210, 214
Southern Airlines, 165
Soy beans, 53–56
Spangenberg, Craig, 99, 101
Staggers, Rep. Harley, 123
Stamps, 21, 22
Standard Airlines, 165
Standard of living, 16
Standard Oil of New Jersey, 22
Starr, Dr. Frederick, 74, 75
State Farm Mutual Automobile Insurance Co., 235
State Life Fund, 272, 273
Steen, Charley, 183
Stefanelli, Theresa, 144
Stefanelli, Anthony, 144, 145
Sterling Drug Co., 83
Stonex, Kenneth A., 217
"Strategy for a Livable Environment, A," 8
Stratton, Rep. Samuel S., 62
Strickman, Robert, 124, 125, 126
Sugar Research Foundation, 70
Sullivan, Rep. Leonor K., 11, 261
Sunasco, 143
Supermarkets, 21–25
Swift & Co., 55
Syntex Co., 94

Tate, James H. J., 143
Teledyne, 251
Thalidomide, 98–103
Thermoelectron, Inc. 224
Thomas J. Lipton Co., 53, 55, 56, 65
Time, 83
Tobacco Associates, Inc., 115
Tony Jacquett Compliance Plan, 267
Top Flight Club, 169
Transamerica Corp., 255

Trans-Bay Construction Co., 268
Trans-Continental Agency, 154
Trans International Airlines, 165
Trans World Airlines, 155, 161, 168
Trichinosis, 5
True cigarettes, 117, 120
Truman, Harry S., 189
Truth-in-Lending Bill, 261
Truth-in-packaging, 24, 26–27
Tsai Mutual Fund, 251

US Overseas Airlines, 154
Uniroyal, 67
United Airlines, 161
United Auto Workers, 212
United Mine Workers, 181
United Planning Organization, 24, 31
United States Pharmacopoeia, 82, 83
Universal Airlines, 165
University of Southern California, 266
Unsafe At Any Speed, 201, 206, 208
Upjohn Pharmaceutical Co., 92, 93, 107
Usury, 141–145

Vertrees, Orman, 238
Veterans Administration, 133, 134, 274
Vinson, Fred M., 214
Virginia Dark-Fired and Sun-Cured Tobacco Export Association, 115
Volpe, John, 246

W. J. Jeffrey Co., 23
Wakefield, Lowell, 40
Wall Street Journal, 263
Wallace Laboratories, 90, 92
Walsh-Healey Act, 184
Walter Kidde and Co., 251
Warner Bros., 115
Warner-Chilcott Laboratories, 93
Washington, D.C., 24, 31; merchants' survey, 27; Ridgeway in, 33
Washington Post, 19, 21
Water pollution, 6
Watt, Charles M., 263, 264
Weekly Recall Report, 6
Wells, Dr. Hawley A., 177
Western Airlines, 161
Western States Meat Packers Association, 45
Wheat, 65
White, Major Edward, 130
White potatoes, 65
Wiggens, David, 272–274
Wm. S. Merrell Co., 98, 99
Williams, Sen. Harrison A., 217
Williams Bros., 224
Wills, Dr. J. Henry, 71
Wilson Research Foundation, 107
Wilson, Dr. Robert A., 104–108
Wilson, Robert A., Jr., 107
Winchell, Frank, 207
Wirtz, Willard, 179, 186
Wolf, Robert A., 217
Wolgin, Jack, 143
Woodall, S. Roy, Jr., 238
Woodward, Warren, 163
Woodward and Fondiller, 232
Worcester Foundation for Experimental Biology, 76
World Airlines, 165
World of Pleasure, 115
World Health Organization, 51, 78
Worthington Foods, 53, 55
Wyeth Laboratories, 90, 93

X-rays, 197–200

280